Beth Elon has lived in Tuscany for thirty years and is the author of three successful cookery books.

D0238539

TASTING TUSCANY

Beth Elon

BANTAM BOOKS

LONDON • TORONTO • SYDNEY • AUCKLAND • JOHANNESBURG

TASTING TUSCANY
A BANTAM BOOK : 9780553816907

First publication in Great Britain

PRINTING HISTORY
Bantam edition published 2006

5 7 9 10 8 6

Set in 10/13pt Stone by
Falcon Oast Graphic Art Ltd.

Addresses for Random House Group Ltd companies outside the UK can be found at: www.randomhouse.co.uk
The Random House Group Ltd Reg. No. 954009

Printed and bound in Great Britain by
CPI Group (UK) Ltd, Croydon, CR0 4YY

For Danae, who properly introduced us to Tuscany
when she was two, and for Amos who shares it all.

And for Tristan who will grow in these
places we love so much.

Contents

Acknowledgements

I COULD NOT HAVE written this book without the enormous help of many others. The restaurateurs I write about have been generous, with both time and recipes. My many friends and neighbours have shown me the way to both beautiful places in Tuscany and its food. To the many local vendors and producers of the products of Tuscany who have clarified local traditions and specialities for me, I offer my thanks as well. Among them are Sonia Balducci in Montecatini, Sauro Signori in Pistoia, Nando Quattrone and Daniela Zamorra in Filattiera and Rosetta Petra in Lamporécchio.

A special grateful acknowledgement to Daniella DeNur and Yossi Riback who discussed the concept of the book with me before it even began. Amos Elon read the manuscript as I wrote and, as always, was invaluable in his continual attention. Marta Braun and Yossi Riback also made many helpful suggestions. Many other friends have helped me to discover Tuscany's rural traditions and joined me in my travels. Among them are Lina Ercolessi, Paola Canepari, Luciano and Vanna Disperati, Miranda and Paolo Giuliani, Gabriella Mazzoni, Massimo and Giovanna Duranti, Sussi Pundik, Michal Pundik-Sagi, Lior Sagi, Clarissa Pryce-Jones, Penny Fantacci, Adrianna Milla, Silvia Servi, Ingrid Harbeck, Paul Gervais, Gil Cohen, Michael

Schluter, Milly Passigli, Nehama and Peter Hillman, Ellen Blair, Tobia and Melina Milla-Moss, Ghiberto Piccini, Amit Matarasso and Anna Lisa Tempestini.

My thanks to the helpful people at Slow Food Italy who care so much about reviving and maintaining the genuine quality of traditional food: Nino Ricci in Florence, Walter Nunciatini in Grossetto and Franco Utili in Vicchio.

Two food writers have inspired both my feeling for food and how I would like to present it. As for so many others, Elizabeth David long ago opened my eyes and my appetite to what Mediterranean food could be. Elizabeth Rohmer's *The Tuscan Year* was a book I read only after I'd been in my own small *podere* for a number of years, and could enjoy and empathize so completely with her kitchen adventures with Silvana and her family in their Val d'Orcia farmhouse.

In addition, I'd like to express my deep appreciation to all those who helped bring this book into print; my agent Abner Stein and his office staff; my editor at Transworld, Francesca Liversidge, who has been such an encouragement from the beginning; Nicky Jeanes for her generous and her ongoing support and Mari Roberts whose careful reading of the manuscript filtered out some glaring errors. Needless to say, if any remain, the responsibility is mine.

And of course my thanks and gratitude go to Amos and Danae, both of whom have encouraged me in my pursuits over the years, and without them both, I would not have known Tuscany.

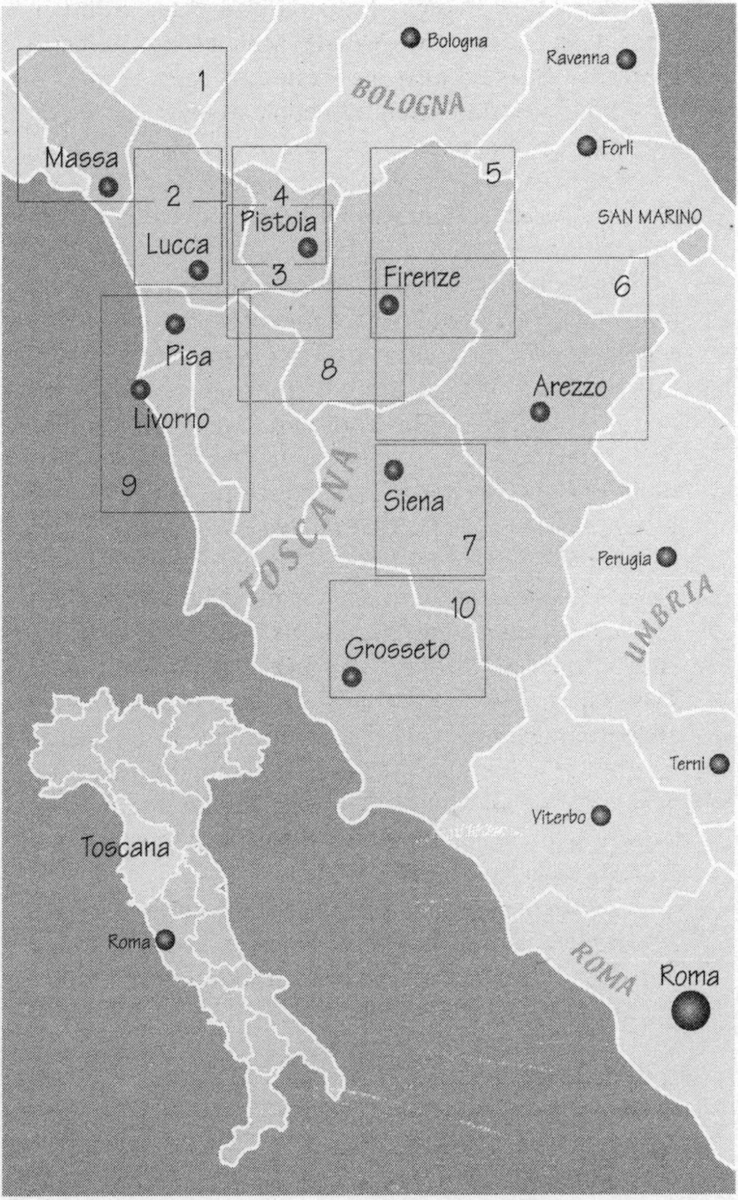

Bologna
Ravenna
BOLOGNA
Forlì
SAN MARINO
1
Massa
2
Lucca
4
Pistoia
3
5
Firenze
6
Pisa
8
Livorno
Arezzo
9
TOSCANA
Siena
7
Perugia
UMBRIA
10
Grosseto
Terni
Viterbo
Toscana
Roma
ROMA
Roma

◆ A Personal Note ◆

TUSCANY – AND ITS FOOD – came into our lives more than thirty years ago when a chance encounter in a lovely little village in the Apennine foothills led to our purchasing a small abandoned farm on its edge. It would be for many years a vacation home, and eventually became our only home as we comfortably settled into a life of Mediterranean enchantment and discovery. This book is a retelling of some of my most pleasurable finds: the rich and diverse Tuscan landscapes, the wonder of isolated, architecturally perfect ancient hill towns, and the culture of natural and traditional food that continues in the face of modernity and fast-paced living to this day. I've tried to combine all of these aspects in the small itineraries I've chosen here; I hope the reader will find his or her way to their own enjoyments too.

Beyond the better-known, larger cities that attract ever growing hordes of tourists, souvenir and fast-food shops, Tuscany is made up of hundreds of small clustered hill towns, each with a singular way of doing things. Throughout the Tuscan countryside, with its lovely churches, piazzas and ancient architecture, you'll find a rural art that is often worthy of the finest city museums. There's also a population that clings obstinately to a sensual way of life that includes an authentic experience of food as one of its most wholesome elements. No great chefs, just great tastes.

We chanced upon our little farm in 1972. On what seemed like a lonely hillside, local acquaintances led us to an old, bramble-covered, heavily beamed ruin of a farmhouse, older even than my native United States and as much in need of repair. With the house came the obligatory farm – too much of it and seemingly abandoned – and an amazing view of vineyards and olive groves, mountains beyond and distant medieval towns sprinkled across the landscape, a view that had not changed dramatically in hundreds of years. Looking at an old map of our village some years later, I was startled to see that pretty much everything was still as it had been in the seventeenth century.

We weren't very particular about restoration, which I now regret. (Once you don't add a fireplace to your living room, it never gets done.) We patched up the house casually, covering the barn and storage-room floors with bricks, adding only bathrooms and central heating. We realized that we weren't located on a lonely hillside but appended to the hillside below the highest point of a small village. Having a village at our backs meant that we could have our little corner of privacy among vineyards, olives and forests, yet still walk up the short path to a perfect Renaissance piazza where our neighbours welcomed summer evening breezes and the children played ball. Our daughter grew up here and the Italian language became part of her heritage. And I had an entire village of invariably kind neighbours who became friends and invited me into their kitchens to gossip and learn all about the Tuscan way with food: the combination of fresh vegetables with the wild and cultivated herbs that grew all around us, the quick and precise way in which meals were prepared, the lasting power of tradition, the festive foods that came with celebrations and the most important rituals.

The house had been lived in by tenant farmers who shared its ample spaces with livestock and farm produce. At one end was the barn where chickens, goats, pigs and sheep had fed and slept. At the other end was the large kitchen with a huge open fireplace where the family cooked, ate, socialized and stayed warm through the winter months. A hole in the wall next to the fireplace opened on to an outside oven where the daily bread was baked, and where on festive occasions game and other succulent casseroles were slowly roasted to perfection. From the large open hood of the fireplace hung a heavy iron chain with a hook to hang the large iron pots in which food was cooked and kept warm.

Between the kitchen and the stalls was the *cantina*, where wine was made and stored. When we first saw the house, an enormous chestnut wine cask still stood in the corner. (We had to dismantle it to clear space for our dining room. Luciano Disperati, our ingenious local carpenter, whose grandfather had made the cask, turned it into a desk for my husband; he's since written several books on it.) We found large, green, hand-blown demijohns resting in rotting straw baskets lined up against the wall. Olive oil had once been stored here too, in big-bellied terracotta jugs; alas, neither oil nor jugs had been left behind.

A hand-chiselled stone staircase, well worn and precipitous, led to the second floor where all the rooms looked out on to the hills and the Apennine mountains beyond. As far as I could tell, the sleeping area for the family was limited to two upstairs rooms, one at each end of the house. I don't know how they did it; the last to occupy the house was a family of twelve. Between the two family rooms were open spaces for hanging and drying herbs, sausages and other meats for eating during the winter months. Clusters of grapes would be hung here too, until Christmas, when they were sealed inside a small barrel to eventually become *vin santo*, the traditional dessert wine served with hard biscuits at the end of most meals. Our farm, I would later learn, also had some of the best fig trees of the entire village; we counted six different varieties among some thirty trees. Figs must also have been hung to dry in the open spaces of the second floor. The chestnuts that grew in our forests and the walnuts and hazelnuts from the trees around the house would all go into the same upstairs larder, as did potatoes, onions and garlic harvested during the summer.

Our house was a *casa del pastore*, a shepherd's house. No doubt heavily scented *pecorino* cheeses – made from the milk of their sheep – had permeated the air of what would become our upstairs guest room. In a corner of this room, which lay directly over the *cantina* on the ground floor, was a trap door through which harvested grapes were thrown down each autumn into the wine cask below. We could imagine the farmer lowering himself as well, to crush the grapes with his bare feet, dancing around inside the barrel. We learned later that this would have been a dangerous practice; the poisonous fumes of the fermenting grapes could overwhelm and kill. It was more likely that large battering poles were used to crush the grapes. (Or that, like with us later on, the grapes were crushed first in large open tubs – indeed with bare feet – and only later thrown into the barrel.)

The last occupants, the Teglia family, had left some twenty years earlier, to find work in the new small industries down in the valley. Many families had abandoned their farms at the time for the same reason. Tenant farming allowed a certain frugal security but was otherwise oppressive. A farmer could not dream of bettering his lot. Age-old paternalism had shaped village life – and Italian cuisine – for centuries. Up to 50 per cent of a farmer's olive oil, wine and other produce went to the *padrone*; the remaining part was consumed at home, and traded or sold in the local marketplace. When land reform came in, farmers had the opportunity – rarely taken up – to buy their farms. Making a living from a farm was a daunting prospect. And so most farmers left.

Nice things began to happen almost as soon as we arrived. I was still unpacking our bags when Giuseppina appeared, having heard about the new foreigners about to move in. She had arrived a few months earlier from Benevento, an impoverished province high into the hills above Naples, to join her sister and brother who were already improving their lives in a more prosperous Tuscany. Might I want someone to help in the house, and with the farm as well? Our meeting that first day led to a warm familial relationship that lasted more than seventeen years, until Giuseppina retired and bequeathed us her loquacious daughter-in-law.

Giuseppina taught me the ways of the field, how to plant what and where. She pointed out edible wild greens, broccoli, rape and fennel, prickly nettles and borage, and showed me how to use them. She taught me how to look for *nipotella*, the wild mint that makes courgettes taste like wild mushrooms, to preserve tomatoes in used beer bottles the way they did in the poorer south, to dry and shell beans and chickpeas. As we picked green beans she would admonish me not to look wearily at the unending line awaiting, but to concentrate on the plant at hand. She insisted on planting full crops of potatoes, onions and garlic at the right moment in order that we might store them for the winter. It did no good to point out that the market could provide me with the same things at a lower cost.

I discovered our capers during my first summer. Early one morning, around 6 a.m., I looked out of my bedroom window to discover a rather grumpy-looking old villager carefully plucking every bud from a bush on the wall below. I'd thought it was a beautiful bush, with graceful pink and white flowers, and wondered aloud to Giuseppina why he wasn't letting the flowers bloom. She explained they were capers and that it was the habit to pick clean the hardy plants each morning. Hesitant American that I was, I didn't very much want to confront the crankiest of locals, and so took the easy way out. I got to the wall each morning by 5.30 a.m. to beat our trespasser, and plucked enough to satisfy my new urge to live off the land, leaving plenty for the old man as well. Giuseppina taught me how to pickle the buds in our own vinegar, and I continue to make little presents of them to grateful friends each winter.

We worked and learned about Tuscany together; although I was more the student, she the teacher. Together we acquired a taste for unsalted Tuscan bread. Together we distrusted a major commandment that rules the Tuscan farm: chores one does or does not do with the rising and setting of the moon. Giuseppina had not followed the moon rhythm in Benevento, nor had I in Larchmont, New York. But we both gave in, Giuseppina muttering that the moon was different here than in Benevento and I simply accepting the local lore. Since then both of us have become convinced. My first experience in being contrary began with my preserving tomatoes before the moon began to descend. It ended one night with an explosion of bottled tomatoes all over the kitchen. Apart from the fright at being woken by the explosion, the scene was one of carnage. We had to repaint.

I had so much to learn. Late in our first summer, I was sitting in the doorway of what was not yet our paved terrace when an enormous pig ran by, almost brushing my knees. My only previous encounters had been of the 'three little pigs' kind. I screamed to my husband upstairs that we were being attacked by wild boars. At that moment a farmer and his two sons came racing around the corner of the house armed with broomsticks and pitchforks. *'Scusi, Signora,'* they apologized as they ran by, *'li voglia bene le mele dietro la casa.'* ('He loves to eat the apples behind your house.') I hurried around to the back of the house to find the pig happily munching the young fruit that had fallen from the apple tree. Emilio – he had been one of the last Teglias to live in our house and the only one still to farm nearby – prodded him home. I'd had my first experience of an enormous Italian pig. (I was later to have my share with wild boars as well, mostly competing with them and huge porcupines for delicious sweetcorn I'd brought from America to plant. Needless to say, I lost.)

Signor Biondi arrived at our door not long after Giuseppina. He told us he'd been working a small piece of our land during the years the property was abandoned. Surely we wouldn't mind if he resumed planting on that insignificant corner. We knew nothing of Signor Biondi but were pleased to agree, and to know that our lower terraces would be profitably used.

As it turned out, Signor Biondi became a lot more to us than just a farmer working a piece of our land. I learned a lot from him too. He helped me to plant the essential rosemary and sage and to pick the wild sour cherries that we could preserve in grappa. He explained and planted *cavolo nero* (black cabbage or kale) and *bietole* (swiss chard) that are so much of the Tuscan table, and brought me artichoke plants that would give us tender baby artichokes each spring. And it was Signor Biondi who all but forced me to overcome a natural revulsion to eating adorable little furry rabbits; I could never reject the warm skinned carcass he presented me with every now and again, lovely dappled fur still clinging to its four paws. The entire Biondi family became good friends. Signora Biondi and their daughter Franca were among the first women in the village I came to know well. With them I first smelled, tasted, envied their skills and learned to make *crostini di fegato, zuppa di contadini* and so many other local special dishes.

Over the years, as our relationship developed, Signor Biondi tended to chores around the house that we could not do ourselves. He did it all in the old-fashioned way. Mechanized tools were not yet in regular use. Every morning before six I could hear beneath our bedroom window the swishing of his little hand-held sickle, the *falce*, as he stooped to cut vines and overgrown grass along our path. He carried the rusting little tool everywhere, tucked into his well-worn leather belt, along with a whetstone to sharpen it. The blade was worn to a width of a few centimetres. He patched it when the handle broke, welded it if the metal cracked. There was no thought of replacing it. He carried one other tool, a *zappa*, an iron-headed short hoe with which to turn the earth and dig up unwanted vegetation. Newfangled tools were not for this old curmudgeon; I expect he would not have known what to do with a strimmer. The quick swish became our early morning sound as much as the crowing of the nearby rooster.

Signor Biondi brought us a few litres of olive oil and wine each year; we did not ask for it, he was working our land for himself. But it was pleasant to receive what he brought, the fresh, fragrant oil especially. His wine grew better with the years, and even won a much-coveted prize as the best vintage in the village one year. We began to make our own wine and collect the olives ourselves only after Signor Biondi, at eighty-five, was no longer able to get around and we began to live here all year round.

He was a natural grump and continually warned against impending disaster, especially when things looked good, every time we hoped that we might see fruit on our trees or a good crop of vegetables. He was usually right. The fruit buds had arrived too soon; frost would kill them. Not enough rain had fallen; we could give up on beans. I later read that this was indeed the curse of Tuscany. Ferdnand Braudel tells us in his history of the Mediterranean that between the fourteenth and eighteenth centuries there were only eleven seasons without at least one disaster: drought or too much rain and flooding, hail, epidemics and other horrors. Signor Biondi was often sour about Giuseppina's capabilities in the vegetable garden. She came from the south, *da giu* ('down there'), where they didn't really know how to farm properly. He corrected, admonished and grouched. It was some years before she began to fight back and defend her own way, and he finally admitted that even though she came from 'down there' she was really OK. In the end they had real affection for one another, each in his or her cranky way. And I loved them both.

We slowly came to know our other neighbours too.

We lived just below the church. Don Giuliano, the village priest, was attended by his bent but spry old mother, who often wandered down our path on her way to find herbs in the forest below. She'd inevitably return with various weeds methodically arranged between her fingers and explain patiently what each was for: to cure a stomach ache or cough, help digestion, to add a taste to the *frittata* or a soothing scent to the bath.

I remember one grim day when I arrived home to a happy Henry, our dog, his tail wagging excitedly, greeting me at the door with a dead chicken he'd killed and proudly brought home for us. To my dismay, the ever practical Giuseppina was already preparing to pluck the poor limp thing. I went off to the village to enquire vaguely if someone might be missing a chicken; in those days it was 5000 lire to reimburse a farmer. No one claimed the chicken, and so Giuseppina prepared it for eating, wrapped it in newspaper and put it into the fridge. Not long after, Don Giuliano's mother wandered by, peering here and there, obviously looking for something. 'Oh, signora,' I said, 'is it a chicken you're missing?' We went into the house and Giuseppina brought the head up from the garbage pail and asked somewhat petulantly if this was him. 'Oh indeed,' she replied, and it wasn't Henry's fault at all. The chicken had escaped from the coop. And thank goodness it was Henry who had gotten it. This way she knew it was safe to eat. And so she trundled off with the day's lunch.

In the beginning our neighbours could not understand why we were here at all. Few foreigners wandered by in those days, and the villagers themselves travelled no further than the local sea coast for vacation. Why would a stranger want to settle in such an out-of-the-way small town? Many Italians were still undervaluing themselves in the aftermath of defeat in the Second World War, and couldn't understand that an American might prefer to settle into an ancient, worm-eaten farmhouse rather than enjoy the splendours of fat, rich America. It was useless to attempt to explain our admiration. We slowly learned how a small Italian village works as a social unit and extended family, people taking care of one another, nurturing the lame, succouring the bereaved, and, often as not, being mean to one another too. Most of the old families in the village are related; in fact, there are only two or three old clans in all. Small rituals, yearly festivals, church processions are all organized within the closed circle of old-timers.

Traditional foods, their preparation and eating are a large part of life and all its rituals. Planning and carrying out various public *festas* during the year is a major task for the village women. The parties happen, mostly in summer months, in the piazza. For each *festa*, the men roast the meat and grill the steaks, the women prepare the rest of the meal: the *antipasti*, soups and bread salads, side dishes and desserts. Over the years I've been there to offer help, but usually local tradition faces me stonily, rigidly. I'm allowed to watch and taste, but not actually to cook. The expression, '*non si fa cosi*' ('that's not how it's done') meets any innovation I might suggest. Every time I've tried to chop something differently or recommend the slightest variation or even stick my fingers into the dough, there it is: '*Non si fa cosi.*'

On *Ferragosto*, Assumption Day, the midsummer holiday on 15 August, an informal picnic takes place on the piazza. Everyone brings something. My hummus – a mash of chickpeas, garlic, olive oil and salt

– has become part of the local lore. I knew that Tuscans savour a salad of chickpeas in a dressing of olive oil, garlic and salt. My mash, I claimed, was the same thing, just prepared differently, a new sort of *crostini* topping. When I brought it to the picnic, only a few courageous souls were even prepared to taste it. The most complimentary comment was '*Hmm, interessante.*' Mostly I just heard '*Cosa sarebbe?*' 'What in heaven's name is it?' Same ingredients, but not the same at all.

Making fresh pasta was something I needed to learn although it remains a challenge. When I heard that Luciano Disperati, our master carpenter and good friend, made fresh pasta for Sunday lunch, I asked him if I could come and watch. I had to see if it was as easy as he assured me it was.

One of the most traditional fresh pasta dishes here is *tortellini in brodo*, little meat-stuffed rings in broth, often served on festive occasions, especially at Christmastime. This was to be the dish on the Sunday I joined Luciano and his wife Vanna for pasta-making. Vanna greeted me at the door at 9 a.m. and took me down to their bright kitchen. Luciano was already busy laying out the ingredients. First thing was to prepare the dough, which would rest while they worked in tandem to prepare the filling. Into the food processor went 300 grams of plain white flour, a pinch (½ teaspoon) of salt, 3 fresh eggs and a tablespoon of olive oil. The processor took less than two minutes to form a solid paste. Luciano scraped it all out and worked it some more on the marble tabletop over a dusting of flour for another five minutes. Then Vanna covered it with a cloth to lie quietly while they prepared the filling.

The filling was 80 grams of prosciutto (with its fat), 80 grams of mortadella sausage and another 80 grams of grated Parmesan cheese. We weighed it as we went, but that was mostly for me; normally they would go *al occhio,* by eye. The ingredients went into the food processor with a good grinding of nutmeg and an egg. The result was a delicious mass, a grainy paste.

Luciano began to roll out the pasta. First he dusted the marble tabletop with some more flour. He worked with his own hand-fashioned rolling pin, a thick round piece of wood about half a metre long. His method seemed easier than any hand-cranked or electric pasta machine. He simply rolled here and there, stretching the sheet out, adding more flour. Every now and again, he rolled up the dough on the rolling pin and flipped it over to its other side. He continued working in this way for about 15 minutes, until the large thin sheet of pasta was almost as wide as the working space, a full metre long and 70cm wide.

Tortellini are little discs of dough, stuffed and folded in half, then pulled round your second finger and pinched to close, ending up as funny-looking fat little rings. To prepare them, Luciano used a glass of about 5cm in diameter to cut discs from the dough. Vanna put half a teaspoon of filling on each. We all folded them and pulled them around the appropriate finger to close the circle, leaving a little flap to stick up. Within minutes we had more than a hundred, enough to generously serve about ten. They went into a home-made meat broth that Vanna had prepared earlier. There was some leftover dough, and that was quickly rolled out and sliced into thin tagliatelle, enough for another meal. We were finished within an hour. An invaluable lesson was over, and eventually I became almost as adept as Luciano.

Preserving olives in the Tuscan way was another lesson picked up from village friends. Olives here are soaked for fifty days in water that's changed daily and then pickled in an elusive combination of spices that can include cinnamon, cloves, nutmeg, allspice, anise and other exotic flavourings. Such spices – that most certainly found their way along the Silk Road into Italy – flavour almost everything preserved in Tuscany, vegetables as well as olives.

Summertime activities in the village piazza, as everywhere in Tuscany, are diverse, ranging from band concerts, operatic offerings, art exhibitions and local theatre performances to just having fun. On the last Saturday in July is a big planned party, with almost 200 paying guests helping to finance other events. The lovely small square is filled with colourful tables with a long buffet of savoury local dishes down the middle. Demand has grown over the years; reservations must be made early. The meal itself has become more elaborate, and more elegantly served too. Now we have rented linen tablecloths rather than paper sheets, cloth napkins, and real cutlery has replaced the plastic. The atmosphere is festive, the piazza dramatically illuminated. The meal is entirely made by the villagers: preparations go on for days in many kitchens and the final assembly takes place in the old crest-encrusted Palazzo Pretorio that fronts the square. Different *crostini* toppings are smeared on to sliced baguettes and placed on large platters. *Ribolitto* (well-flavoured bread soup) and *panzanella* (bread salad) arrive, along with cold meats to slice and tasty side dishes to spoon on to large platters. The proudest display is collected in a back room: a vast assortment of desserts, cakes and fruit tarts, creams, different versions of the acclaimed *torta della nonna* (grandmother's cake, a rich layered cream cake dotted with pine nuts). Every housewife in town makes her own favourite.

The men grill the sausages, pork chops and chicken over a large fire behind the palazzo, just opposite the church. Those who aren't preparing the food lay the tables, precisely and decorously. Much attention goes into the flower arrangements for the tables, and how the service is laid and the napkins folded. The little piazza becomes an elegant outdoor salon. A local band arrives just before the guests, and sets up on the grassy patch along the broad side of the church. After dinner the large buffet table is moved away to make room for dancing, traditional dancing mostly.

When it's all over, the clean-up begins, tables and chairs are gathered, tableware divided for washing up at home. The piazza is left spotless, ready for church-goers the next morning. The following evening is for *avanzi*, leftovers, shared by everyone who's helped.

Like most foreign newcomers to Tuscany, we became enormously proud of our home-made wine, and are now almost the only wine-producing family around. Our Italian neighbours turned long ago to buy at the local *cantina*, where inexpensive wine can be bought by the demijohn for bottling at home. It was Signor Biondi who kept us at it. He never ceased trimming the vines to make wine at the end of September. A few bottles always awaited us when we arrived the following summer. When Signor Biondi could no longer do it, we continued. Now we have Stefano. The demographic nature of our village – as in all of Italy, indeed Europe – has changed over the years. African, Vietnamese and eastern European children have joined the games on the piazza. Stefano arrived with his wife Flora and two lively daughters – Giulia and Melena – from Albania a few years ago, and live in the small *dependenza* that adjoins our house. They tend the dogs when we're away (as we do theirs when they are off somewhere), plant and weed the *orto* (vegetable garden) and keep the produce coming for all of us. Stefano also tends the grapes and the olives, and we all join to make the wine and collect the olives that go for pressing at the local cooperative mill.

My favourite festivities are the ones occasioned by the new wine and freshly pressed olive oil. At *vendemmia*, the grape harvest, in late September, we invite friends to help pick the grapes and I prepare a hearty and festive Tuscan lunch. I remember *vendemmias* from years back, real feasts with a lot of drinking and too much eating. We do it more simply. With help from friends it doesn't take more than a few hours to cut and gather all our grapes. A few years ago Signor Biondi was still crushing the grapes with his bare feet in large plastic tubs. Now we have an aged hand-cranking press that does it just as well. The process is simple. Everything – crushed grapes, seeds, juice – is dumped into the *botte*, these days no longer a chestnut barrel but a large fibreglass vat. The fermenting juice separates from the dregs and, after a week, when the boiling stops, is decanted into demijohns. We take a sampling over to the local *cantina* for analysis; if the alcohol content reaches 11 per cent, we don't have to add anything. If it's less, we add a bit of *mosto*, a heavier wine usually from the south, to give it a bit more alcohol content as well as body and taste. Nothing else ever goes in; no preservatives or other enhancers. We transfer the wine from demijohn to demijohn a couple of times during the winter, to drain off the sediment, but don't otherwise pay it much attention until we bottle it the following spring. It may not be a fine Chianti but we never wake up next morning with a headache.

Making olive oil is even less of a science than

winemaking. I've tasted better oils and worse. One thing is certain: fresh olive oil that you – or a friend – have made is nothing like the stuff you buy in bottles, no matter how expensive and *extravergine* it claims to be. I love the ritual that goes along with making oil. If the smell of fermenting figs fallen from the trees is my September and the odour of burning charcoal the first sign of winter, November brings the overwhelming aroma of crushed olives at the *frantoio*, the mill where we bring our olives to be ground into oil. I loved it even more when our *frantoio* was still an old mill powered by the river next to it. The olives were crushed as they had been for centuries, by two massive revolving grindstones. The oil oozed out through pads of felt squeezed by a giant screw. A big open fireplace in a large beamed room was available; while we waited our turn we could prepare the meal that ritually went along with olive pressing. Friends were invited to gather at the long chestnut table. The air was rich with smells of centuries of oil. Carafes of your own oil, still warm and bubbling from the press, arrived at regular intervals.

The traditional *frantoio* meal always began with a simple *fett'unta*, a thick slice of farm bread gently toasted on the open fire and saturated with the new thick golden-green oil. Everything that followed demanded yet another topping of the fresh oil: the *farinata*, a bean and kale soup thickened with polenta, salt cod – *baccala* – and boiled potatoes, grilled chicken, meats and sausages, roast potatoes, salad with a dressing of only salt and fresh oil. To finish was the traditional chestnut flour cake – *castagnaccio* – made with rosemary, pine nuts, a little sugar and, of course, more fresh oil. It was heavenly.

Our *frantoio* moved some fifteen years ago to a modern cement-block enclosure, a cold affair. In the beginning it smelled only of cement. Over the years the centrifugal extraction – now through big stainless-steel processors – has brought rich aromas to the new place too. The nostalgia-evoking old machines are displayed like museum pieces, along with a few ancient terracotta vats that manage a bit of atmosphere. Your olives get weighed,then dumped into a dark opening in the floor. After a lot of button pushing, in about ten minutes the oil begins slowly to pour out through a spout. It's certainly more efficient, but I still miss the old press. (Today some mills even feature machines that separate out the pits before beginning to crush the olives; this break from the past I've so far refused to consider.) The level of acidity in the oil is measured immediately; if we get no more than 2 per cent acidity, it's a good year. Most years ours measures less than 1 per cent.

In the new mill a large side room still has its open fireplace but the long tables are covered with plastic tablecloths. Elaborate meals are rare nowadays. Our festive supper has become more of a tasting, a light meal of *fett'unta* and sausages, with lots of bread and wine to wash it all down. No longer do lots of friends join in, just a few neighbours, Stefano, Flora, the girls and us. I still think of it as tradition.

Such have been my particular adventures in Tuscany. I hope the traveller will partake of some of our pleasures in the ten itineraries that follow. The restaurants I've chosen all serve traditional food. You can count on a good meal in any of them. Their cooks have generously shared recipes with me. Nothing has been altered or changed, not even ingredients that might be difficult to come by. Careful substitutes can certainly be made. I've tried all their recipes at home; those included in the book have succeeded well, with friends, family and other prejudiced critics. Most often they are dishes of local tradition. Occasionally there's something innovative; I've included those when they've been interesting and good.

The greatest legacy of the old tenant-farming system is what is now – all too fashionably – called the *cucina povera*, the poor kitchen. *Cucina povera* is a misnomer. Tuscan food may be simple, but it isn't poor. It can be amazingly imaginative, occasionally even innovative, and always based on the freshest local produce. This cooking is still widely available in rural trattorias and unpretentious restaurants throughout the region. It is the basis for this book.

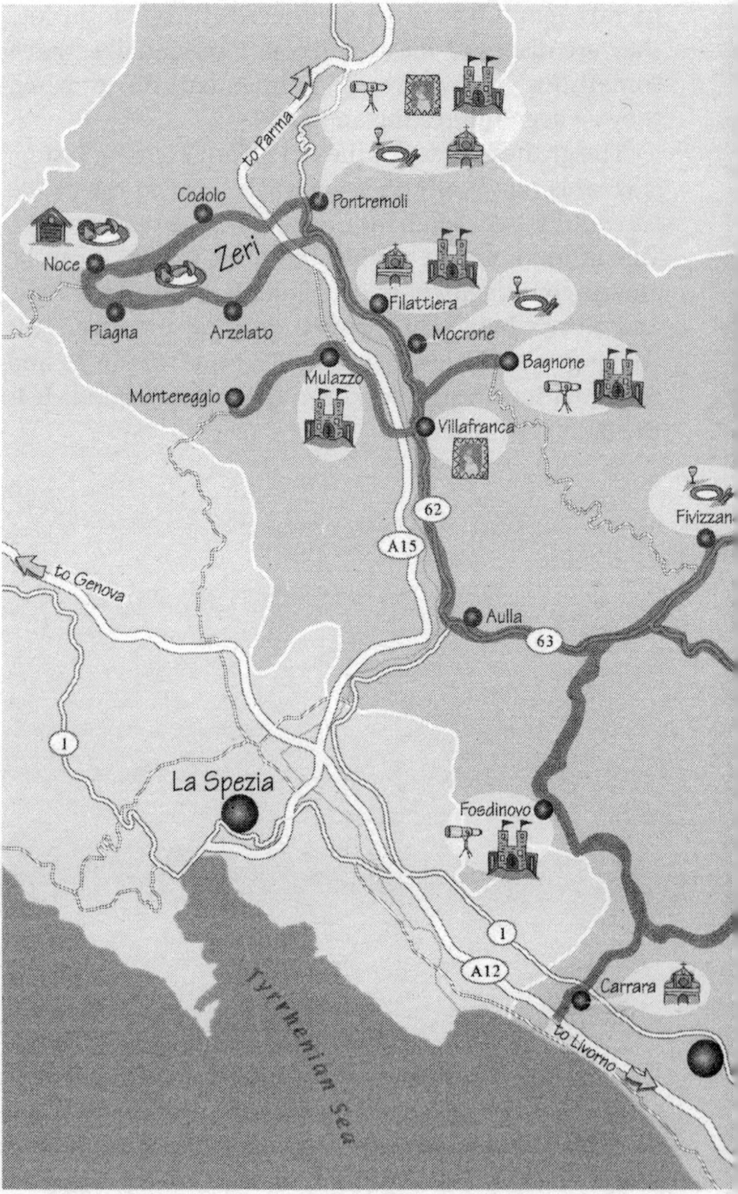
to Parma
Codolo
Pontremoli
Noce
Zeri
Piagna
Arzelato
Filattiera
Mocrone
Bagnone
Mulazzo
Montereggio
Villafranca
62
A15
Fivizzan
to Genova
Aulla
63
1
La Spezia
Fosdinovo
1
A12
Carrara
Tyrrhenian Sea
to Livorno

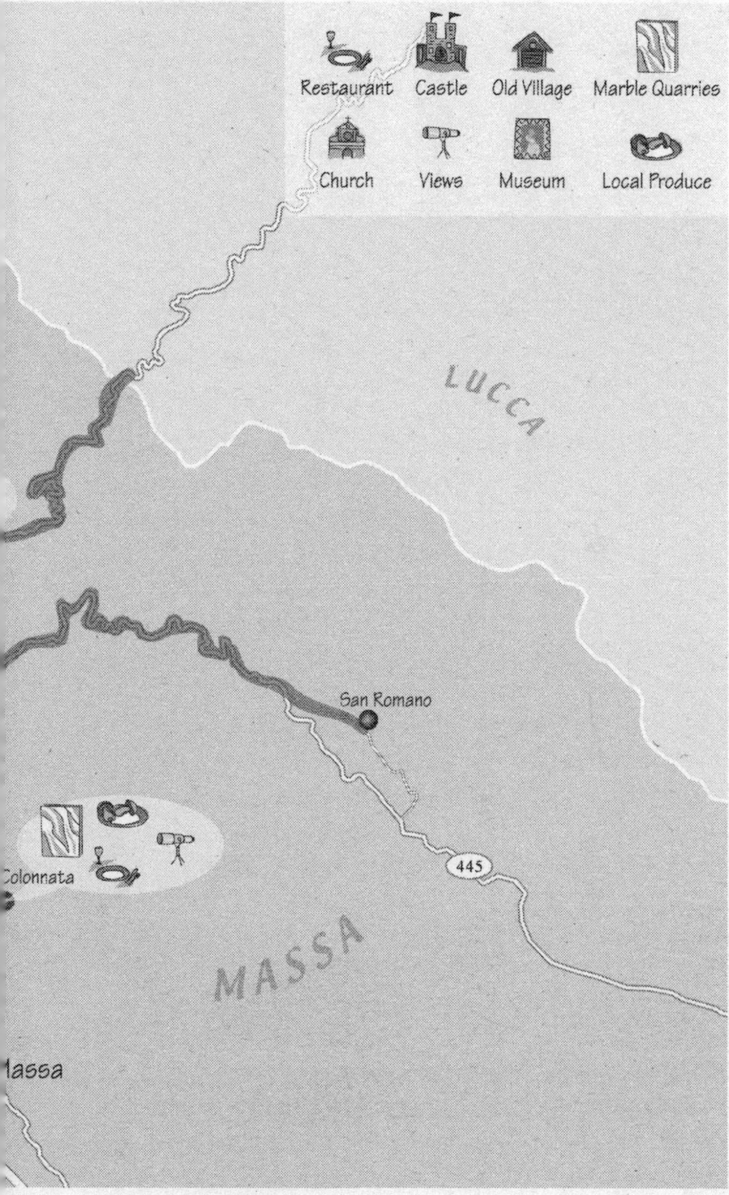

Restaurant
Castle
Old Village
Marble Quarries
Church
Views
Museum
Local Produce
LUCCA
San Romano
445
Colonnata
MASSA
Massa

1

The Lunigiana and the Mountains of Carrara

MYSTERY, LEGEND and a touch of paganism surround this most north-western area of Tuscany, in and around the Magra valley, giving its craggy mountains and looming castle ruins the feeling of an Italian Land of Dracula. Even its name – which translates loosely as Valley of the Moon – has a slightly ominous cast. An assortment of local legends evokes witches, ghosts and goblins that inhabit moonless nights, wander about castles and hang from lonely trees. Spirits of the medieval ruling Counts Malaspina still haunt evocatively named towns such as Fosdinovo, Bagnone, Fivizzano, Licciana Nardi, Filattiera, Minucciano, Filetto and Pontrémoli.

Tuscan names often seem designed to flex power or ward off the evil eye, especially those beginning with 'mal', which means 'bad' or 'evil'. The name of the man in charge of restoring our house was Malforte, or 'evil strength'. The name is quite popular in these parts. Evil he certainly wasn't, but strong, yes. We still encounter names like Malatesta ('evil head'). Maltagliati ('badly cut') designates the brand name of a well-known local pasta factory. It also happens to be the name of a local dressmaker . . . I once even met a lawyer in Pistoia called Malconsiglio ('bad advice').

Malaspina, the name of the leading noble family of the Lunigiana during the Middle Ages, means 'evil thorn', a particularly nasty surname, allowing for all kinds of interpretation. In fact, the family had two branches, locally known as the Malaspina Secca, the dry thorn, or bad Malaspina, and the Malaspina Fiorita, the flowering thorn or good branch. Dante, who spent some time with the Malaspina Secca, locked them into his Purgatory. The flowering Malaspina could be pretty awful too; a ruling count in Filattiera – his castle still sits in the main square – shot an unsuspecting suitor coming to woo his daughter.

A werewolf is said to terrorize the old *borgo* in Pontrémoli. The ghost of a maiden abused by Francesco Malaspina plays practical jokes in an old family fortress that is now a school in Mulazzo. On the road to Villafranca – no one knows exactly where – goblins and witches are said to dance around in a mysterious oak. The most famous spirit is that of the young Marchesa Malaspina of Fosdinovo, who haplessly fell in love with a stable hand and was imprisoned by her father in a windowless room of the castle. Under a full moon her long-haired ghost is still said to wander about the *castello* in a floating white gown. Such are some of the macabre old tales of the Lunigiana.

The Lunigiana is actually a lovely small mountainous corner of Tuscany, touching upon Liguria along the coast, Emilia in the north and the Garfagnana to the east. The food here is often different from the rest of Italy, dishes you won't find anywhere else. For a long time, from the tenth century on, the Lunigiana was the northern gateway to Tuscany and Italy's south. Pilgrims passed through from France along the Francigena, on their way to Rome, pausing to build churches and hospices. The church grew here on the ruins of a pagan past. Ancient stone pagan icons continue to be dug out from under old Romanesque churches; pagan legend still mingles with church tradition.

The Lunigiana includes some of the most unspoiled landscapes of the region, the Zeri valley and the foothills of the Apuan Alps. In recent years, castle ruins have been turned into museums that give a real feel of the place and its past. In Pontrémoli and Villafranca they are well worth a visit. The ancient castle in Pontrémoli displays extraordinary stelae – flat stone slabs with figures carved on to them – dug up in various parts of the Lunigiana. Interestingly enough, most of the figures have moon-shaped heads that resemble the geographical shape of the Lunigiana itself, and from where the name Luni comes. In Villafranca an old water mill has been turned into an ethnological historical museum. Popular tradition throughout the Lunigiana mingles Christian traditions with a pre-Christian religious past in festivals, amulets and superstitions.

There are several ways to approach the Lunigiana. When time is of no import, the most dramatic approach is over the Passo del Cerreto from Lucca and the Garfagnana, down the mountain through the Apuan Alps, where you never lose the dramatic view of the cold white marble mountains of Carrara. The nicest way to reach the pass is a small road that leads off from the Garfagnana main road between Castelnuovo and Castelvecchio. A lovely winding old way takes you past two pretty hill towns – Silicagnana and San Romano – and under the fortress of Verrucola, which stands on a high hill defending the entire valley. From below, it looks like a piece of the Great Wall of China. Continue along this road into the Lunigiana, down to Fivizzano, an old Medici town and today a mountain summer resort. In the restaurant of an old inn there,

Il Giardenetto, you'll find some fine traditional fare of the Lunigiana. From here you descend into the valley.

A more comprehensive way to see much of the Lunigiana is to exit the Cisa Pass *autostrada* between La Spézia and Parma at Pontrémoli, and travel the main road down through Filattiera and Villafranca to Aulla (or reverse, exiting at Aulla and heading up to Pontrémoli). Detours along the way take you to some impressive hill towns and imposing castle ruins.

Leaving the *autostrada* at Pontrémoli, a small side trip before heading into the town will take you into the valley of Zeri, an unspoiled landscape with vast vistas of the Apuan Alps and luscious green nearby hills. Among the shepherds' huts and pastures, you'll come upon a little town called Noce, a tiny centre of old stone houses with ragged slate roofs that might have been fashioned by elves. It is totally harmonious. The sound of a rushing river below enhances an eerie quiet. This is poor land, characteristically independent and proud, known for an indigenous white sheep named after it, the *zerasca,* which looks something like a cross between a small llama and a goat. A local adage tells us of the *zerasca* that the people of the valley 'eat its bread and clothe themselves with its skin'. You can circle the entire area and return on a different road to Pontrémoli.

Pontrémoli is actually a peninsula, snuggled in between the Magra and Verde rivers. Two ancient walking bridges span them, once the only way to approach the town. Today there's a modern bridge joining both sides, from which you drive up the main Via Cavour to reach Piazza del Duomo and some limited parking. From the piazza it's a short walk to Da Bussë, one of the most welcoming restaurants of the Lunigiana.

Pontrémoli has been an important strategic market

town since feudal times, under the patronage of one feudal family after another. In the seventeenth century it became part of the republic of Genoa. It is a noble little city, interesting and pretty, with baroque palaces and churches, and a castle ruin overlooking it all. The Castello del Piagnaro was never one of the Malaspina fortresses; rather it was built sometime in the ninth and tenth centuries, and later reinforced to bar the way – unsuccessfully – of northern armies passing through. Today the climb up to the castle and its archaeological museum is a splendid trudge through an ancient past. The old stone houses are supported by arches that stretch from house to house. The crest, at the gateway to the museum, affords views of the town below. Just look straight ahead, avoiding the popular housing estates and the monster of an *autostrada* looming over the landscape to the right. The way into this small museum that houses some of the important ancient finds of the area can be a bit slippery on wet days, so take care.

The big cathedral on the main square is a gaudy rococo seventeenth-century splendour, with gilded chandeliers and candelabras, in sharp contrast to the austere Romanesque churches elsewhere in the Lunigiana. It was built, a notice tells us, as 'a sumptuous noble temple, capable of holding as many people as possible'. Just off cathedral square, in the heart of old Pontrémoli, you can find some of the area's food specialities at Salumeria Angella. Owner Andrea Guiduglia has his own laboratory to season and age his pork products. Especially good are the *filletto* (paper-slim slices cut from the leanest part of the pork), the undersized mortadella and the dried *spalla* (pork shoulder). They are all seasonal products, not always available.

The road from Pontrémoli to Aulla brings you soon to Filattiera. Just before the town you'll come upon one of the loveliest Romanesque churches in Tuscany, the Pieve di Sorano sitting quietly on the edge of an old cemetery. It's a monumental granite-grey complex of a church, built over an old pagan temple. Pre-Christian idols and urns have recently been excavated. The inside is as simple and neat as the outer complex itself.

Filattiera calls itself the gate to the pilgrim's road; during the sixteenth century the little town was a major power in the area. In the cobblestoned borgo, three main roads lead from the main piazza and its perfectly proportioned fifteenth-century mini-castle of the Flowering Malaspinas. This was where the afore-mentioned 'good' Malaspina shot his daughter's suitor coming to claim her hand. The young principessa's tears are said to still flow along the wall into a carved basin. There is a handsome round bell tower in Filattiera, with a terrace on top, from which approaching enemies, as well as more amenable pilgrim groups, could be seen. At the bottom of the town the perfect little Romanesque chapel, San Giorgio, is well worth a visit. The Ospedale di San Giacomo is another old building, built to house pilgrims arriving along the Francigena on their way to Rome.

Filattiera, like so many small Tuscan towns, celebrates its food and other traditional pleasures during the summer months with a local *sagra* or *festa*. The *festa* here is appropriately called a festival of *la Fame e la Sete* (Hunger and Thirst). It takes place on the first four days of July every year. The entire town busies itself in preparation and execution. I once persuaded some friends to join me at the festival in order that we might taste just about everything offered. We came early. The smell of meat grilling on a large open wood fire at the entrance to town was already in the air. The beautiful little village square, filled with tables, was alive with what one friend likened to hobbits, dozens of small children in bright T-shirts preparing to serve all comers. Filattiera is a small place. Most of the villagers were either busy cooking at home for the event or getting ready to serve some particular dish. Local specialities included a fritter of courgette flowers, a light pancake of chestnut flour topped with the freshest ricotta cheese, pastas and fried little fresh anchovies. Freshly made local bread, called *tigelle*, was ready, waiting to be eaten while still warm.

Maria Angela Pagani had invited me into her kitchen to prepare with her a Lunigiana favourite: a vegetable pie. The Filattiera version was filled with grated courgette, green onions and potatoes, chopped chard and a lot of grated cheese. In simpler days it used to be a hardened goat's cheese, today she uses a more elegant Parmesan. The pie was made with the simplest of pastries surrounding the vegetables, top and bottom. Maria Angela worked quickly and efficiently, making it all seem effortless. It was a dish she made in one form or another almost every day, she told us, especially during seasons when fresh vegetables are available in her kitchen garden. The pie was delicious. It was a perfect lesson: an ingenious dish of the so-called *cucina povera*. The pie developed over the years to become a sophisticated, authentic delicacy. (See Maria Angela's recipe among others below.)

A small detour along the road between Filattiera and Villafranca leads to the little medieval hamlet of Bagnone, a harmonious cluster of granite houses on an almost vertical hillside. You come upon it through the gracious portal of the lower town. As you drive through the arch, the town on the hill sits directly before you. At the very top is the ever-present castle, and from its terrace you can look down at the entire valley and the mountains beyond. Along the road to Bagnone, a kilometre or so from the main road between Filattiera and Villafranca, there's a very pleasant garden restaurant, Gavarini, around a bend in the small nondescript town called Mocrone.

Villafranca in Lunigiana is a valley town almost destroyed during the Second World War; the ruin of yet another Malaspina castle dominates it. Villafranca was often recorded by pilgrims passing through. The area ethnological museum is here, a good introduction to the culture and ethnology of the Lunigiana, its Christian and pagan past, its symbols and charms against illness, danger and the ever threatening risk of bad harvest. Amulets protecting against 'the evil eye' abound. (Ethnological Museum of the Lunigiana, Via Ponte Vecchio. Tel. 0187 493417. Summer 4–7, winter 9–12/ 3–6. Closed Monday.)

Other towns off the main road to wander through include Filetto, an ancient little walled borgo with a single main street ending in old arches on both ends; the remains of a castle form part of the surrounding wall. Go by foot along the main street and you'll note a small, perfect urban design, a fine piazza at its centre. Here a lively festival takes place every August, usually the second week. The local population dresses in costumes of past centuries; food specialities and a medieval artisan market fill the streets.

Mulazzo is off the north/south axis. To reach it from Villafranca you pass under the *autostrada* that cuts through the Lunigiana. You find yet another Malaspina castle, more notable because Dante Alighieri spent part of his exile here working on *The Divine Comedy*. The

Malaspina in Mulazzo were of the Secca branch, the bad Malaspina; Dante locks them into his Purgatory. One Malaspina, Alessandro, was a well-known seventeenth-century scientist and explorer. The Spanish claim, as they do with Christopher Columbus, that he was one of them.

A bit further up the same road is totally isolated old Montereggio, seemingly tucked away in nowhere, but strangely enough bearing in street and piazza names all the greats of modern Italian publishing: Mondadori, Rizzoli, Einaudi. In this little mountain village during the sixteenth century, a great Lunigiana cultural tradition of bookselling was born. Somehow, villagers here took on the role of itinerant booksellers, and from Montereggio went on to become major publishers and booksellers all over Europe. One of Italy's major literary prizes – the Premio Bancarella – is awarded here.

Aulla, at the southern end of the Tuscan Lunigiana, has always been a transit point, mostly for pilgrims and armies. It boasts the obligatory Malaspina castle but otherwise little else. From Aulla you can travel over the mountains to Fosdinovo, where the most complete and imposing Malaspina castle sits on a hill ruling the entire landscape. It is, in fact, still the summer home of the Counts Malaspina. (The castle, with many of its ancient rooms still intact, is visitable by appointment: 0187 68891.) The ancient town ambles down from the castle.

From Fosdinovo there is another spectacular mountain road down to Carrara.

Massa/Carrara

It's a moot point as to whether the twin towns of

Massa/Carrara, south of Aulla, are part of the Lunigiana. When one thinks of the Lunigiana, the two towns don't come to mind, and yet Massa has the biggest Malaspina castle of them all.

Carrara has its great marble mountain looming over the town to the east. Drive through the centre of Carrara and up the mountain, eight kilometres through cascading white marble to some of the oldest quarries. Here Michelangelo personally supervised cutting the blocks he needed for his sculptures. Each sculpture meant months of scouring the quarries for the perfect block. The marble for *David*, the *Pietà*, *Nicodemus*, *Moses* and other major pieces came from here. The close-up view of the spectacular mountain begins soon after you leave Carrara. The vista opens. The marble mountain lies just opposite. You can visit the quarries from where Michelangelo and others sent the great blocks down to the sea on carts pulled by up to twenty oxen. Loaded on to barges, the blocks were carried along the coast to the mouth of the Arno and from there to Florence. From the Lungarno in Florence, teams of labourers carted them off to the nearby studio.

From the quarries, continue on up to the almost hidden little hamlet of Colonnata. Quarry workers have lived here for centuries, nourished by a local speciality, *lardo di Colonnata*, the seasoned and aged lard of Colonnata. For centuries almost unknown outside of here, these delicious hunks of fat have been discovered by food lovers in recent years, and the food is now cherished all over Europe. The little town has thrived on its new notoriety. The little piazza of Colonnata has been smartly paved in decorated marble slabs. Near the square a small staircase leads on to a theatrical setting that affords an awesome view of the marble mountain opposite; the little terrace also includes a rather startling modern marble tribute to the quarry workers of past centuries.

◆ Specialities of the area ◆

Lardo di Colonnata is only one of the special foods of this area. The Lunigiana is probably the most autonomous of Tuscan areas in how it eats, and its specialities are mostly unknown elsewhere in Tuscany. One notable dish is *testeroli al pesto*, the particular pasta of the area eaten in the familiar basil-based sauce. It's not really a pasta, but more like a quickly baked crêpe that's then sliced into little squares and boiled, drained and smothered in the special pesto of Lunigiana.

Testeroli take their name from the pan in which the first baking happens, the *testo*, a large round baking dish with a tightly fitting domed cover. I've seen them mostly in copper or even tin; the original *testi* were of earthenware. I searched in vain for a *testo* – even an old one – all over the Lunigiana; it seems to be a utensil of the past, although I did see one or another in almost every restaurant and home I happened upon. *Testeroli* are still made in the old way; in the Lunigiana the finished product can be bought in every food or bread shop.

The *testo* was the major cooking utensil of the farmhouse. It could be used to make *crescente*, the round loaf of Lunigiana (bread is salted here, unlike in other parts of Tuscany), the large vegetable pies so typical of the area and various chestnut-flour flatbreads and cakes. All were cooked in the ashes of the big open fireplace, both the plate and cover maintaining a uniform heat. The *testo* first came into use long ago with shepherds and woodsmen who went off for periods to live in huts in arable grazing land or forests. The *testo* they took with them cooked a splendid variety of dishes from the simple provisions they could muster.

As in other mountainous regions of Tuscany, chestnuts and chestnut flour have provided basic sustenance throughout history. It is estimated that two-thirds of the daily intake of calories once came from chestnuts. In our own days of more easily milled wheat and corn, chestnut flour has become something of a luxury. The simplest preparation is called a *pattona* in the Lunigiana: chestnut flour cooked to a soft paste in salted water, mixed with milk and served as an accompaniment to roasts. *Panigacci* are 'wet bread' baked with the same mixture.

There's also a fine oversized bean here, tasty and tender, its local cult status testament to the value Tuscans invest in their beans. This particular bean doesn't get much further than the hills of the Lunigiana. I discovered it quite by accident. A waiter in Fivizzano mentioned that a famous local bean came from the village of Bigliolo, on the way from Fivizzano to Aulla. My husband is a bean lover; a search for the village was irresistible. Unfortunately the small road that was marked for Bigliolo seemed to lead nowhere. I stopped at the first cluster of houses where a few people were in evidence. It was Bigliolo. An open doorway led me into a wine storeroom and a family absorbed in the monthly transfer of their new wine from one demijohn to another. When I asked about the bean, they looked perplexed. Then one of the women ignited with a spark of recognition. A farmer just down the road might have the bean, she said. It was more than just down the road, but we did find Luigi Perdrelli, his wife Giulia and the bean, along with some young farm lamb that Giulia was chopping into cuts for the Easter market.

There was also a slew of farm animals and some splendid olive oil. We went off with a package of the little-known Bigliolo bean along with some very tender lamb. The bean was perfect in a *farro* soup. (There's more about *farro* later; see page 78). I'm still looking for another reputedly fine bean in the Lunigiana, *fagioli con il grembiule* – beans with a vest. It grows in the Zeri valley, but we've not yet found it.

The real speciality of the Zeri valley is the aboriginal zerasca baby lamb, which is raised only in this small valley north-west of Pontrémoli. The little animal is almost unknown elsewhere in Italy, and probably the world as well. It pastures during the entire year, its milk going only to feed its young, giving it a particular soft and delicate flavour. Ask for it when you're in a Lunigiana restaurant; I found it in Mocrone, at Gavarini. (The lamb we brought home from Bigliolo was tender and tasty, but not Zerasca.)

Lunigiana is also special territory for beekeepers. For more than 500 years they have been producing honey in the same valley woods between the Apuan Alps and the Apennines, an area with low humidity and lots of varied wild flowers for bees to suckle on. Acacia and chestnut honey from the Lunigiana are among the most desirable in Tuscany.

Vegetable tarts, ubiquitous in the Lunigiana, come in many variations according to local whim and season. They are a speciality you won't find elsewhere in Tuscany, except perhaps in the nearby Garfagnana. A product of the farm kitchen, they encase a variety of vegetables in simple pastry. The vegetables that go into the tart come right from the garden, mostly potatoes, Swiss chard, onions, cabbage and kale in the winter and, in the summer, a greater variety that includes courgette, spinach and wild asparagus. In some towns cheeses are added, in others not. The choice of cheese also varies from town to town; originally it was strictly the cheese of the local sheep, ricotta and aged pecorino. In Pontrémoli tarts you'll still find ricotta cheese. Everywhere the tarts are delicious local favourites, home and restaurant staples throughout the area. I've included a number of recipes from various restaurants. Those with just vegetables and some grated cheese are the lightest, those with ricotta are richer. But each reflects the particular taste of the area.

Stuffed baked vegetables are another dish of the Lunigiana. This too was traditionally a way of extending the seasonal provision into a main course. In the autumn there are wild mushroom caps, in winter cabbage leaves and onions, spring and summer bring courgettes and their flowers, peppers, aubergines and Swiss chard. The stuffing is without meat, usually of breadcrumbs mixed with a flavourful combination of garlic, herbs, grated sheep's cheese and soft ricotta, with eggs to hold it together.

As I mentioned above, marble-white *lardo di Colonnata,* slices of pork fat deliciously seasoned and aged, has turned a little town above Carrara into a place of culinary pilgrimage. Once the hearty lunch of the quarry workers – Colonnata was their home – this little slab of shiny white pork fat has become a delicacy. Its fame, and Colonnata's fortune, arrived in a backhanded way. Few had heard of *lardo* before someone suggested – probably in Brussels – outlawing it, not only in Italy but throughout the European Community. As with non-pasteurized French cheeses, San Daniele prosciutto and other treasures of gastronomic Europe, an uproar ensued. *Lardo* became the centre of a controversy that spread through Europe, with all the ensuing attention. The ruling was rescinded. The best result is that now we're all craving and enjoying *lardo di Colonnata*.

My first experience with the seasoned pork fat came some years ago, before all the controversy, at a dinner party in Lucca. A great hunk was sitting in the middle of the table. I couldn't believe that we were expected to eat this slab of fat. 'Taste it,' urged a friend, as he carefully sliced a paper-thin sliver and wrapped it around a piece of toast. I did, not without trepidation, and instantly became a *lardo* fan.

Traditionally the quarry workers of Colonnata went off on winter mornings carrying their lunch: some *lardo*, a sliver of preserved tomato and a crust of bread to ward off the chill of the stone with calories. It is a tradition that dates back to the eleventh century. Pigs were raised here then, skinny and underfed. No longer. The fat comes from rich pigs now, mostly from Parma, and much more gets produced. Since the uproar, the little quarry-workers' town has turned its attention from marble to *lardo*. The two original *lardo* producers in Colonnata have expanded to include almost all the families in the little village. Thousands arrive for the *Sagra di Lardo*, celebrated here in mid-August.

The fat is heavily seasoned in layers of salt and a great number of herbs and spices that includes black pepper, rosemary, garlic, sage, oregano, cinnamon, coriander seeds, nutmeg and anise. Once seasoned and layered, it is bathed in a water and salt solution, covered and allowed to age in heavy marble vats for a minimum of six months. The end product resembles a slim block of streaked white stone. It's sliced paper thin, and wrapped around an olive-oiled slice of toast, then heated gently, to make the most delectable little bruschetta imaginable.

Typical restaurants and their recipes

FIVIZZANO: Il Giardinetto

Il Giardinetto, Via Roma 155, Fivizzano.
Tel. 0585 92060. Closed Mondays. Priced moderately.

WALK UP THE STAIRS at this charming little hotel and you feel as though you've entered someone's parlour. But for the extraordinary odours emanating from the nearby kitchen, the dining room at Il Giardinetto could be somewhere in England. It's a family home from the early twentieth century; stained-glass doors lead into the old wood-lined gracious dining room, complete with the urn of silk flowers that sits at one end, and various family portraits and drawings that cover the walls.

Il Giardinetto is owned by the Mercandini family. The grandparents of the current Mercandinis opened the restaurant some eighty years ago. With each generation the place has expanded a bit, and it is today a decently sized hotel. The same traditional kitchen still serves the dishes of all those years ago.

You'll find many of the area's traditional dishes at this little hotel in the mountains of the Lunigiana. *Testeroli al pesto* is the traditional starter, after some local salami and prosciutto that comes with preserved vegetables. If a vegetable tart has been made in the morning, that's on the menu as well. Lamb is served with *polenta incatenata*, polenta in chains. A speciality of the house is *bomba di riso*, the festive rice dish of the Lunigiana. It can be ordered in advance. It's a celebration, a true bomb: a large mould of deliciously flavoured rice filled with game birds (pigeon or quail), sausages, various cuts of veal and innards.

Wild berries from the surrounding mountains are

always on the menu, fresh during the summer, preserved during other seasons. House speciality is *semi-freddo di myrtille*, a soft ice-cream mould with wild blueberries.

RECIPES FROM Il Giardinetto

Testeroli with pesto / *Testeroli al pesto*

Testeroli are rarely made at home these days. They are available everywhere in the Lunigiana, either fresh or vacuum-packed from the local grocer. There are those who claim this as the first Italian pasta; archaeological discoveries lend credence to the idea. The traditional method, in the covered *testo*, required no turning. This method does. Use the largest frying pan available.

Serves 6

500g flour
Enough water to make a batter that can slowly pour into the frying pan to cover: about 600ml
Pinch of salt
1 tablespoon extra virgin olive oil
½ potato
Olive oil, for frying

Put the flour into a bowl and slowly add the water, mixing all the while, to make a thick liquid batter. Add the salt and the tablespoon of olive oil, and mix again.

Dip the potato half in some olive oil and lightly oil a large frying pan. Heat the pan, and pour in just enough batter to make a disc about 1cm thick. Lower the heat, cover the pan and cook for about 2 minutes. Turn and cook for another 2 minutes. Repeat to use all the batter.

Roll up each *testerolo* (to save space) and allow to cool. They will keep, wrapped and refrigerated, for several days. To prepare, cut each disc into diamond shapes or squares of about 10cm, and toss into boiling water to cook for another few minutes. Drain and serve with a thick sauce of pesto.

Pesto

2 large bunches of fresh basil leaves
2 tablespoons pine nuts
2 garlic cloves
½ teaspoon salt, or more to taste
50g freshly grated aged pecorino cheese
25g freshly grated Parmesan cheese
180ml extra virgin olive oil

Combine the basil leaves, pine nuts, garlic, salt, cheese and oil in a blender or food processor and process to a smooth paste. It should be creamy, but not too thick. Add a bit more oil and some of the testeroli cooking water if necessary.

Polenta in chains / *Polenta incatenata*

When I asked my young host at Il Giardinetto why this substantial dish was 'in chains', he said he wasn't too sure, that perhaps it was such a heavy bundle that it could be tied. This would be a tough thing to do, but I lack any other explanation. It may be heavy, but it's very tasty.

Serves 6

150g dried borlotti beans
1 small bunch kale leaves
2.5 litres water
1 teaspoon salt
120ml extra virgin olive oil
400g corn meal (polenta)
Parmesan or aged pecorino cheese to grate at table

Soak the beans overnight. Chop the kale leaves well, removing any large core pieces. Drain the beans and put into a large pot with the water. Bring to a boil, lower the heat, and cook at a simmer until almost tender, about 45 minutes. Add the salt, chopped kale and olive oil, and slowly pour in the polenta, a handful at a time, stirring all the time to ensure no lumps. When the polenta has been added, turn up the heat a bit and cook until the entire mash is thick and smooth, about 45 minutes.

If you are using instant polenta, allow the beans to cook until soft and tender before adding the polenta.

Serve with lots of grated cheese at the table.

PONTRÉMOLI: Da Bussë

Da Bussë, Piazza Duomo 31, Pontrémoli.
Tel. 0187 831371. Closed Fridays and first three weeks of July. Open for lunch daily, weekends also dinner. Reservations recommended. Priced moderately.

TALKING ABOUT FOOD with Antonetta Bertocchi at Da Bussë is great fun, a pleasure surpassed only by the eating. She practically fondles the pesto that will accompany her *testeroli*. She pounds the fragrant basil by hand, with just the right amount of garlic. Perfectly aged pecorino cheese comes next, and finally a precise amount of fresh olive oil from a nearby mill, 'never any other'.

She spoons out a taste of her soothing *salsa verde* that goes with the special young beef *bollito* served daily at Da Bussë. In the winter she adds a *cotechino*, a sausage-like stuffed shin of pork, to the *bollito*. She manages it all by herself in a sparse well-organized kitchen. But for a simple mixer, the small space is unencumbered by machines. The great earthenware casserole she uses for most of her dishes sits on the old stove. She talks with a mother's love about the ingredients she handles, giving a taste here, a demonstration there.

Antonetta plans her menu as you might at home. On the front door is a sign announcing, 'We serve no funghi here.' When I asked her why, she told me it just isn't her thing. She plans her menus the evening before; wild mushrooms are not something she can plan for next day, so she doesn't serve them.

Testeroli and *bollito* are always on the menu, as are traditional vegetable pies, delicately stuffed cabbage leaves and, on Wednesdays and Saturdays – market days in Pontrémoli – Da Bussë's famous *la zuppa*, a ragú in broth served over the thinnest slice of *pagniaccio*, a local, lightly salted bread. The stew is topped with a grating of aged pecorino.

The restaurant is open on weekdays only for lunch, but its small stand-up bar becomes a kind of men's club at dusk. The men stop by after work for their evening glass of wine. No food is served at this hour, but the talk seems mostly about it. Enquire of a particular dish and they'll know everything about it, and talk with great lust about the preparation of *testeroli* and the meats that go into a *bollito*.

The restaurant consists of four small appealing rooms, with walls frescoed in gentle floral patterns by Antonetta's sister-in-law. Da Bussë has been in the family for years. It was begun by Antonetta's father in 1930, with her mother as cook. Today Antonetta and her sister, who helps out with the serving, continue the traditions of their parents.

RECIPES FROM *Da Bussë*

◆ Vegetable-stuffed cabbage / *Carolo ripieno*

Serves 6

1 Savoy cabbage
1.25kg Swiss chard, with hard white core removed
1 bunch parsley leaves
½ clove garlic
200g ricotta cheese
2 eggs
2 large handfuls freshly grated Parmesan cheese
Olive oil
Salt and freshly ground pepper

FOR THE SAUCE:

2 cloves garlic
1 bunch parsley leaves
2 tablespoons olive oil
1 x 800g tin tomatoes, removed from juice and chopped
250ml meat stock

Carefully separate the cabbage leaves. Chop 2 or 3 of the outer leaves finely together with the chard, the parsley leaves and garlic. Salt well and place in a colander to drain.

Boil the remaining whole leaves for 5 minutes and drain in another colander.

Squeeze dry the chopped vegetables, and add the ricotta, eggs and grated cheese. Dry the cabbage leaves and place a tablespoon of filling into each. Fold each stuffed leaf into a loose bundle and tuck them all together, with the fold underneath, in a well-oiled flameproof earthenware casserole. Pour over the following sauce.

For the sauce, chop the garlic and parsley together and sauté them with the oil in a large pan. When the oil around the garlic begins to bubble, add the chopped tomatoes and cook over a medium heat until the sauce thickens, about 10 minutes. Pour the sauce over the cabbage, add enough meat stock to cover, and simmer over a low heat for 1 to 1½ hours. Serve warm.

Swiss chard or spinach pie / *Torta di verdure*

For this and the following pie, you need a 40cm baking dish.

Serves 8 generously

FOR THE PASTRY:

500g plain white flour
Salt
2 tablespoons extra virgin olive oil
Warm water

FOR THE FILLING:

1.5kg Swiss chard or spinach
2 eggs
2 big handfuls freshly grated Parmesan cheese
200g ricotta cheese
Large handful breadcrumbs
Salt and freshly ground pepper
Olive oil

Wash and chop the chard or spinach into thin strips. Salt well, place in a colander and allow to sit for at least an hour. Squeeze out the water, put back in the colander and let it sit some more. Squeeze again as hard as possible.

Place the chard or spinach in a large bowl, add the eggs, cheeses, breadcrumbs and lots of freshly ground pepper. Taste and add salt if needed.

To make the pastry: put the flour and a good amount – about a tablespoon – of salt in a mound on a working surface, make a hole in the middle and add the oil. Slowly add warm water, working the flour into it. Knead well until the dough has reached a consistency that is soft but malleable, and easy to roll out. Divide into two balls. Heat the oven to 180°C/Gas 4.

Flour a work surface and gently roll out one ball of pastry into a paper-thin round that will fit into the bottom of the well-oiled baking dish. Fill the dish with the vegetables and spread evenly. Roll the second ball into another paper-thin round and cover. Brush the top surface with olive oil and bake for about an hour. Serve warm. Leftovers can be heated and served again.

Rice and onion pie / *Torta di riso e cipolle*

This is another perfect example of the inventiveness of *cucina povera*. You need a 40cm shallow baking dish.

Serves 10
Pastry as on page 57

1.5kg onions
Coarse salt
200g rice
200g ricotta cheese
2 big handfuls freshly grated Parmesan cheese
3 eggs, beaten
Salt and freshly ground pepper
2 tablespoons olive oil

Slice the onions, not too thinly, sprinkle well with coarse salt and place in a colander to drain off their bitter juices for about an hour. Squeeze out the water well, wash the onions and squeeze dry again, this time in a kitchen towel.

In a large bowl, mix the raw rice with the onions. Add the two cheeses, mix well, then stir in the beaten eggs. Add salt if needed and lots of freshly ground black pepper.

Make the dough as on page 57 and prepare the tart in the same way. Brush the top with olive oil and bake at 180°C/Gas 4 for about an hour.

Piquant green sauce for bollito / *Salsa verde*

Makes about 240ml

1 large bunch parsley leaves
3 hard-boiled eggs
5 anchovy fillets, washed
2 tablespoons capers in vinegar, drained and washed
1 thick slice country bread, soaked in red wine vinegar
Salt, if necessary, and freshly ground pepper
About 180ml extra virgin olive oil

Chop the parsley leaves finely together with the hard-boiled eggs, anchovies and capers. Squeeze the bread dry and add in grain-like pieces to the sauce. Add freshly ground pepper and salt to taste, and cover with olive oil. Can be stored in the refrigerator for several days.

FILATTIERA
Maria Angela Pagani's vegetable pie / *Torta d'erbe*

This is a recipe that I watched Maria Angela Pagani prepare in her Filattiera home. The vegetables came from her garden that morning. She makes the tart in a large 40cm pan; I've done it in a paella pan of about 35 cm.

Serves 8 generously

5 medium-sized courgettes
1 bunch Swiss chard
6 large spring onions, with the edible green
Salt
500g plain white flour
Warm water
4 tablespoons extra virgin olive oil
3 large potatoes, peeled and grated
150g freshly grated Parmesan cheese

Grate the courgettes into a colander. Chop the chard and add to the courgettes. Mix well with a good amount of salt, and leave for an hour or two to eliminate as much water as possible. Into another colander, grate the onions, including as much of the green as is fresh. Salt well and leave to drain.

Make the pastry. Put the flour with about a table-spoon of salt and 2 tablespoons of olive oil into a bowl and add water slowly, working it into the flour. When it reaches a sticky but firm consistency, start to work it into a pastry, kneading and adding more flour as necessary. Work the dough for about 5 minutes, until it has some elasticity.

Wash the grated vegetables well and squeeze out as much water as possible. Mix them all together. Add the potatoes, cheese and remaining oil and mix well. Add salt to taste.

Heat the oven to 200°C/Gas 6.

Roll out the dough into two very thin discs, one a bit larger than the other. Line a large baking pan with baking paper, and place the larger disc on the bottom. Spread the filling evenly across the bottom. Place the smaller disc on top and fold the edges of bottom disc over, closing the tart. With wet hands, slap the top all over. With a fork, prick holes all over the top.

Bake the tart for about 40 minutes, until the top is slightly brown and the vegetables cooked. Serve hot or warm. If there are leftovers, heat them again before serving.

MOCRONE: Restaurant Gavarini

Gavarini, off the road to Bagnone, between Filattiera and Villafranca.
Tel. 0187 493115. Closed Wednesdays, except in August when it is open every day. Closed February. Priced moderately. Best to reserve, especially in summer months.

THE LITTLE TOWN of Mocrone lies just off the main provincial road between Filattiera and Villafranca. Turn at the sign to Bagnone, and you'll soon see a sign on the left for Mocrone and the restaurant Gavarini. Follow the road around (it becomes frighteningly narrow) and on the small Piazza Benedicenti you'll find the inauspicious entrance to Gavarini, behind which a large and welcoming restaurant with an adjacent garden for summer dining awaits.

Even in winter it's cheery. Large picture windows framed with sheer orange draperies look out to the garden beyond. Gavarini has been a family restaurant for four generations. It is currently run by Nadia Folloni, her husband Pierangelo and their son Fabio. Nadia's grandmother actually turned her popular little *forno* (*forno* actually means oven, and is the name by which bread bakeries are called in Italy, traditionally it was a wood oven and called *forno a legna*) into the restaurant. It was expanded by mother Elvezia and the menu hasn't really varied since. It is seasonal and features specialities of the region: *testeroli* with pesto, vegetable tarts, *farro* soups and a chestnut flour pasta. *Sgabei,* little quickly fried puffs of bread filled with bits of ragú, are served with the *antipasto*. A favourite *antipasto* is the *torta di cipolle,* a thin pastry with lots of fresh onions sliced right into it. Twenty-two vegetables go into the *minestra di verdure* – vegetable soup – in a six-hour preparation. *Chicchere della nonna* are little gnocchi, swimming in a tomato cream sauce. A *bomba di riso* is the festive dish of the region and can be pre-ordered. I first tasted the notable lamb of the Zeri valley here; it was tender and succulent. Lamb chops are always on the menu; sometimes an entire crown is as well. The dessert not to miss is *pasticcio della nonna,* crumbled amaretto cookies with whipped cream and melted chocolate on top.

The restaurant has recently expanded into a small guest house and has added an atmospheric wine bar, where a different menu is offered. There you'll find a good selection of cheeses and wines from all over Italy.

RECIPES FROM *Gavarini*

Fried bread / *Sgabei*

Makes about 30 fried rolls

500g plain white flour
10g beer yeast
1 heaped teaspoon (10g) salt
Enough water to form soft dough: about 240ml
Vegetable or peanut oil for frying

Combine all the ingredients in a bowl and leave in a warm place to rise for an hour. Roll out into a width of about 1cm, and cut into strips about 2–3cm wide and 5cm long.

Heat about 4–5cm of vegetable or peanut oil in a heavy pan, until hot. Throw in the strips and fry until golden and puffed up. Drain on to a paper towel and serve hot, with any number of fillings. I like them best with ricotta or another soft white cheese.

Polenta and onion tart / *Torta di polenta e cipolle*

Serves 6

4 large onions, sliced thinly
200g polenta (not instant)
50g plain white flour
50g freshly grated Parmesan cheese
1 teaspoon salt
About 500ml milk
2 tablespoons olive oil
Freshly ground pepper

Put the sliced onions in a large bowl with cold water to cover for about an hour. Heat the oven to 180°C/Gas 4. Drain and dry the onions, pressing out the liquid in a dry cloth. Mix the dry ingredients well, and add the milk and oil to make a fairly thin batter. Add the onions and mix well. Taste and add more salt if needed. Line a shallow baking dish, about 30 by 40cm, with baking paper, oil lightly and pour in the batter. Spread evenly, and bake until golden and firm, about an hour.

◆ Winter vegetable tart / *Torta d'inverno*

Another version of the Lunigiana tart. Make a simple pastry with 500g flour, 2 tablespoons olive oil, salt and enough water to make a dough that can be easily rolled out. Let it rest while you prepare the filling.

Serves 6–8

500g Swiss chard (or borage, if available)
2 leeks, finely chopped
2 potatoes, cubed
150g freshly grated Parmesan cheese
180ml olive oil

Wash and salt the chard and lay in a colander for half an hour to release its water. Squeeze well to remove as much water as possible. Chop and place in a bowl. Add the leeks, potato cubes, cheese and oil.

Heat the oven to 200°C/Gas 6.

Roll out the dough large enough to line and re-cover

an oiled rectangular baking dish, about 30 by 40cm. Lay the dough over the pan, and fill with the prepared vegetables. Bring the dough back over the vegetables to cover as much as possible. Punch a few holes with a fork into the covering dough and drip some more olive oil over.

Bake for 30–40 minutes, until the top is golden.

COLONNATA: Ristorante Venanzio

Ristorante Venanzio, Piazza Palestro 3, Colonnata, Carrara.
Tel. 0585 758062; fax 0585 758033. Open every day lunch and dinner during the summer; other months closing day is Thursday, as well as Sunday evening. Also closed from Christmas Eve to 10 January. Best to call first; reservations are necessary during the summer months, especially August. Priced moderately. The *menu degustazione* is also moderately priced.

VENANZIO WAS THE FIRST owner of this little gem of a restaurant on the main piazza of Colonnata. Thirty years ago, quarry workers would end their days with a drink and something to eat here. Two long-time employees took it over a few years ago and kept the name. Today, rather than workers, owners and managers of the great quarries arrive with their foreign business associates – buyers and agents – for a lunch that's a touch more sophisticated.

He is still in his twenties, but chef Alessio Lucchetti has already been working in the kitchen for twelve years. He began to work summers for Venanzio while still in hotel school in nearby Massa. Roberto Ferlini, the genial manager and host, has been at Venanzio's for twenty years. He works the *lardo*, seasons and stores it in the marble vat. He has become a master of the art. Restaurateurs from all over Europe, and even, surreptitiously, from the United States – where it is indeed prohibited – come to buy chunks of *lardo* from him. He delights in discussing the process of ageing it, and showing off the marble vat in which it soaks up all the goodness. He's also developed a carpaccio of beef that's put for a week or so into the seasoning. The restaurant is still pretty much a family affair. Roberto's wife Anna is in the kitchen with Alessio – she makes the light delectable pasta – while Alessio's fiancée Pamela is out in front with Roberto.

This is a restaurant where I'd go for the *menu degustazione*, a taste of everything. The great variety and taste of all the starters makes it hard to choose, so it's easier to choose them all. There is, to begin with, the paper-thin slices of *lardo* served on warmed, almost toasted, bread. From there go on to delicately stuffed courgette flowers, the *torta di zucchini* and the simple platter of single-layered *melanzane alla parmigiana*. Pasta arrives next, ravioli stuffed with meat and Swiss chard, enhanced with a bit of chopped fried *lardo* and topped with a fresh tomato sauce. Another pasta is *lasagnetta*, thick green noodles made with borage – a wild green much used in the northern Tuscan home kitchen – and served, in autumn and winter, with a sauce of wild mushrooms. Main courses include a rabbit, boned and stuffed with *lardo*, or a guinea hen stuffed and served with a truffle sauce (black in the early autumn, white when they come into season later).

Desserts are the only thing that come out of the freezer; Alessio and Roberto boast that almost everything – save the *lardo* – in their little out-of-the-way restaurant is absolutely fresh, brought up to Colonnata in the morning to cook for lunch. They live down the mountain in Carrara, so it's less of a feat than it might seem. But I liked it when Roberto told me they make their own olive oil. This is not olive country, it's much too high. So Roberto buys his olives from a farmer he knows in nearby Lucca and takes them to the *frantoio* to be crushed into oil. He wants to know the oil he's serving.

The desserts are good. My favourite ending to the meal is a local sheep's cheese that's also been aged in a marble vat and is served with a candied-fruit mustard. Other desserts are seasonal; there's a coconut or chocolate mousse served with fresh-fruit sauce or an apple tart made with calvados. Others come according to the whim of the day.

RECIPES FROM *Venanzo*

Ravioli in fresh tomato sauce / *Ravioli con salsa pomodoro*

Serves 6

100g *lardo di Colonnata* (or solid lard), finely chopped
3 tablespoons olive oil
1 onion, finely chopped
4 cloves garlic, finely chopped
1kg mixed chopped meat, including beef, pork and veal
1.5kg Swiss chard, cooked, squeezed dry and chopped
1.5kg fresh ripe tomatoes
25g butter
100g Parmesan cheese, freshly grated
Pasta made from 500g flour, 4 eggs, 1 teaspoon olive oil, salt

To make the filling, fry the lard in 1 tablespoon of the oil, then add the onion and garlic. As the lard becomes crisp, add the meat, to brown it. When the meat has lost its redness, add the chard and 2 of the tomatoes, chopped. Add salt and pepper to taste, cook for another few minutes and set aside. If necessary, chop all the ingredients together roughly in a food processor using the pulse button.

Prepare the pasta, kneading well, and roll out thinly (using a pasta maker if available) into strips about 6cm wide. Dot teaspoons of filling along each strip, leaving 5cm between each one. Cover with another strip of pasta, and cut – with a ravioli cutter – into squares. Separate, making sure each is closed well.

Drop the remaining tomatoes into boiling water to skin them. Squeeze out the juice, chop and sauté gently in the butter and remaining olive oil.

Drop the ravioli into a big wide pot of boiling salted water. Remove with a slotted spoon about 30 seconds after the ravioli have risen to the top on to a serving dish, pour the tomato sauce over them and add the Parmesan cheese.

Stuffed courgette flowers / *Fiori di zucca ripieni*

These are about the most delicate stuffed flowers I've tasted.

About 30 flowers, serves 6–8

100g ham, cubed
250g ricotta cheese
2 eggs, beaten
3 tablespoons freshly grated Parmesan cheese
Salt
Freshly grated nutmeg
30 courgette flowers
1kg tomatoes, squeezed of juices and seeds and chopped
120ml vegetable stock

Mix the ham with the ricotta and eggs. Fold in the grated cheese, and add salt to taste and a good grating of nutmeg.

Carefully open the flowers along the side without breaking them completely and take off the yellow pistil inside. Oil a large baking dish in which you can lay the flowers side by side. Spoon a teaspoon of the filling into each flower and close it into an envelope, first the sides, and then by folding the top over. As you work, lay the flowers in the baking dish. Heat the oven to 250°C or as hot as it will go.

Pour the stock over the flowers, add the tomatoes and bake for no longer than 10 minutes, when the stock begins to bubble. It is important not to allow the flowers to overcook; you don't want to cook the filling. Remove carefully and serve.

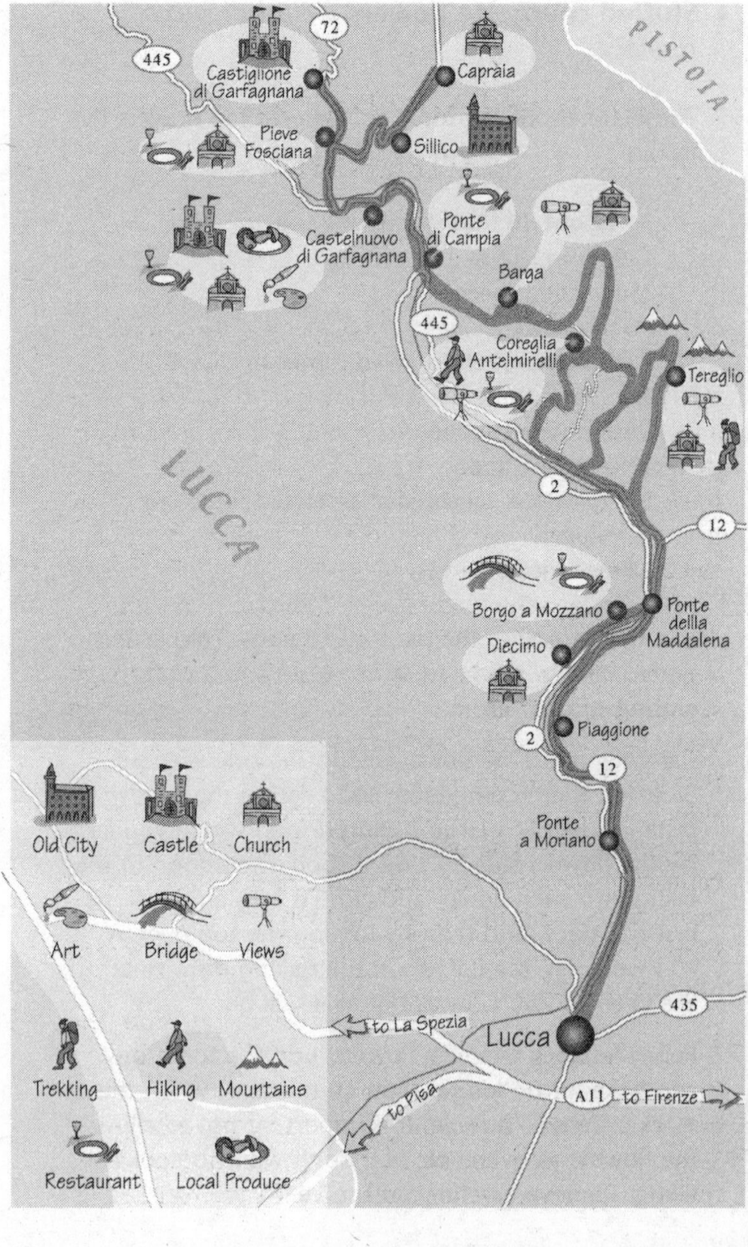

72
445
Castiglione di Garfagnana
Capraia
PISTOIA
Pieve Fosciana
Sillico
Ponte di Campia
Castelnuovo di Garfagnana
Barga
445
Coreglia Anteiminelli
Tereglio
LUCCA
2
12
Borgo a Mozzano
Ponte dellla Maddalena
Diecimo
Piaggione
2
12
Ponte a Moriano
Old City
Castle
Church
Art
Bridge
Views
to La Spezia
435
Lucca
Trekking
Hiking
Mountains
A11
to Firenze
to Pisa
Restaurant
Local Produce

2

Valle del Serchio and the Garfagnana

THE GARFAGNANA, always a fascinating place with its impressive castle ruins and precipitous hills, has lately become especially inviting for food lovers. In this area north of Lucca, the sweet plump *farro* and coarse savoury polenta made from overlarge corn kernels have brought the area well-deserved celebrity. In the past, both *farro* and polenta were poor man's food, the area less alluring to the outsider.

The Garfagnana lies in the wildest part of the Apuan Alps, where old fortified towns hang over narrow valleys, skinny roads wriggle their way up through seemingly unsurpassable mountains. A few hundred years ago, the area was little more than a strategic passage, continually occupied by overbearing outsiders, robber barons, bandits and mercenaries for hire; a gloomy place. The poet Ludvico Ariosto, a fifteenth-century governor of the area, wrote rather grimly about 'tears, voices and life in the cold white marble mountains of Castiglione . . . [where] man wins over death and disarms it.'

These days the 50-kilometre excursion into the forests and hills along the Serchio river that meanders down from the Apuan Alps to Lucca is a lot more enticing. Agriculture and small industry along the Serchio have given the area a new prosperity. Nowadays the roads are decent. It's a special pleasure to head up from Lucca along the twisting riverbank road that slowly winds into the hills. The magnificent marble mountains to the rear of Carrara suddenly emerge looking like pure snow. The softer Apennine hills curve off for ever in the other direction. Within this endless forest of great green chestnuts, oaks and pines lie not only castles and fortress-towns, but a little-known wealth of local produce as well.

Its intimidating landscape kept the Garfagnana poor and isolated for many centuries. Until Italian unity in the nineteenth century, the area was controlled at varying times by the warring lords of Ferrara, Florence and Lucca. Their castles and fortresses are still there, marking the landscape, etched into the towns. Armies passing through picked up their fighters from available mercenaries along the way, and armaments too.

The right-hand side of the Serchio is the best way to travel up the valley from Lucca, even though signs point to a bridge crossing at Ponte Moriano. On the other side you may encounter truck traffic to and from the many paper factories and other industrial plants that have sprung up indiscriminately in recent years.

As you travel up, a first worthwhile detour is at Borgo a Mozzano, and the church of Santa Maria Assunta in Diecimo. Cross the river at the bridge indicating Borgo a Mozzano and head back toward Lucca for a few kilometres on the other side; you'll notice a sign to the church on the right-hand side of the road. Follow the signs that bring you to Santa Maria Assunta, sitting on its unassuming site since the sixth century. What you actually see is the finished twelfth-century church. Its massive bell tower is one of the most impressive of the area. The simple harmonious Romanesque church, like so many others you encounter in this area, is built of soft, seemingly pliable *pietra serena* – a deep grey travertine stone with a particular depth and beauty. Most are graced within by marble and wooden sculptures of the primitive early gothic style that is pervasive here. The Diecimo church is a perfect example. Inside – along with an early Roman sarcophagus found nearby – is a collection of early medieval wall sculptures. My favourite is *Re Pippino,* a seemingly headless horseman. There's another of the Prophet Isaiah, looking sternly medieval.

Travel back to the right side of the river at Borgo a Mozzano. Just past the town – where a very pleasant meal can be had at Osteria I Macelli – you'll soon be struck by the sight of an unusually high-arching walking bridge. It is the Ponte della Maddalena, better known as the Devil's Bridge. A feat of fourteenth-century engineering, it spans the river in three gracefully asymmetrical arches. A first sighting takes the breath away. On a sunny day the arches are reflected in the river, making three perfect diminishing circles. At night, it's smartly lit. There are a few parking places, and a walk over the bridge is a heady experience.

It's here, at the Devil's Bridge, that the flat Valle del Serchio begins to edge up into the Garfagnana. A few kilometres further on, a leisurely detour takes you up through nine kilometres of curved mountain road to Tereglio, a remarkably long and narrow little town, built along a steep ridge that falls off into deep gullies on both sides. I discovered Tereglio some years ago with Giovanna and Massimo Durante, Luccan friends who owned several decrepit houses and were slowly, almost brick by brick, putting together a little inn – La Fagiano – no doubt in the hope that visitors who had come so far, so high up the steep mountain, might want to spend the night. Hundreds arrived for the festive opening to celebrate the new inn and enjoy the rich offering of Garfagnana special dishes, thick *farro* and bean soup, savoury sausages, polenta and funghi, and more. The inn – during its season from May to October – is as popular as its owners (tel. 0593 762179).

Tereglio may strike you as one of the most unusual mountain villages you've ever seen. Once a remote mining town, it consists of a single, long narrow lane. The meandering pedestrian walk of several kilometres begins and ends with two portals, built centuries ago to protect the place. Ancient stone houses line the way, effectively blocking a view of what lies behind them. A lovely surprise waits just beyond the halfway point. The street curves gently down to an ancient rounded staircase. Directly below is the graceful red-tiled roof of another medieval Santa Maria Assunta church fronting a little piazza. Looking down at the church and over the rooftop at the surrounding mountains, you can believe you've reached heaven. The silence is penetrable, the feeling awe-inspiring.

From Tereglio you can follow a rather long and tortuous narrow road to another mountain town, Coreglia Antelminelli. Look right as you enter the town; there's a little ninth-century church of San Martino, a squat three-aisled rectangle. A strange lopsidedness adds to its harmony. On one of the main squares of the town, there's a delicious full-sized statue of figure-maker Mario Pisani, a *figurinaio* who sculpted portraits in plaster of Paris that give Coreglia its bit of notice. From here spread the popular art of making gesso figures, little white plaster shapes to paint and decorate. A small museum nearby is dedicated to the art. The sculpture of figure-maker Mario is smartly dressed, ready to emigrate (which he did) in a suit and little cap, standing determinedly with a rather Egyptian-looking cat sitting on one shoulder and two saintly heads held in the other arm. Nearby there's a little inn called L'Arcile, which during wild mushroom season can sate you with a full meal of funghi. *Farro* dishes are also a speciality.

From Coreglia, an almost untravelled mountain road leads you down to Barga and its majestic cathedral. This approach is special in that you come upon the majestic dome from above. Barga's cathedral, a grand travertine-faced structure, dominates its surroundings. It sits at the top of the old town, its large porch grandly overlooking the landscape of rooftops and the dramatic mountains beyond. The cathedral was badly damaged in an earthquake in 1897 and later tastefully restored. The impressive statuary inside survived intact. Most remarkable is the thirteenth-century Romanesque pulpit by the Lombard sculptor Guido Bigarelli, held securely in place by two serene lions.

On the road north from Barga to Castelnuovo di Garfagnana you pass through Castelvecchio Pascoli, named after a beloved nineteenth-century poet who enjoyed life here a good deal more than Ariosto. His home has become a museum. The *canti di Castelvecchio* (songs of Castelvecchio) evoke the landscape and aura of the Garfagnana:

Al mia cantuccio, donde non sento
Se non le reste brusir del grano
Il suon dell'ore viene con vento
Dal non veduto borgo montano

In my corner I hear nothing
But the rustle of the bearded grains.
The ringing of the hour comes with the wind
That sees not the mountain town.

Ariosto, author of Italy's great classic *Orlando Furioso,* may have been a better poet, but Páscoli was well enough thought of to have the town named after him. Al Ritrovo del Platano, an evocative restaurant directly on the road, is filled with Páscoli memorabilia. The poet took breakfast here daily with his host, present owner Gabriele de Prato's grandfather.

As the road winds gently up to Castelnuovo, the Apuan Alps emerge more and more dramatically, a scene marked as well by distant spires and castle ruins. The hub of activity that is Castelnuovo di Garfagnana comes almost as a surprise. Here is the small capital of the Garfagnana, and as you arrive at its main crossroads, a fortress built by the Este dukes of Ferrara appears on the left. Inside the city walls, there is a simple Romanesque cathedral to visit. It has the usual travertine *pietra serena* facade, and an impressive thirteenth-century crucifix inside. Thursday morning is market day here, the town bustles with shoppers and visitors from all over the Garfagnana. At the edge of the market, along the main road, look for the overwhelming food shop L'Aia di Piero. It is crammed with every sort of speciality that the Garfagnana has to offer: breads, stoneground grains, chestnut flours and polenta, preserved vegetables, jams, honeys, *farro* tarts and cheeses from goats and sheep grazing in the hills above. Around the corner is Andrea Bertucci's Osteria il Mulino Vecchio, a little bar and lunch stop that overflows on every wall with specialities, wines, olive oils, photographs, posters and everything else that speaks of Garfagnana.

From Castelnuovo, the road continues up toward Castiglione di Garfagnana. The mountains on both sides take on an awesome beauty as you climb. If there is time, take the small road on the right that leads to Sillico, an ancient Garfagnana hill town with a local trattoria – Locanda Belvedere – whose terrace affords some of the most spectacular views of the surrounding landscape. Drive beyond Sillico to Pieve Capraia, where you'll find the lonely little church of Santa Maria. It sits in the middle of a wood. A few stones are all that's left of the castle that once stood here. The church and its adjoining little stone house became a settlement of hermetic monks; today it emanates a timeless serenity, the quiet broken only by a melodic rushing of the river below. The church gives you a surprising example of arts of earlier times: several large stunning hand-painted Florentine wood-carved frames of the fifteenth century.

A short drive brings you back to the main road and on to Pieve Fosciana, where there is yet another beautiful simple church, San Giovanni Battista. The facade is of the usual soft grey stone, but the imposing tower was created not from *pietra serena* but from the ancient building stones of a nearby fortress ruin. Inside is a lovely annunciation by Luca della Robbia. At Pieve there is also the ancient old water-driven mill where chestnut flour and polenta are still stone-ground (call to visit, tel. 0583 666095), as well as Il Pozzo, one of the finest restaurants of the area.

The road from Pieve Fosciana continues up the mountain to Castiglione di Garfagnana, a great fortress with ramparts and watchtowers presiding over the surrounding landscape. Take the 'new gate' in, walk up the ancient street to the left along the wall to find the handsomest little church of them all, Chiesa di San

Michele with its sculpted twelfth-century facade of layered *pietra serena* and pink marble.

◆ Specialities of the area ◆

Life was hard in the Garfagnana. Each ruler in his turn extracted heavy taxes from the local population, and as a bonus forced them to keep up the defences within the territory as well. The food specialities are those of the poor, and are all the more interesting because of the area's isolation.

Farro is a good example. When we first arrived in Italy thirty years ago, few had even heard of it. Now *farro* is being exported in greater and greater quantities. It is a hearty grain, similar to the spelt or emmer mentioned in the Bible and given as a yearly tithe to the Roman emperors. *Farro* has been found in Etruscan tombs, but was not so long ago all but lost to the West. Were it not for a few hardy farmers of the Garfagnana, who grew it in this amenable soil mostly as animal feed, the grain might have been lost to us completely. In this small corner of Tuscany, this mother of all grains has been resuscitated and refined to its current plump and crunchy desirable sweetness.

These days *farro* has come back into fashion. Visitors to local trattorias in Lucca, impressed with its earthy taste and ability to retain both shape and firm bite when cooked, carried it to the world. Garfagnana farmers took advantage of this new interest and developed a solid export trade. *Farro* is also grown in mountain areas elsewhere in Tuscany, but the soil in the Garfagnana seems to favour it best. A puréed bean soup, in which *farro* has been cooked, is best eaten here, made with an intensely flavoured bean that has also been grown for a long time in the Garfagnana. The bean is called *gialliorini,* because of its yellow colour and small shape.

While these mountains nurture a good amount of *funghi porcini,* game and wild berries, other interesting food products have found their way into domestic production. Early on, the farmers of the Garfagnana discovered their mineral-laden earth was perfect for the growing of grains. Alongside *farro* a very special corn – *granturco di Garfagnana* – is grown here to produce savoury polenta and corn bread. The long skinny cob of this special corn was brought from the Americas in the sixteenth century and, with a certain pride, is called *otto file di Garfagnana,* the eight rows of Garfagnana, because of its eight rows of large hard kernels rather than the usual twelve or thirteen. It is not a corn that one wants to nibble; the kernels can break a tooth. But ground into polenta or into flour for bread, it produces a robustly flavoured result.

As in other mountainous areas of Tuscany, the ubiquitous chestnut forests were once a primary means of sustenance. You can still find stone-grinding chestnut-flour mills on private farms. Constant threat of war – right up until the latest – kept sending the local population into the forests to eke out sustenance from chestnuts. Blight after the Second World War temporarily cut off the supply, but chestnuts are now again collected in large quantities to be roasted, boiled and turned into flour for bread and cakes. The flour is known as sweet flour, *farina dolce,* and combined with normal grain for bread. Small pancakes called *frittelle* or *necci,* served with fresh ricotta, are a favourite finish to a winter meal. While chestnuts are also roasted over an open fire, Tuscans seem to prefer them boiled in either milk or water flavoured with fennel until they are soft and the meat can be squeezed out.

Often stone-ground chestnut, *farro* or *otto file* flours are added to wheat flour to make a variety of other breads that in the past helped to make precious wheat go further. Mashed potatoes are often added as well, to give longer life to the loaf. Each kind of bread is delicious, and each is eaten with different specialities. Pasta too is made from *farro* and chestnut flour. In this non-wine-producing area, the local alcohol is a tasty *farro* beer.

The *salumi* or cold sausages of the region are diverse and spicy, and go well with the different breads. The most noteworthy is the *biroldo della Garfagnana,* made with what the local population calls 'the least noble parts of the pork': head, heart, lungs and tongue, all cooked together for hours and spiced generously with cloves and anise, cinnamon and nutmeg, a few wild fennel seeds, salt and pepper. Blood holds the ingredients together as they are packed into the stomach lining of the beast. It's quite delicious when seasoned, aged, sliced and eaten on a slab of one of the rough local breads, especially bread made with chestnut flour. The most elegant sausage is *mondiola,* made with the choicest pork meat, seasoned with laurel, stuffed into a broad intestinal sac and folded in half to make a big round sausage tied with a laurel twig. The home-cured prosciutto of the area – *prosciutto bazzone* – is made from fat old pigs raised on wheat, corn, whey and, in the last months, chestnuts; it tastes of all of them. Spiced well, *prosciutto bazzone* is more savoury and succulent than the elegant prosciutto of Parma and San Daniele. I recently tried a newly concocted sausage called *linchetto,* made of beef that has been aged wrapped in a coat of dried *funghi porcini* that imbues the meat with the heavy musty perfume of the dried mushrooms. All the *salumi* are made in an acclaimed artisan *norcineria* – maker of pork products – in Ghivizzano, just before Barga on the road up to Castelnuovo. If you'd like to see them at work, call Rolando Belandi at L'Antica Norcineria (tel. 0583 77008).

The cheeses of the Garfagnana come from both sheep and cows that graze in the highest mountain pastures. The most favoured pecorino, or sheep's cheese, ripens firmly for six months to a year in a wrapping of straw. The most valued cow's cheese, *vacea*, comes from cattle grazing above 1500 metres, on the highest peaks of the Apuan Alps. *Vacea* is available only from September through until May, but another fine cow's cheese — *vaccino Bertami* – is more frequently available, fresher and pleasingly eaten with fresh marmalade or the fine local honeys.

◆ Typical restaurants and their recipes ◆

BORGO A MOZZANO: Osteria I Macelli

Osteria I Macelli, Via di Cerreto, Borgo a Mozzano.
Tel. 0583 88700. Reservations recommended, especially weekends. Closed Sundays. Inexpensive to moderately priced.

OSTERIA I MACELLI sits behind the main street of old Borgo a Mozzano above the municipal parking lot, in a bright-yellow building that was once a slaughterhouse and is now one of the more enticing restaurants of the area. Owners Patrizio DeServi and Alberto Lina returned to Borgo a Mozzano some time ago after years spent making New York City a better place to eat. Patrizio is a pastry specialist (and owns a delectable pastry shop – DeServi – in Fornaci di Barga, on the road to Barga); Alberto knows wines. The confidence that the two acquired in New York is evident from the well-placed tables, the knowledgeable waiter and the freshness of every dish. Opened in 2002, it has become a popular eating place at lunchtime for local business people. In the evening, white tablecloths are laid and a more elaborate menu is offered.

Specialities include the *salumi* – cold meats – of Lucca and Garfagnana, local soups – a light vegetable *zuppa alla frantoiana* is peerless, and a *passato di verdure* that adds various grains is especially good. It feels as though the freshly made ravioli has been made just for you. Main courses are unusually varied. Rather than the normal list of grilled meats, you'll find wild boar or venison stewed in an olive-laden sauce, beef simmered in Chianti wine, and roast baby veal in a milk sauce. And because Patrizio is a pastry chef, a list of delicious desserts is offered.

The menu changes by the day; lunch is listed on a blackboard in each of the restaurant's two pleasant rooms. You can also buy Lucchese olive oil here, but the house wine is from Chianti. All this goodness is remarkably inexpensive.

RECIPES from Osteria I Macelli

◆ Mixed vegetable custard / *Sformato di verdure miste*

Serves 6

2 carrots
100g fresh young green beans
2 courgettes
2 carrots
1 onion
1 leek
2 tablespoons olive oil
Breadcrumbs
3 eggs
50g freshly grated Parmesan cheese
500ml bechamel
Salt and freshly ground pepper
Good grating of nutmeg

Chop the vegetables into bite-sized pieces and cook gently in the olive oil with water to cover. When the water evaporates, add a handful of breadcrumbs to absorb the remaining liquid. Remove from the heat.

Heat the oven to 180°C/Gas 4. Beat the eggs with the grated cheese and mix with the bechamel. Add the cooked vegetables, salt, pepper and nutmeg. Mix well and put into a deep ceramic baking dish. Cover with more breadcrumbs and bake for about 30–40 minutes, until the custard is firm and the top golden.

Beef braised in wine / *Brasato al Chianti*

Serves 6

1 sprig rosemary
2 sprigs sage
3 cloves garlic
Salt and freshly ground pepper
1kg beef for roasting
2 carrots, thinly sliced
2 stalks celery, thinly sliced
1 large onion, halved and thinly sliced
2 tablespoons olive oil
1 bottle Chianti wine

Chop the rosemary, sage and garlic well, place in a mortar – or a high-speed small chopping machine – with about a teaspoon of salt and a teaspoon of pepper and pound or grind finely together into a paste. Rub the entire roast with the mixture.

Put the sliced vegetables together with the olive oil into a large heavy pan and sauté gently until soft and aromatic, about 10 minutes. Add the beef to the pan and, over a lively flame, brown on all sides. Pour the wine over and bring to the boil. Lower the heat and barely simmer for 2 to 2½ hours, until the wine has reduced to a thick sauce and the meat is well cooked. Allow to rest, then slice fairly thinly and serve with the sauce.

COREGLIA ANTELMINELLI: L'Arcile

L'Arcile, opposite the duomo in Coreglia Antelminelli. Tel. 0583 78401. Open every day during the year, lunch and dinner. Priced moderately.

L'ARCILE'S restaurant (it's also an inexpensive pension) sits on a flower-filled terrace just opposite Coreglia's main church. The bell tower looming over the narrow street below is in close view as you dine.

Owner and chef Giustina Paladini didn't have much patience when we chatted about authentic traditional food in the Garfagnana. I'd eaten several meals at L'Arcile, and they were all notable for a strict adherence to local products and traditions. I was pretty sure she'd open up with some enthusiastic response. But it wasn't to be. It was full season, and she was probably too tired from running the quirky little nest of rooms she calls a pension. Or maybe because she was up to her elbows in newly gathered porcini mushrooms preparing an all-funghi dinner for forty-five diners from Lucca, who were travelling up to Coreglia for her special meal. When I asked her about traditions and finding genuine food, she snorted. 'Who cares about tradition any more? All kids want today are pizzas and McDonald's. No one cares about whether foreign funghi [i.e., mostly Croatian] invade our markets. They all come from somewhere else, and nobody cares.' She continued to rail against what she calls the loss of tradition. My protests went almost unheeded. How was it that she was still serving only the most local of products to her guests? Why would they come all the way up to Lucca for funghi from the nearby woods? Wasn't it local *farro* that made her seafood salad so special?

At this, she grunted a small assent and agreed she was just too tired to be agreeable. I asked her what her all-porcini meal would consist of. I'd just eaten her salad of fresh grated funghi and Parmesan cheese dressed with balsamic vinegar and olive oil, served on a thin slice of *bresaola* – dried beef – which certainly would be a part of such a dinner. What else? For *antipasto*, there'd be the addition of *crostini di funghi*, small toasted breads with chopped sautéed mushrooms. For *primi*, or first courses, *malfatti*, an oven dish of funghi and ricotta, a cream of mushroom soup, and *pappardelle di funghi*, wide home-made pasta with *funghi trifolati*, or chopped mushrooms in a garlic, oil and parsley sauce. She'd then serve another funghi dish I'd enjoyed at L'Arcile: slices of large porcini caps dipped in a batter of polenta meal and flour, quickly fried in olive oil and served with a large slab of moderately aged pecorino cheese. All this was a 'light' version of her all-funghi meals; another might include large meat-stuffed and baked mushroom caps. Or a main course of wild boar with funghi. Giustina prepares such a meal only on order, for at least five diners. But she is happy to spend her day preparing it during the months when porcini arrive daily from the woods: from the last days of August through to November.

There are plenty of non-mushroom dishes at L'Arcile, depending upon the season. The tomato bruschetta has a touch of balsamic vinegar along with the usual coating of extra virgin olive oil; the *farro* and seafood salad is a staple when there's time and good seafood around. Home-made ricotta and spinach-filled tortelli are rustic and served with large sage leaves fried crisp in olive oil. A walnut sauce covers freshly made tagliatelle.

Her meat courses are the usual grilled and roasted meats, with game added when it's available. Desserts are varied. The most 'typical' would be something she claims the young don't care about any more: *frittelle di castagne*, fried chestnut-flour fritters with a topping of ricotta cheese.

RECIPE FROM L'Arcile

◆ *Farro seafood salad / Insalata di farro e frutti di mare*

Serves 6

250g *farro*
Juice of ½ lemon
150g small fresh prawns, peeled
150g calamari, sliced thinly
500g mussels
500g clams
120ml white wine
12 large crayfish
120ml extra virgin olive oil
1 bunch parsley leaves, chopped finely
60 ml balsamic vinegar
Salt and freshly ground pepper
1 bunch rocket

Cook the *farro* in boiling salted water until it is easily biteable but still firm, about 20 minutes to half an hour. Drain and run under cold water. Douse with the lemon juice and set aside.

Prepare the seafood. Chop the prawns into three pieces each and cook in boiling salted water for 2 minutes. Remove and cook the calamari in the same water for 5 minutes. Drain and add to the prawns.

Steam the mussels and clams in the white wine, with 1 tablespoon of the olive oil. When they are open, remove, cool and shell.

Boil the crayfish in a pot of boiling salted water for 5 minutes. Drain and set aside.

Mix the *farro* with the shrimp, calamari, mussels, clams and chopped parsley. Add the vinegar and remaining oil, mix well. Taste and add salt and lots of freshly ground pepper.

Chop the rocket and spread it over a large platter. Spoon over the *farro* salad, and lay the crayfish on top.

PONTE DI CAMPIA: Al Ritrovo del Platano

Osteria al Ritrovo del Platano, Ponte di Campia. Tel. 0583 766039; fax 0583 76642. Priced inexpensively. Reservations recommended evenings and weekends. Closed Wednesdays.

AT A TURN in the road, between Castelvecchio Pascoli and Castelnuovo Garfagnana, just over the bridge called Ponte di Campia, you'll bump into Al Ritrovo del Platano, the oldest inn in the area. Two large plane trees (*platoni*) sitting in front and the name of the trattoria clearly painted on the outer front wall indicates you are there.

The interior of Al Ritrovo del Platano is dedicated to poet Giovanni Páscoli, who was one of its first habitués in the nineteenth century. The small bar/trattoria is cluttered with memorabilia of times gone by, its walls covered with large photographs and manuscripts.

Interesting old wooden farm machinery takes up a good amount of floor space.

The trattoria has passed from generation to generation. Gabriele's father Luigi and mother Maria Grazia are still cooking, although the restaurant now belongs to the younger generation. Maria Grazia is there first every morning preparing the various breads and pasta. The food hasn't changed much here since Páscoli ordered ravioli and fresh river trout for lunch. Gabriele and his wife Michele are enormously proud of their ties to the local food and literary culture and a way of life that becomes obvious the minute you begin to order.

Home-made pastas at Ritrovo del Platano are of a well-kneaded full-wheat dough called Grano Torrenova, another venerable old grain special to the Garfagnana. The pasta, *granscuro*, is thicker and chewier than normal pasta, with a heartier flavour. The *tortellaccio* of *granscuro* is a single large ravioli, filled and sauced with wild *funghi porcini*, a speciality of the restaurant and heavy with earthy tastes.

Two thick soups also show off local products. Both the *passato di fagioli* and the *minestrone di farro* are made with the seemingly skinless *gialliorini* beans special to the area.

Like so many small trattorias in Tuscany, the first courses are the most interesting; meat is meat, and while preparations vary, it's still just meat. My choice for a main course would be a local river trout dish that dates back to the time of Páscoli, *trota marinata del Corsonna*. It's best in spring and autumn, when fresh trout fishing is permitted and the trout comes not from a fish farm but from the heights of the river Serchio before it gets to all the paper factories in the valley. One interesting main course is a platter called *pascoliano*, a selection of local cheeses and cold meats served with a variety of breads that Gabriele's mother bakes each day at the restaurant. There is chestnut-flour or *farro* bread, local *biroldo* sausages and other samples of Garfagnana cold meats. Sweets in winter include chestnut-flour crêpes with a topping of ricotta cheese.

On Sundays a fried roll is added to the offerings, usually for a take-away lunch bought at the front bar. It is lightly crisp outside with a soft dough filling, something like a puffed-up focaccia. It serves perfectly for any of the sausage or cheese fillings on hand.

At Easter you'll find a special sort of dry cake, the *panettone Pasimata*.

Gabriele de Prato's zest for old food traditions of the Garfagnana has been joined by his new passion for recreating the wine that was once made here. He began the first new commercial vineyard of the area, with its premier vintage in the year 2000. Melograno is not yet widely available, but if you find it, it's the perfect accompaniment to a meal at Al Ritrovo del Platano.

RECIPES FROM Osteria al Ritrovo del Platano

Trout with rosemary and wine / *Trota marinata del Corsonna*

For each serving:

1 fresh trout, about 300g
1 sprig rosemary
1 clove garlic
2 tablespoons extra virgin olive oil
Juice of ½ lemon
1 glass white wine
Salt and freshly ground pepper

Clean and wash the trout. Chop together the rosemary and garlic. Heat the oil in a pan large enough to hold the entire fish, add the rosemary and garlic and then the trout. Brown the trout for a minute, and gently turn, taking care not to break the fish. Add salt and pepper to taste.

Add the lemon juice, then the wine. If necessary, add a bit of water towards the end of the cooking, which should be no longer than five minutes. It is served here at room temperature, with the soft polenta of the Garfagnana, but can be served with boiled potatoes and fresh vegetables as well.

Easter cake / *Pasimata*

30g anise seeds
30g beer yeast
Pinch of salt
Grated peel of 1 lemon
Grated peel of 1 orange
700g white flour
8 eggs
300g sugar
Vermouth
200g butter
200g currants or small black raisins
4 tablespoons extra virgin olive oil

Soak the anise seeds in water for 20 minutes. Dissolve the yeast in 100ml warm water in a large bowl. Add the salt, drained anise seeds, the lemon and orange peels, and mix. Add just enough flour gradually, mixing it in as you go, to make a soft pliable dough. No kneading is necessary, simply put the dough to rise in a warm place for 2 hours.

Add 4 of the eggs, 100g of the sugar and a tablespoon of vermouth and mix well. Sprinkle over a layer of flour and allow to rest for another hour.

Add the remaining ingredients to the dough. It should be soft and sticky. Pour into a buttered 18cm springform baking tin and leave to rise in a warm place for another 45 minutes. Heat the oven to 170°C/Gas 3 and bake for 50 minutes, until the cake has reached a deep brown and the aroma wafts through the entire house. Remove from oven, and allow the cake to rest for 5 minutes before removing the sides of the tin.

The cake is eaten during the Easter period. Closely wrapped, it can last for more than a week. Served with a glass of *vin santo.*

CASTELNUOVO DI GARFAGNANA: Il Vecchio Mulino

Il Vecchio Mulino, Castelnuovo di Garfagnana.
Tel. 0583 62192. Meals are wooden plates of local cheeses and cold meats served along with tarts and other specialities of the Garfagnana. Prices are inexpensive, depending upon how much you eat and drink. No reservations are necessary; if the single large table inside is all taken, there are tables outside. You can also stand. Closed Mondays.

YOU'LL FIND THE perfect choice of local products at this small inauspicious bar/osteria at the entrance to Castelnuovo di Garfagnana. Owner Andrea Bertucci is called the Indiana Jones of the Garfagnana, not out of a particular quest for tombs or holy grails but for his excavating of food traditions and local produce. A good sampling of what he has uncovered lies on the shelves at Il Vecchio Mulino. The place is packed with jars, bottles and dry goods; not an inch of wall space is left unoccupied, a cluttered *Wunderkammer* of Garfagnana delights.

The major attraction at Il Vecchio Mulino is not of the Garfagnana, but from nearby Emilia: a huge mortadella sausage, looking like a ballistic missile and weighing 200kg upon arrival, lying on its own fitted table next to the hams and sausages in a corner of the tavern. Slice by slice, it lasts about 3 months. Directly next to it sits a large *prosciutto bazzone*, the succulent fat prosciutto of the area, its juices almost dripping.

To all who have encountered him, Andrea is the guiding light of the Garfagnana culinary experience and his little osteria provides samplings of all the specialities he has uncovered. He serves no hot food – a lukewarm *farro* and bean soup, or the very Luccan spring soup called *garmugia* are about as hot as it gets – but rather an assemblage of Garfagnana specialities that he has collected from small farmers and bakers, meat curers and cheese makers. The sampling of what the Garfagnana means to its food lovers arrives at the table on a thick wooden board. On the board, you'll find *lardo di Garfagnana*, a thin slice of seasoned pork fat, a cured carpaccio called *manzo di pazzo* (beef for the crazy), various sausage samplings and some wonderful cheeses of the Garfagnana. All are accompanied by thick slabs of *farro*/potato bread.

RECIPES FROM Andrea Bertucci's Vecchio Mulino

Andrea has more *farro* recipes than anyone I've met, and it's a pleasure for me to share them with other fans of this plump little grain.

◆ *Farro* and bean soup / *Il farro della nonna*

Serves 8–10

This is a classic version of *minestra di farro*, the traditional *farro* in a bean purée. The soup tends to thicken; add water until you reach the consistency you want.

300g dried borlotti beans, soaked overnight in still mineral water
5 cloves garlic
1 full sprig sage
2 tablespoons extra virgin olive oil, plus extra to serve
1 large onion, finely chopped
1 carrot, finely chopped
1 stick celery, finely chopped
4 Italian plum tomatoes, skinned and chopped
2 medium potatoes, cubed
300g *farro*
2 sprigs rosemary
Lots of salt and freshly ground pepper

Cook the soaked beans in the water in which they have been soaked, plus enough extra to cover by about 5cm. Bring to the boil, reduce the heat as much as possible and simmer with 2 peeled cloves of garlic and a large sprig of sage. Add more water as necessary. After about 2 hours, the beans should be cooked.

Meanwhile, chop the remaining 3 cloves of garlic and sauté in the olive oil in another pan. Add the chopped onion, carrot and celery. Cook for about 10 minutes over a low heat. Add the tomatoes and continue to cook until the tomatoes soften into the other vegetables. Add the potato, mix well and cook for another few minutes. Put the contents of the pan into the cooked beans and their water, and continue to cook for another 40 minutes. Purée the entire contents, and add enough water to make a creamy, thick consistency. If it looks too thick to absorb the *farro*, add more water. Add salt and pepper to taste.

Put the blended soup back into the pot. Add the *farro* and the rosemary and cook for another 30 minutes. Allow to stand for at least an hour. If the soup becomes too thick, add some more water. Serve warm with fresh olive oil and a grinding of pepper.

Farro risotto / *Farrotto*

Serves 2

100g *farro*
½ onion, thinly sliced
2 tablespoons extra virgin olive oil
500ml vegetable stock
1 small potato, cubed
1 carrot, cubed
3 tomatoes, skinned and chopped
Salt and freshly ground pepper
50g freshly grated pecorino cheese

Wash and drain the *farro*. In an earthenware casserole, soften the sliced onion in the olive oil and add the *farro*. Toast for a minute or two. Add the stock, salt and pepper, and allow to cook slowly. If necessary, add more stock if the *farro* absorbs it all. Stir often. After 15 minutes, add the vegetables and cook slowly until they are softened, adding stock just to cover as needed. It should have the consistency of a risotto. Allow to rest for 5 minutes, and add the grated cheese before serving.

Farro pudding / *Budino di farro*

Not too different from an English rice pudding, but rather more firm. *Farro* has a special nutty flavour, and retains its bite. This also serves as a tart filling in the Garfagnana.

Serves 6–8

200g *farro*
1 litre milk
Pinch of salt
2 egg yolks
1 whole egg, beaten
200g sugar
50g flour
200g ricotta, preferably sheep's
2 tablespoons cherry liqueur, or amaretto or rum
Icing sugar for coating

Cook the *farro* in 350ml lightly salted milk until the milk is entirely absorbed, about 15 minutes.

In the meantime, prepare the cream. Whisk the egg yolks together with the whole egg. In a large saucepan, put the eggs, sugar and flour. Whisk together over a low heat until the sugar begins to melt. Add the remaining milk and bring to boiling point. Remove from the heat and whisk in the ricotta and the liquor. Add the *farro* and mix well.

Heat the oven to 180°C/Gas 4. Butter a large oval baking dish (about 33 x 20cm) and pour in the mixture. Bake until the top begins to brown and the pudding is firm. Sprinkle with icing sugar and serve warm.

Luccan spring soup / *Garmugia*

This is Lucca's welcome to spring, unknown outside of the province. I once asked a vegetable seller in a neighbouring province about *garmugia*, but the term was totally unknown to her. Rich with bits of spring vegetables, it's a thoroughly comforting dish for a light supper. It's usually made on the hob in an earthenware pot.

Serves 4

3 small onions, thinly sliced
3 tablespoons extra virgin olive oil
30g pancetta, cubed
100g lean minced beef
500g fresh broad (*fava*) beans, weighed with their pods and shelled
3 fresh artichoke hearts, cubed
100g shelled small fresh garden peas
1 small bunch asparagus, chopped
850ml vegetable stock (more if needed)
Freshly ground pepper
Small knob of butter
4 slices Tuscan bread, toasted

In a deep earthenware flameproof casserole, soften the onion in the olive oil. Add the pancetta and beef. Break up the beef with a fork, and cook the meats together for 10 minutes. Add the podded and chopped vegetables, mix well and cook for another 5 minutes. Add the stock and continue cooking for 20 minutes. At the end, taste for seasoning, add pepper and a small knob of butter and serve from the casserole over a slice of toasted bread.

PIEVE FOSCIANA: Il Pozzo di Giordano e Maurizio

Il Pozzo, 2/A Via Europa, Pieve Fosciana.
Tel. 0583 666380. Open for lunch and dinner. Closed Wednesdays. Priced moderately.

ENTER THE LARGE dining room of Il Pozzo any day after the bells strike twelve and you'll find the large, rustic, beamed dining room full, each table with five, six or ten men quietly and intently finishing a meal. They are local labourers, who crowd into the restaurant every day for their main meal. Giordano Andreucci is genial host to them all. A little later, after 1 p.m., white-collar workers from nearby banks and offices arrive, and perhaps a few women from Lucca out for an afternoon. Evenings, it's just as crowded with families and groups of friends. Il Pozzo seems to be a local treat for everyone. During summer, there is a garden full of tables as well.

While he claims Sienese origins, Giordano's family has been in the Garfagnana for eight generations. His grandfather was a local *mugnaio*, a miller of the three main Garfagnana flours – wheat, corn and *farro* – that have always been the staples of the area. He is the first of the family to become a proper restaurateur, deciding early on it was a decent and quick way to earn a living. He also developed a timely philosophy and determined his restaurant would maintain and revive the traditional dishes of the area. He presents them well, so well that the restaurant has been awarded a 'snail' for quality/price, one of thirty-two in all of Tuscany bestowed by the fastidious Italian branch of the Slow Food organization.

Giordano's partner, Maurizio Romei, is chef at Il Pozzo. He makes his *tagliarini*, thin fresh noodles, when he arrives every morning. His truffled *tagliarini* – with local truffles – are as celestial a dish as you'll find in the more popular truffle areas of Tuscany. They are a recent luxury in the Garfagnana; in the past, truffles were never sought out. They were a delicacy that had little to do with the local taste or purse. In time, as in other areas of Tuscany, the brownish truffle has become widespread, its most flavourful moment in late autumn and early winter.

Antipasti include the special cured pork products of the region, the elongated, succulent prosciutto and delicately spiced *biroldo* and *mondiola* sausages, all served with a choice of the splendid breads that are so particular here. *Primi* – pastas and soups – include a *minestra di farro* and *pappardelle rustiche* of *farro* pasta with a venison ragú that's almost sweet.

A special main course puts chestnuts and chestnut flour to good use: a roast pork loin with chestnuts and a sauce thickened by the flour. Ask also for *fagioli scoppiati*, cooked borlotti beans roasted in a hot oven until they burst.

The dessert of the house has the irresistible name *la torta squisita* (the exquisite tart), and is a crunchy mélange of pastry, ricotta and caramelized sugar. Giordano is also a qualified sommelier; his wine selections can be well relied upon. The simple house wine is also fine.

RECIPES FROM Il Pozzo

◆ Pork tenderloin with chestnuts / *Maiale con castagne*

Serves 6

1 onion
1 carrot
1 stick celery
1 clove garlic
1 handful parsley leaves
50g pork fat, in one piece

4 tablespoons olive oil
600g loin or tenderloin of pork
240ml white wine
Meat stock if necessary
200g preserved non-sweet cooked chestnuts, chopped
2 tablespoons chestnut flour, fused with 25g butter.

Finely chop together the onion, carrot, celery, garlic and parsley leaves to make a *soffritto*. In a large pan with a cover, combine the *soffritto* with the pork fat (lard) and olive oil and cook for a few minutes over a medium heat to soften the vegetables.

Add the meat and brown on all sides. Add the wine. Cover and cook for 30 minutes, adding meat stock if it becomes dry. Add the chopped chestnuts, and mix the fused chestnut flour/butter into the broth. Cook for another 30 minutes.

Exploded beans / *Fagioli scoppiate*

More a curiosity than a dish, but fun to eat. The beans burst open, get a bit crisp, and with some good olive oil and salt make a nice side dish.

200g borlotti beans
3 sprigs sage
1 sprig rosemary
4 cloves garlic
2 tablespoons olive oil
Salt
Extra virgin olive oil, to serve

Cover the beans with lots of cold water and soak for 12 to 18 hours. With a slotted spoon, remove the beans to a small pot, and add 1 sprig of sage, the rosemary and 2 of the peeled garlic cloves. Cover with some of the soaking water and cook slowly over a low flame, covered, until the beans are well cooked but still whole. Add water as they cook to keep them just covered. Add salt at the end of cooking, and allow to cool in their own water.

Heat the oven to 250°C or as hot as it will go. Drain the beans into a shallow pan with a few tablespoons of the water and add the oil and the remaining sage and garlic. Place in the hot oven for about 10 minutes, until they burst open. Salt well and serve either warm or at room temperature with fresh extra virgin olive oil to drip over at the table.

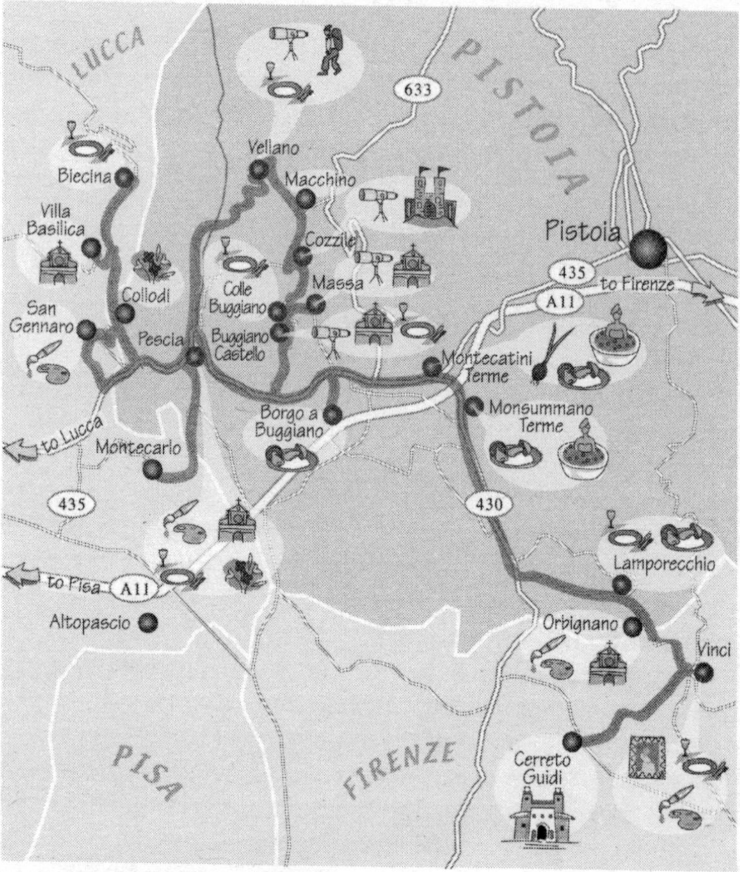
LUCCA
PISTOIA
PISA
FIRENZE
Biecina
Villa Basilica
Collodi
San Gennaro
Pescia
Vellano
Macchino
Cozzile
Massa
Colle Buggiano
Buggiano Castello
Borgo a Buggiano
Montecatini Terme
Monsummano Terme
Pistoia
to Firenze
to Lucca
to Pisa
Montecarlo
Altopascio
Lamporecchio
Orbignano
Vinci
Cerreto Guidi
633
435
A11
430

Restaurant
Trekking
Castle
Art
Museum
Church
Flower Market
Views
Market
Local Produce
Spa
Villa Medici

3

La Valdinievole and Svizzera Pesciatina

THE VALDINIEVOLE, or Foggy Valley, is a vast basin in the province of Pistoia, prosperous, busy, surrounded by mountains and hills. It was once a vast swampy lake with steam fogging up the entire plain, hence presumably its name. To the north soar the craggy Apennine mountains. In the east lie the gentler green hills of Monte Albano. Amid the terraced hills of olives and vineyards are small inviting hill towns called *castelli*, the former strongholds of aristocratic families ruling over the entire wet valley. In many, you can still see vestiges of the great castles. The young Leonardo da Vinci wandered through these hills sketching the *castelli* and later mapped the entire valley in an attempt to devise a water-control system. A copy of his map hangs in the little Leonardo museum in Vinci.

Today brightly refurbished old farmhouses reflecting the general prosperity of the area are scattered through the hills. There's an ever increasing international demand for good olive oil, and farms that were abandoned in the 1960s are again thriving, many of them with foreign owners.

The Valdinievole begins in the west around Péscia, includes the once fashionable spas of Montecatini and Monsummano Terme, the wine centre of Montecarlo and the small historic town of Fucécchio with its lovely old centre. The marshes (*padule*) of Fucécchio are the largest wetland in Tuscany, all that's left of the muddy lake that was once the scene of raging battles between the navies of Florence and Pisa. Today the swamp is a national park, a feast for bird lovers and rare flora enthusiasts.

Péscia, Valdinievole's principal town tucked comfortably under its surrounding hills, is the flower-growing centre of central Italy. An eighteenth-century portal – the Florentine Gate, built by the last rather decadent Medici who controlled Péscia – welcomes you into an old town filled with lovely old surprises. Among them is a great oval main square, a backstage set almost hidden behind the Péscia river which divides the two sections of the old city centre. An impressive thirteenth-century city hall rises at one end of the oversized square and a little chapel crowned by a magnificent coffered ceiling stands at the other. Noble buildings line both sides. The long oval is packed every Saturday morning for the weekly market.

On the other side of the river, opposite Péscia's hospital, a dramatic thirteenth-century painting of San Francesco hangs in the gloom of a church of the same name; nearby is another little treasure, the tiny chapel of the Oratorio di Sant' Antonio, where you'll find a twelfth-century group of carved figures depicting the Deposition of Christ.

Péscia is also home to the wondrous display of citrus plants in the greenhouses of Oscar Tintori. Shaped lemon trees in pots have been grown in Tuscany since before the Medici. At Tintori you can still find enormous pots of fruiting 500-year-old lemons. Once a small citrus orchard, Tintori has become the largest exporter of ornamental citrus in Italy. They've recently inaugurated Il Giardino degli Agrumi, a landscaped 'hesperidarium' of more than 200 different kinds of citrus. You can visit at any time, but check visiting hours for guided tours. (Tel. 0572 427928; small charge for guided tour.) You can also buy from a choice selection of citrus jams and citrus-based honeys, some of them unlike any I've seen elsewhere. Oscar's son Giorgio and his two sons are usually there to show you around.

In the heart of Péscia you'll also find the best-known trattoria of the area, Cecco, a restaurant that prides itself on having offered almost exactly the same menu for the past hundred years.

From Péscia to the west along the old provincial road to Lucca are a few more surprises. Just past the turn-off to Collodi, a town to which we'll return, is a sign on the right to San Gennaro. A long stretch of tall umbrella pines and cypresses leads you to this small town, with another hidden treasure inside the small eleventh-century church of San Gennaro. If the church is closed ask next door for the key. Inside, a wondrous Angel of the Annunciation stands along the wall. Only a few years ago, when it was attributed to Verrocchio, you could still freely touch the lovely sculpture. Today it is acknowledged to be an early work of Leonardo da Vinci, and has gone behind glass.

From San Gennaro there's an inside road to Collodi and the place where Pinocchio was born. The castle town cascades down a mountain hillside into the Villa Garzoni, a splendid house that seems to hold the village on its back. The tales of Pinocchio were woven in the kitchen of this large villa. Today a bustling Pinocchio tourism is the town's mainstay. The main square below the villa is filled with stalls selling Pinocchio replicas of every size and function, thousands of bright-red little dolls to welcome you into Pinocchio land. The general confusion is increased by the large wrought-iron gate leading into the seventeenth-century baroque Garzoni gardens off the same square. They are a fine example of the imported French landscape architecture of the time. Nearby is a Pinocchio theme park, unlike most in that there are no rides, but rather a landscaped series of mosaic figures and stories from the original story, executed by a group of Italian artists. A large whale invites children into its gaping mouth.

A few kilometres into the hills from Collodi, the road curves up to the town of Villa Basilica, a cul-de-sac ending in an odd little square that has at its heart a small twelfth-century church most remarkable in its Luccan/Pisan gothic style. Its stone is the soft grey *pietra serena*. Four tiers of columns, each column with a different capital, make it almost as imposing as Lucca's cathedral. The interior is pristine with little ornament to mar its tranquillity.

As you go back down towards Collodi, a sign will indicate a left turn for the inauspicious Trattoria Aldo at Biecina, which offers the simple classic dishes of the area.

Return to Péscia, where, along the western bank of the Péscia river (the side of the river with the long, oval piazza), a narrow valley road runs up into the lower Apennines. The hills and thick chestnut forests are known as the Svizzera Pesciatina (Péscia's Switzerland), but *le dieci castella* – a collective singular meaning ten castles – is the official and more attractive designation. Both terms describe the area well. Capping the peaks of dramatic hills, ten tiny medieval hamlets today attract few but discerning travellers. Although almost every one of the ten hamlets offers an attractive church and ancient lanes, few number more than fifty inhabitants. The Swiss essayist Jean Sismondi who lived in Péscia in the early nineteenth century and wrote a celebrated history of the Italian republics apparently gave the area its Swiss nickname. The ten *castelli* better resemble remote mountain villages of Sicily, perched on top of each peak in the area and totally independent from one another.

Vellano is the largest, the *capaluogo* or main village, and the only one still featuring any sort of commercial life. On the main road below this medieval borgo you can sit on the terrace of a little inn, Antica Locanda del Borgo (via Matteotti 32; tel. 0572 409137), eat a fairly typical meal (try the *trippa della casa*, a saucy version of the well-known Florentine plate of tripe) and look down on the valley below. The Antica Locanda brings some life into the village with Saturday-evening jam sessions and little theatrical productions both inside and on the large terrace across the way. During summer months, Vellano takes on a resort air; Italian and foreign – mostly Swiss and German – vacationers come to enjoy the breezy hills.

The road circles up to the top of the village and its medieval wall, from where you can look down at several of the other little hamlets. A tiny portal in the wall brings you into a warren of old streets and tunnelled alley that lead into a well-preserved mini-square. The square is the heart of a chestnut festival held in the town each October.

Leaving Svizzera Pesciatina at Vellano, continue through the mountain landscape to Macchino, where a right turn takes you back towards the valley and the most inviting hill towns between Péscia and Montecatini, four little towns that remain an oasis of well-guarded calm. It wasn't always so; in earlier times they were either warring with one another or caught in the cross-fire of battling Luccans, Pisans and Florentines. The Florentines won the day in the fifteenth century and the Medici took over the whole area for several hundred years. Highest of the towns is Cozzile, fronted by its remodelled old castle. Cozzile is known as the balcony of the Valdinievole. On a clear day you can see the entire basin almost to the sea. A local saying claims that all of Tuscany sits at the foot of silent and tranquil Cozzile.

The sister village to Cozzile is Massa, with an impressive old portal leading to its eleventh-century tower and porticoed church of Santa Maria Assunta. Inside the church is a trove of precious church objects, including a lovely old wooden Madonna, and a carved inlaid wooden sacristy. A walk up through Massa's narrow streets brings you to the medieval city hall and an impressive view.

Below Massa are two hill towns, Colle di Buggiano, where you can enjoy a rustic meal at Antica Trattoria di Colle directly on the lively piazza, and, just below it, Buggiano Castello, perhaps the loveliest of them all. Buggiano Castello spreads out against the hill, with a tenth-century Romanesque abbey at its top. The church is fronted by an undisturbed little Renaissance square, dominated by its Palazzo Pretorio, encrusted with dozens of coats of arms. It's an idyllic playground for the children of the village. Sporadic cultural activities – plays, concerts, a traditional festive dinner – take place on the piazza. The harmony of Buggiano Castello is accentuated by the deep brick-red or ochre colour of so many of its homes.

Just under the old gate of Buggiano Castello is Sant' Elena restaurant and its terrace, where on a sunny Sunday afternoon you can have a glass of wine accompanied by what owner Mario Cortesi calls his Tuscan *merenda* – tasty bruschetta, *crostini* and other snacks – on a pleasant terrace. (It's also a nice restaurant, tel. 0572 30548.) Borgo a Buggiano, the commercial centre below, was once the central meat market of Tuscany.

The *mercato del bestiame* (the animal market) still carries the name, and today houses a remarkable old country store – Michelotti & Co – which not only supplies the needs of local farmers and granaries, but can provide you with some of the fine products of the area. Their beans, lentils and other legumes are sold from sacks, and guaranteed to be the freshest of the season.

Just across the valley, on a hill of its own, is the wine-growing centre of Montecarlo, an imposing medieval red-brick hill town with a broad main pedestrian street linking its two old gates. Montecarlo is well known for its white wines; less known is a perfect tiny little seventeenth-century court theatre – still used for summer concerts and plays – just off the main street. There are a number of impressive restaurants in Montecarlo; if you want to join local farmers for a simple meal, try Trattoria di Natale in a pine grove just under the town.

Nearby is Montecatini Terme, where a variety of thermal waters are proffered in a Roman-style spa filled with romantic gardens; a roving Viennese quintet plays in the background. Montecatini has all the stylish hotels and shops that elegant spas demand. It's also home to a compact marketplace, and a teeming weekly market that takes up a good portion of town every Thursday morning. The vegetable market is impressive every day, divided between wholesale suppliers and local farmers selling to local buyers.

The marketplace has the added attraction of a fine artisan pasta shop: P&P, named after its proprietors Paola and Piero Zucconi (no relation to another less remarkable pasta shop called Zucconi down the street). Neither Paola nor Piero ever miss a day in their busy shop. Seven days a week they and their staff work at hand-rolling and stuffing the most melt-in-the-mouth ravioli and tortelli imaginable. The variety of fillings is vast. Beyond the usual you find fillings of truffle, nettle – the delicious nutritious weed grows wild all over Tuscany – squash, wild mushroom, orange, artichoke and a host of others. The shop has been in business for almost sixty years, ever since Piero's mother, Marietta Romani, began hand-rolling pastas for neighbours. (Via Mazzini 60; tel. 0572 773511.)

Monsummano Terme is another spa, next door to Montecatini Terme, known less for its waters than for the blistering thermal grottoes in the quarried mountain visible from everywhere in the valley. Just beyond Monsummano on the road to Lamporécchio and Vinci is an enticing small cafe and chocolate shop that is definitely worth a visit. Slitti has a fine array of handmade chocolates – sold throughout Italy and Europe – and the best coffee around. Out of a small bar that Luciano Slitti opened in 1969, the family enterprise has grown to become a major exporter of fine chocolates and coffee. Some time ago, Luciano turned over the production and distribution of products to his sons Andrea and Daniele. You'll still find Luciano manning the cash register every day. Andrea manages the production and Daniele the marketing. Daniele tells me that Slitti's chocolates contain a good deal less fat than French or Belgian. Coffee spoons and old Tuscan farm tools made from chocolate are hand-fashioned here in soft moulds. If you're anywhere in the area around Easter time, don't miss a stop. The large, elaborately decorated chocolate Easter eggs are the status gift of the season, and despite their steep price manage to disappear completely before Easter Sunday.

It is mostly because of Slitti's fame that Monsummano plays host to a feast of chocolate – the *Cioccolosita* – every January, a heady fair that features handmade chocolates from all over Italy.

The long low mountain of Monte Albano lies just beyond Monsummano and completes the half-circle of hills surrounding the Valdinievole. Castle remains at Larciano overlook the valley. The nearby hill town of Lamporécchio is the home of *brigidini*, thin, crisp sweet wafers that find their way to street fairs all over Italy. Along Lamporécchio's main street you'll also find a friendly restaurant – Antico Masetto – with a large inviting menu of local dishes.

Vinci, Leonardo's birthplace, is nearby. The best approach is from Monte Albano over a mountain road from Lamporécchio: Via Pistoiese, the old route Leonardo undoubtedly travelled back and forth on from Vinci to Pistoia (now the provincial capital). His father had an accounting office there. Santa Maria del Pruno, a little church along the road, in Orbignano, has some lovely late fourteenth-century frescoes; one is a most unusual Madonna that has been attributed both to Giotto and the school of Donatello. Ask the keeper next door to open the church as you pass by; it's a nice surprise.

This mountain road descends to Vinci from the hills above the town. An angle of Vinci strikes you suddenly as you descend, protruding like the bow of a ship above the olive-covered landscape below. I visited Vinci in 1986, the year of the big frost, when the olives were burned black, and remember how the little walled town stood sad but proud above the devastation around. The recovered full-blooming olive groves now look as they'd never known disaster. Vinci has become the centre of a busy well-tended Leonardo industry, with Leonardo replicas, Leonardo cafes, Leonardo restaurants, tobacco shops and even laundries. The farmhouse where he is said to have been born is on view, along with two small museums that feature his inventions. Both demonstrate the genius of the man, his imagination and his contrasting dreams of advanced armaments and a better life. The main museum – Il Museo Leonardo da Vinci – sits in the Castello Guidi, an imposing structure rising in the middle of the old town. The second more recently opened Museo Ideale also contains examples of his machines for olive-pressing, winemaking, and a working rotisserie that may seem a bit archaic these days but would have been an amazing culinary advance in the fifteenth century.

Just across the street from Museo Ideale is the busy little restaurant Il Restoro del Museo, a favourite lunch-time trattoria of museum workers and their guests.

Further on, just beyond Valdinievole into the valley of the Arno river, is Cerreto Guidi, a small cluster of a town surrounding the impressive Villa Medicea of Cerreto, once a Guidi family stronghold and later – redesigned – of the Medici. Here the daughter of Cosimo, Isabella, was strangled by her husband for an alleged infidelity. The room where it all happened is a major attraction.

Specialities of the area

Spring and autumn are the moments to sample the best of this area's specialities. Fragrant wild porcini mushrooms and chestnut dishes are the menu of the autumn. From late September to November, the hills are packed with families out in the earliest hours of the morning scavenging for funghi and *castagne*. Funghi have lately been arriving from all over Europe, but the locals wait for *nostrale* ('our own'), from the nearby woods. As the season draws near and the firm dark mushrooms with their pure white flesh begin to arrive, shoppers will always ask, 'But are they local?' Strangely enough, there's little cheating. It's assumed the buyer can actually see and taste the difference. We are warned away from buying from the large trucks filled with funghi along the main roads; who could know where they come from and who is selling them?

Large porcini caps are grilled like steaks; smaller ones and their stems are generally served *trifolati*: chopped and sautéed in olive oil with garlic and parsley. Chestnuts are roasted or boiled with a sprig of wild fennel, eaten whole or squeezed from their shells. The smaller ones are ground into flour – called *farina dolce*, or sweet flour – to produce two of the favourite winter desserts: *castagnaccio*, a flat unleavened cake of chestnut flour, pine nuts, rosemary and olive oil, which takes some getting used to; and *necci*, chestnut-flour crêpes deliciously served with a topping of fresh ricotta cheese.

A very special, velvety, small white bean is harvested in late August and September along the Péscia river under Sorano, one of the little mountain towns of the Svizzera Pesciatina. The Sorano bean is treasured throughout Tuscany, but the harvest is small and precious. (There's such a thing as Sorano-type beans, meaning they are grown elsewhere; the real Sorano is a DOP controlled appellation.) The beans are quickly dried and quickly sold; you can find them here only from autumn through to the following spring. Their notable texture results from a mini-climate in the narrow river valley: the sun reaches it only for a few hours each day, thus keeping the plants moist and cool. The beans, gently simmered, with some sage leaves, smashed garlic and a bit of oil, feel almost skinless and have a perfectly smooth consistency. They're eaten with just a sprinkling of salt, a fresh grinding of pepper and a drizzle of newly pressed extra virgin olive oil, sometimes with *bottarga* (fish roe) grated over. Sorano beans are hard to come by outside of the Valdinievole, and expensive when you do find them. Bean lovers should look for them in the markets here in September and October. Many restaurants in the area also serve Sorano beans and list them as such on the menu.

Spring brings the fine, fat pale-green asparagus of Péscia, served abundantly in restaurants throughout the Valdinievole. The season is short; it is worth taking advantage when it is offered. The same is true for the tiny local spring artichokes and fresh green peas. A risotto with either or both, or a veal escalope under a covering of thinly sliced sautéed artichoke, makes a fine main course. The little artichokes are also served raw, with a topping of sliced Parmesan cheese, fresh olive oil and salt, as part of an *antipasto*.

The small trattorias of the area well reflect their peasant past. Beyond sheep and goats, few animals graze here; home-bred pork, rabbit and chicken are still the main meats. The *caccia*, or hunt, in the past reserved for the rich is more popular now. From the first days of September, when the hunting season begins, a popping of rifles spattering shot randomly into flocks of sparrows, thrush and blackbirds is as much a weekend disturbance as the roaring of motorbikes. You won't find the shot-laden little birds – mostly thrush – on restaurant menus, but wild boar and hare are offered throughout the winter. Simple little home-made pasta squares called *maccheroni* are served with a sauce of either. Another local speciality you'll find only in the typical trattoria is *cioncia alla Pesciatina*, not a dish for the weak of heart, or stomach. It is best described by its origins in the tanneries of

Péscia, the *concerie*. It was a poor time, with little meat. Tannery workers, so the story goes, stripped off whatever bits and pieces of meat they could find on the fresh skins, to mix with a few herbs and boil into a stew. Needless to say, the dish has been gentrified over the years; today it is made from the most edible and gelatinous parts of a beef muzzle, a savoury stew cooked for hours and hours. *La concia* is a great winter favourite among local inhabitants.

Bread in the Valdinievole is a precious staple and is never thrown away. Entire winter meals are constructed from different porridge-like soups poured over a slice of day-old bread. In summer, *panzanella* – stale bread soaked in water, flavoured with vinegar and extra virgin olive oil and mixed with summer vegetables – is a major *antipasto*. Corn meal, *farina giallo*, is also well used. *La farinata* – which elsewhere in Tuscany can be a corn-meal crêpe – is the almost regal local appellation for a favourite winter soup of kale, beans and polenta. It is a dish to savour.

Like elsewhere in Tuscany, two favourite traditional Friday dishes are made from preserved types of cod: salted *baccalà* and dried *stoccafisso* (stockfish), which, for hundreds of years, have been imported from Norway. They can be found side by side in local markets. (I've been told that 80 per cent of the Norwegian yield each year is exported to this part of the world.) Both are well soaked before being fried or served in a tomato sauce.

Other specialities are the sweet *brigidini* of Lamporécchio, wafers that look like potato crisps although they are baked, not fried. In Montecatini Terme, you'll find similar wafers, *cialde*, a pair of large paper-thin discs pressed together with a hazelnut-paste filling. Tins of *cialde* can be bought in bars and at speciality shops throughout the spa. Both sweets have their origins, oddly enough, in the communion wafer.

Brigidini originated – some say as a cooking mistake – in the convent of Santa Brigida in Lamporécchio in the sixteenth century. A nun was preparing the host for communion and somehow sugar and anise fell into the edible little wafer. They are still produced today in Lamporécchio and transported fresh in cellophane wrappers all over Italy to be sold from stands at street fairs and church festivals.

To end a meal in the Valdinievole most will choose a small glass of local *vin santo*, fortified sweet wine, dipping the little half-moon-shaped hard biscuits called *cantucci* into it.

Typical restaurants and their recipes

PÉSCIA: Trattoria Cecco

Cecco, Via Forti 96/98, Péscia.
Tel. 0572 477955. Cecco is located between Péscia's river and its main square; you can enter from either side and go by the immaculate open kitchen in the middle to find dining rooms on either side. It is moderately expensive. Reservations are recommended. Closed Mondays.

Cecco has been serving the best of local food since the end of the nineteenth century, when Francesco Pacini opened a little inn of six rooms. He was the grandfather of cousins Dino and Francesco, who retired in 2005 to leave the restaurant in new local hands. Cecco is still thought of as the most reliable in the area. Such is its reputation that new owner Federico Schiavelli – himself a Pesciatino and scion to another restaurant family – is determined to maintain the tradition and standard just as it's always been.

The menu has hardly changed over the years; old dishes of the area remain as staples. Sorano beans are usually on the menu, either as a side dish with a sprinkling of fresh olive oil and salt, or as an appetizer sprinkled with grated *bottarga* or small pieces of octopus. *Bottarga* can be made from the roe of tuna or grey mullet; here it's usually that of tuna. Asparagus in season comes from a single trusty farmer, who divides it for the restaurant into bunches according to size. The slimmest go into a tagliatelle pasta sauce or a risotto; thick stalks are served either with oil and lemon dressing or over a fried egg. In autumn and winter, there is fresh tagliatelle dressed with butter and a generous scraping of San Miniato truffles, a dish that must be one of the world's most heavenly.

The preparation of *cioncia alla Pesciatina,* offered throughout the winter, is almost a rite. The stewing and solidification of the beef maw takes days to prepare. *Pollastrino al mattone,* a crisp and juicy baby chicken sautéed under a weight, seems to have originated at Cecco. A more recent addition – perhaps only a generation old – is a fresh *branzino al sale,* a sea bass baked under a thick coating of coarse salt. The *branzino* turns out moist, succulent and not at all salty. But Cecco does have a tendency to oversalt other dishes; if you're not crazy for salty things, be sure to mention it. The chef may be in love, but he can serve up unsalted dishes as well.

Desserts are both rich and diverse. One of the more straightforward is a simple pear baked in wine and covered in caramelized sugar.

RECIPES FROM Trattoria Cecco

◆ Baby chicken under a brick / *Pollastrino al mattone*

This dish is traditionally cooked under the weight of a brick in a flat earthenware dish; thus the word *mattone*. But any heavy weight will do. Just make sure the pan in which the chicken is cooked is well covered, perhaps with an inverted cover or another frying pan. This will prevent the fat from splattering too much.

Serves 2

1 baby chicken, not more than 800g, split and opened flat
Salt and freshly ground pepper
About 350ml olive oil, or enough in which to immerse (but not cover) the chicken
Juice of ½ lemon
120ml white wine

Open the split chicken and flatten well with a good hammer. (Or have your butcher do it.) The legs should be tucked in under the thighs, and the wings flattened out. Season well on both sides. Heat the olive oil in a pan just large enough to hold the entire flattened chicken.

When the oil is sizzling hot add the chicken, skin side up. Cover immediately with another pan filled with a weight to press the chicken even flatter. Cook in the hot oil for about 8 minutes. Remove the weight, check that the chicken has taken on a golden hue, and turn it. Cook under the weight again for another

8 minutes on the other side. Turn again, add the lemon juice and wine (this *will* spatter a bit), replace the weight and cook for another 5 minutes. Remove to kitchen paper to dry off any liquid, and serve immediately.

Sea bass under salt / *Branzino al sale*

Why this salt coating of the fish makes such a difference to the taste is difficult to understand; the bass turns out delicate and moist, in no way salty. But the presentation is lovely; the golden-brown crust breaks open easily and the fish is served filleted.

Serves 2

1 800g sea bass
2 sprigs fresh rosemary
Freshly ground pepper
400g coarse sea salt
1 egg, beaten
1 small wine glass white wine

Clean the fish, put rosemary and pepper inside and place in an oiled oval baking dish. Heat the oven to 220°C/Gas 7. In a large bowl, mix the salt together with the beaten egg. Coat the entire top of the fish with the salt, making a thick crust. Bake for 10 minutes, then remove and pour the wine around the fish, not on the salt. Replace, and bake for another 10 minutes. By this time the salt should have taken on a golden colour. Remove from oven and pour off any remaining liquid.

At the table, gently remove the crust in one piece (or

broken, it does not matter), slip off the skin and fillet the fish.

NEAR COLLODI: Trattoria Aldo

Trattoria Aldo, Via delle Cartiere 175, Biecina/Villa Basilica.
Tel. 0572 43008. Best to reserve, especially during the autumn funghi season. Prices inexpensive to moderate. Closed Sundays. If you want a choice meal, reserve for the evening. The restaurant serves a *prix fixe* meal at lunch for workers from nearby paper factories.

TRATTORIA ALDO LIES about five kilometres up into the hills above Collodi, in Biecina past the turning to Villa Basilica. It's one of the more popular local restaurants, hard to find the first time you look. You reach it on an old road that runs alongside a small run-off of the river Péscia, lined with old gothic ruins of once majestic paper plants. It's the largest concentration of paper-producing mills in Italy from the thirteenth century on. To the traveller's eye, the crumbling old ruins are a lot more attractive than the modern plants behind them that function today.

Aldo's unprepossessing green neon sign reading 'Trattoria' greets you on the left. It's also a bar ('Jolly Caffe', says the sign) and grocery, and easy to pass right by in the dark. There are several entrances, and chances are you'll walk into a noisy collection of card-players in the bar. Continue up a flight of stairs and through the kitchen, which also serves as family dining room (television blaring) into a more soothing room filled with chequered tablecloths and family portraits. This is the domain of Mirco Flosi, owner and cook, carrying on the family tradition of father Aldo, now ailing, and his grandfather who started it all. His mother serves; the rest of the family helps. Mirco learned to cook growing up in the kitchen. He has never thought to pick up anything really new. Thus the restaurant remains one of the true *casalinga* – home cooking – places of the area.

The very decent house wine is from a popular *cantina* in Vinci and is served from a carafe; the bread comes from a nearby wood oven; the olive oil is the restaurant's own, fresh and extra virgin. Dishes are simple, beginning with an *antipasto* of local prosciutto and salami and a subtle warm mixture of vegetables in a light vinegar-oil marinade. A basket of toasted bread comes with a garlic clove to rub on it and a decanter of fresh olive oil to inundate it.

To prepare for seasons when mushrooms aren't available, Mirco dries enough funghi to serve the year round. Second courses include handmade thick tortelli stuffed with dried funghi and served in a sage/butter sauce, *farro* and dried funghi risotto (this is an area close to the *farro*-producing Garfagnana) or squares of home-made pasta called *maccheroni* served in a variety of sauces. On occasion you'll find a *maccheroni* made with chestnut flour topped with a walnut sauce. Autumn is the major season at Aldo's, a time when the nearby woods are filled with porcini, and funghi, made in every conceivable way, become the prevalent dish.

Main autumn and winter courses emphasize game: wild boar in a black-olive sauce, hare and venison. The best way to finish a meal at Aldo's is with the home-made *cantucci*, the little, well-known biscuits of Prato, to dip in *vin santo*.

RECIPES FROM Trattoria Aldo

◆ Mixed marinated vegetables / *Verdure sott 'aceto*

This is a lovely smooth accompaniment to first courses, with just the slightest pungency. It keeps in the refrigerator for several weeks.

Makes 1kg

1kg mixed vegetables, including cauliflower florets, celery, carrots, mushrooms, red peppers, onions
10 large whole black olives
1 hot red chilli pepper, finely chopped
500ml white wine vinegar
1 litre water
1 tablespoon salt
1 teaspoon of mixed spices, including cinnamon, allspice and nutmeg
Fresh extra virgin olive oil, to cover

Thinly slice the celery, carrots and mushrooms, and chop the remaining vegetables into small bite-sized pieces. Add the whole olives and chopped chilli.

Boil together the vinegar, water, salt and spices. Add the vegetables and cook for 10–15 minutes. Drain immediately and spread on a clean cloth to dry.

Put the vegetables in a large jar, and cover with the olive oil. Keep in the refrigerator. Serve with a bit of the oil and some bread to soak it up with.

◆ *Farro* risotto with dried mushrooms / *Risotto di farro ai funghi secchi*

Garfagnana *farro* is the best for this dish. It needs no soaking, cooks in 15 minutes and turns into nice round chewy kernels that retain their firmness. (If using another *farro*, follow instructions for soaking and cooking on the packet.)

Serves 6

500g *farro*
30g butter
2 cloves garlic, chopped
50g dried porcini mushrooms, soaked in 250ml warm water for 30 minutes.
Salt and freshly ground pepper
120ml full-fat milk

Cook the *farro* in boiling salted water until it is *al dente.*

Melt the butter with the garlic in a small pan. Drain the mushrooms and add them to the pan. Add 120ml of the water from the soaked mushrooms, taking care not to include any sediment, and cook for 10 minutes.

Drain the *farro,* mix with the mushrooms and stir in the milk. Serve warm.

COLLE DI BUGGIANO: Antico Colle
Antico Colle, Piazza Cavour, Colle di Buggiano.
Tel. 0572 30671. Open evenings, winter Sundays and holidays for lunch. Reservations necessary, especially for the terrace during spring and summer. Priced moderately. Closed Thursdays.

DINERS FROM NEARBY Montecatini and Péscia crowd into this pleasant, very reliable trattoria on the main square of picturesque Colle di Buggiano. Summer evening dining is the best, out on the lively square. Mila Lupori and Piero Belardi are the husband/wife team who own the place. Mila controls the dining room, Piero cooks in a small compact corner kitchen. Their daughter and a few local youngsters serve. The grandchild runs around.

The menu is filled with local dishes, never grand, never complicated. It changes somewhat from season to season. The *antipasto* list includes the usual prosciutto with figs or melon, sliced salami and game sausages, *crostini* and bruschetta with a marinated tomato topping. Piero prepares some interesting traditional dishes, ravioli stuffed with a pear and pecorino filling – odd sounding, but delicious – and *la farinata,* the local polenta-thickened bean and kale soup. *Ribollita, pappa al pomodoro, aquacotta ricca* (a rich man's *aquacotta,* thick and different from that of other areas) and other bread-based dishes are listed as *piatti tipici,* traditional first courses. You can also sample each of them in a single serving. In the summer, *panzanella* (bread salad) is a favourite *antipasto.* Pizza, thin and crisp, is a staple here: there are thirty-five different kinds on the menu and a special wood oven in the back dining room to bake them. During autumn, wild porcini and other mushrooms arrive daily with Mila's uncle who has been out since before dawn searching for them.

Main courses include various grilled meats, sliced steak called *tagliata* served with various toppings, Florentine-style tripe, salt cod served in a spicy tomato sauce and the *cioncia alla Pesciatina* popular here. They've recently added some traditional fresh fish dishes to the menu.

Desserts are simple, different offerings on different evenings. And Mila usually offers a home-made *limoncello* liqueur that can finish off both dinner and diner.

RECIPES FROM Antico Colle

Polenta-thickened bean soup / *La farinata*

Serves 6–8

500g borlotti beans, soaked overnight
4 cloves garlic
120ml extra virgin olive oil, plus extra to serve
2 onions, halved and thinly sliced
2 sticks celery, thinly sliced
4 carrots, thinly sliced
2 bunches kale leaves (about 20), stems removed, thinly sliced
½ small white cabbage, quartered and thinly sliced
3 ripe tomatoes, or contents of 1 small tin
1 vegetable stock cube, or 1 teaspoon vegetable stock powder
350g polenta
Salt and freshly ground pepper

Place the soaked beans in 1 litre of water with 2 peeled garlic cloves and a tablespoon of olive oil. Bring to the boil, immediately lower the heat, and simmer until the beans are soft. Add salt at the very end. Purée half the beans and return them to the pan with the remaining beans and their water.

In a large heavy soup pot, heat the remaining oil and add the onion and the remaining 2 cloves of garlic, thinly sliced. Cook for a minute, then add the celery, carrots, kale and cabbage. Cook for 10 minutes. Add the tomatoes and simmer for another 30 minutes.

Add the purée and beans to the pot with their water. Add the stock cube or powder, mix well and add enough extra water to cover by several centimetres. Bring to the boil, then slowly add the polenta, mixing to prevent lumps forming. Continue mixing for another 20 minutes, until the soup is thick and creamy. If it becomes solid, add water. Taste and adjust the seasoning and serve with a good drizzle of fresh extra virgin olive oil over the top.

Bread salad / *Panzanella*

For this salad you must have a loaf of Tuscan-style bread that does not dissolve into a mass when soaked but rather squeezes into a grainy consistency. The *tropea* is a popular sweet red onion from Puglia.

Serves 6

500g Tuscan bread, at least 3 days old
60ml red wine vinegar, plus a few tablespoons
3 ripe tomatoes, halved vertically and thinly sliced
1 *tropea* or other sweet fresh red onion, halved and thinly sliced
1 cucumber, washed and thinly sliced

1 stick celery, finely sliced
1 large bunch basil leaves, chopped
Salt and freshly ground pepper
120ml extra virgin olive oil, plus extra if needed

Soak the bread for at least 30 minutes in water flavoured with the few tablespoons of red wine vinegar. Meanwhile, combine all the vegetables in a large bowl. Take pieces of the bread, squeeze all the water from them and break them up over the vegetables. Sprinkle the basil over the top, add salt and pepper, the 60ml vinegar and the oil. Mix the entire salad well. Taste and adjust the seasoning, and add more vinegar or olive oil if necessary.

LAMPORÉCCHIO: Antico Masetto

Antico Masetto, Via Gramsci 83, Lamporécchio. Tel. 0583 82118. Open lunch and dinner. Closed Thursdays and all of August. Priced moderately.

A good reason to pause in Lamporécchio would be to visit this diverting little restaurant, which serves some very good typical food of the region. Owner Walter Maccione named it Antico Masetto after a character in a Boccaccio tale that takes place in Lamporécchio. Masetto is an impoverished stranger who arrives in Lamporécchio to seek a living. His search is unsuccessful and a townsman suggests Masetto play deaf and mute to get the nuns at the Convent of Santa Brigida to give him work. The nuns take him on as a gardener. As Boccaccio tells it, when the young Masetto finally departs the convent, he leaves all of the nuns in the 'family way'. From this tale, Antico Masetto was born in 1967. Walter is the host, his wife Sylvia the cook.

The menu is fun, filled with expressions in old Tuscan dialect. Ask for a translation. It is a characteristic menu of the area, an *antipasto* of local Tuscan prosciutto, liver *crostini* or a savoury mix of artichokes and olives from trees on the nearby hills.

Second courses are more special. *Ribollita al fraticello* (a diminutive for monks) is a savoury fresh-vegetable bread soup fashioned by Sylvia. There's also a soup of *farro* and barley in bean broth, and a tasty *risotto co'l cibreo* with artichoke purée and chicken livers.

Daily fresh fish are also on the menu; you can even order a lobster. More typical are the charcoal-grilled Florentine (*Chianina*) beefsteak and the boar with olives.

For dessert, try the delicious tiramisu prepared with a whipped-cream-topped cappuccino instead of the usual coffee.

RECIPES FROM Antico Masetto

◆ Vegetable soup / *Ribollita al fraticello*

Walter Maccione calls this a *ribollita* in the manner of the little monks. It's more a minestrone, with few tastes other than vegetables cooked in their own juices and the half-puréed cooked beans added and served on toasted bread. (Traditionally a *ribollita*, or twice-cooked soup, means the second day of eating a good soup. First day it's just a bread soup; on the second day, it's either sautéed in oil for a second cooking or put into a baking dish with some oil and cheese on top and crusted for another meal; hence its name.)

Serves 6

250g dried white cannellini beans, soaked overnight
5 tablespoons olive oil
2 sprigs sage leaves
Salt and freshly ground pepper
2 leeks, thinly sliced
2 courgettes, thinly sliced
2 carrots, thinly sliced
2 potatoes, cubed
1 bunch Swiss chard, finely chopped
5 kale leaves, ribs removed, finely chopped
½ Savoy cabbage, core removed, thinly sliced
1 bunch parsley
2 garlic cloves, crushed
3 large slices stale Tuscan bread, broken into chunks
Fresh extra virgin olive oil and Parmesan cheese, to serve

Drain the beans and put in a large saucepan with 2 litres water, 1 tablespoon of the olive oil and the sage. Cook over the lowest heat possible until the beans are soft, about 2 hours. During the cooking, keep adding water as it evaporates. Add salt just before the beans are finished.

While the beans are cooking, put all the vegetables together with the remaining 4 tablespoons of olive oil into a heavy soup pot. Add a good amount of salt, and cook the vegetables slowly, covered, mixing often, until soft. This can take almost as long as the beans. Add salt to taste.

Purée half the beans in a food processor with the parsley leaves and garlic, then add the purée and the remaining beans and their water to the cooked vegetables. Mix well, adding more water if necessary, but keeping it a thick creamy soup. Taste for salt and add some pepper as well.

To serve, place a bit of bread on the bottom of each soup plate and pour over the soup. Serve warm, with fresh oil and cheese at the table.

Chicken liver risotto / *Risotto co'l cibreo*

Cibreo is one of the more ancient traditional foods of Florence, a mixed stew of innards and the crest of a cock. Walter Maccione uses only chicken livers in this risotto. It's made with Persian basmati rice, a new addition to the Italian table.

Serves 4

200g chicken livers (about 4)
2 cloves garlic
1 anchovy fillet, or 1 teaspoon anchovy paste
2 sage leaves
3 tablespoons olive oil
3 tablespoons capers
Salt and freshly ground pepper
3 fresh or frozen artichoke hearts
50g butter
300g risotto or Persian basmati rice
1 small wine glass white wine
½ litre light vegetable stock
Freshly grated Parmesan cheese, to serve

Sauté the chicken livers with 1 garlic clove, the anchovy or anchovy paste and sage in 2 tablespoons of the olive oil until the livers are just cooked. Add the capers and cook for another minute. Place in a food processor and blend, but not too finely. Set aside, keeping warm. It should be creamy; if it feels too dry, put a bit of boiling water in a pan and mix the chopped livers into it. Add salt and pepper to taste.

Slice the artichoke hearts and cook them with the remaining garlic and oil. Add water to cover and cook until the water is completely gone. Purée the artichokes, return to the pan and add about a third of the butter and salt well. Set aside, keeping warm.

To prepare the rice, melt the remaining butter in a pan, add the rice, mix well to coat the rice and add the wine. Allow the wine to evaporate and then add the boiling stock slowly, covering the rice with a bit each time as it absorbs. Do it slowly in order to make a fairly dry risotto.

Mix the finished risotto well with the puréed artichokes, add lots of salt and pepper and turn into an oval serving dish. Spoon the chicken livers over and serve with lots of Parmesan cheese.

VINCI: Il Restoro del Museo

Il Ristoro del Museo, Via Montalbano 9, Vinci.
Tel. 0571 56516. Best to reserve, especially during tourist seasons, for both lunch and dinner. Closed Friday evening and Saturday lunch. Prices are moderate, including the very decent local house wine.

ENTER IL RESTORO DEL MUSEO through a small, cosy bar and plunge downstairs into a warm, colourful cellar with a terrace facing a landscape of olives and vines. The staff in this trattoria numbers two: Mariella, breathless hostess and waitress, and her more reticent husband, Maurizio Beretta, who runs the kitchen single-handedly. A surprising number of genuine dishes emerge from this small compact kitchen. Maurizio comes from the mountains of Sicily, but he's learned Tuscan fare well. His dishes are fairly sophisticated reflections of deep ties to both the Tuscan tradition and his own.

A mix of *crostini* appetizers (*funghi porcini,* liver paste and a topping of chopped red radicchio and *tropea* onions, the popular sweet red onion from Puglia) comes first, brought to the table in 'serve-yourself' little candle-heated terracotta bowls. The *zuppa del contadino* – farmer's soup – has a wonderful overwhelming aroma of fresh thyme and rosemary. Don't miss the sliced steak (*tagliata*) topped with aromatized fresh virgin olive oil (a secret Maurizio is not about to part with) and a vegetarian cutlet in a porcini sauce. Il Restoro freezes fresh porcini to serve throughout the year, and it works very well; both the *funghi crostini* and the cutlet sauce are an authentic fresh – not dried – taste.

RECIPE FROM *Il Restoro*

Farm vegetable soup / *Zuppa del contadino*

This uses seasonal vegetables from the garden, the *orto*, with a bit of white wine to give it a slight tang.

Serves 8

200g borlotti beans, soaked overnight
200g cannellini beans, soaked overnight
1 onion, thinly sliced
3 cloves garlic, finely chopped
3 tablespoons extra virgin olive oil
1 bunch kale leaves, stems removed
1 small wine glass white wine
500g ripe tomatoes, peeled (or tinned Italian *pelati)*
3 carrots, halved and sliced
1 stick celery, sliced
3 courgettes, sliced
1 large potato, cubed
200g fresh or frozen peas
1 large bunch fresh thyme
2 sprigs fresh rosemary
Salt and freshly ground pepper
Freshly grated Parmesan cheese and fresh extra virgin olive oil, to serve

Cook the soaked beans in plenty of water over a low heat until thoroughly cooked. Saving their water, purée half the beans and mix them with the remaining whole beans. Set aside.

Put the onions and garlic together with the olive oil in a large soup pot, and cook for about 10 minutes over a medium heat until the onions are soft. Add the kale and cook for another 10 minutes until the kale has completely wilted. Add the wine, and allow to evaporate. Add the tomatoes and cook for another 10 minutes.

Add the remaining vegetables (there should be about 1kg) in bite-sized pieces, the beans and their purée, the herbs and enough boiling water to cover. Taste and a goodly amount of salt and pepper. Cook partially covered over a low heat until the vegetables are cooked, but still firm, about an hour.

Serve warm with Parmesan and fresh oil.

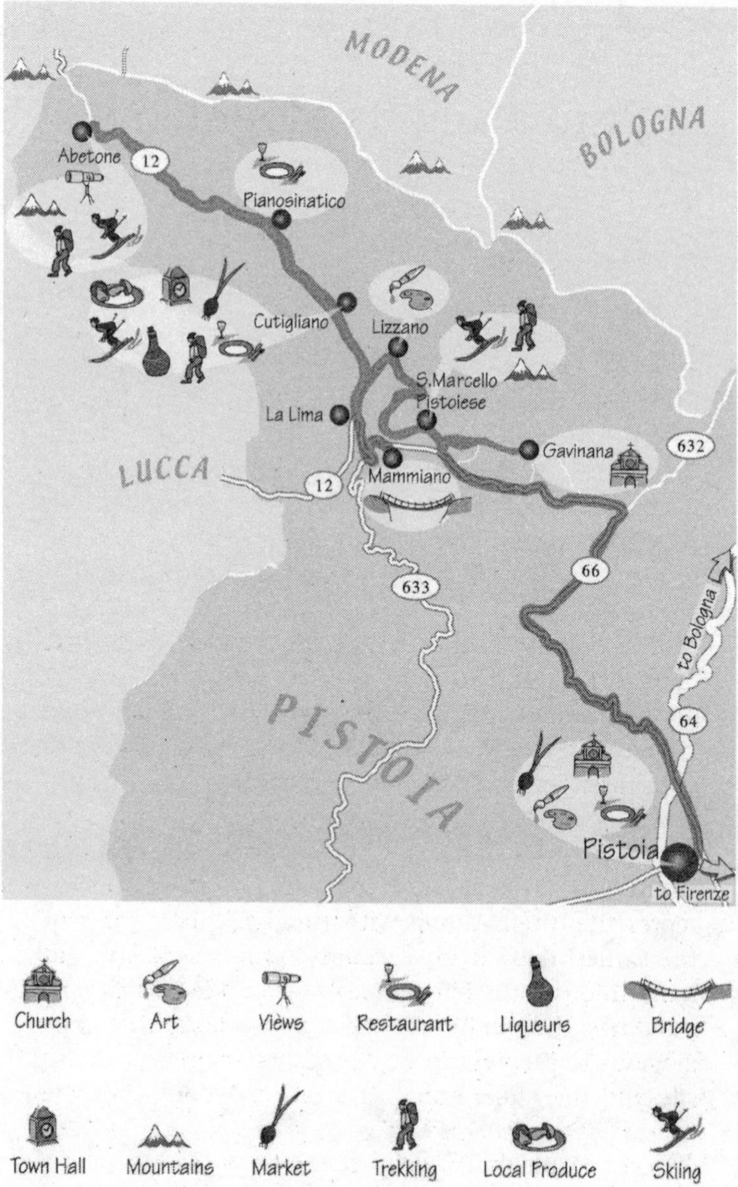
MODENA
BOLOGNA
Abetone
12
Pianosinatico
Cutigliano
Lizzano
S.Marcello
Pistoiese
La Lima
Gavinana
632
LUCCA
Mammiano
12
66
633
to Bologna
64
PISTOIA
Pistoia
to Firenze
Church
Art
Views
Restaurant
Liqueurs
Bridge
Town Hall
Mountains
Market
Trekking
Local Produce
Skiing

4

Pistoia and its Mountains

PISTOIA, ABOUT half an hour west of Florence, is the single sizeable city I've chosen to write about. It is filled with splendid churches and their art, and home to one of the most delicious little marketplaces imaginable. Not many tourists find their way here. Pistoia is also a good place from which to head up into the foothills of the Apennine mountains to the peaks around Abetone, all part of Tuscany that few visitors get to.

The historic centre of Pistoia – within walls that date back to Roman times – is really a small town. A good number of imposing austere Romanesque churches contain a rare richness of pre-Renaissance sculpture. Sculptors Nicola Pisano, his son Giovanni and a lesser-known Giovanni Pesani were the precursors to Renaissance sculpture, much as Duccio and Giotto were to Renaissance painting. All three are well represented here, along with some sublime works of the earliest della Robbia studio. Pistoia's spacious and harmonious cathedral square is surrounded by elegant buildings: the small richly decorated duomo, the large gracious tower next to it, the striped baptistery opposite and the old tribunal, the Palazzo Podesta. In the tribunal you still see the stone seats, so hard, so uncomfortable that the judges must have been anxious to finish the business of meting out justice as quickly as possible. Opposite the tribunal is the austere Palazzo Pretorio, the city hall. Imagine the youthful Leonardo arriving from the hills of Vinci to seek out his father at his Pistoia accounting studio, approaching this grand square through one of the narrow streets that still lead to it. They're now lined with Max Mara and Luisa Spagnoli shops.

To the rear of the large square, behind the baptistery, sits the irresistible little marketplace, appropriately called Piazza della Sala, the square of the salon. In the eighth century the palace of the Lombardian governor stood here, hence its name. A graceful, lion-topped fifteenth-century fountain – Il Pozzino – stands in the middle. Every day the square is packed with food stands. At its edge is a table laid with bundles of fresh herbs and wild greens. Here on Primetta Bartolomei's little table you'll find neatly tied little bundles of oregano, lavender, thyme and *nipotella*, a wild mint growing all over Tuscany that goes into the frying pan with funghi, courgettes and other fresh vegetables. Primetta claims magic powers, and is ready to tell you how to use her greens and where they all come from.

Food and artisan shops surround the square and fill the side streets as well. On the far corner you'll find a cheese shop to dream about. Simone Bovane's Spaccio del Parmigiano (Piazza della Sala 19) has a hygienic glow and carries a wide variety of every kind of cheese. The pecorinos are mostly of *latte crudo* – unpasteurized milk – a Pistoian speciality he brings to his shop from small producers all over the surrounding hills. Parmesan cheese comes from a single producer in Emilia; the buffalo mozzarella is delivered daily from the south.

Near the cheese shop, notice a sign that says 'Norcineria', or pork shop. It's an old-fashioned word, once the appellation of a wandering pork butcher. In the old days, before refrigeration, the *norcino* travelled from door to door and farm to farm, slaughtering pigs and preparing them to feed a family for the year. He would salt, season, stuff, hang and do whatever else necessary to make the meat last, readying prosciutto, *spalle* (shoulders of the pig), different sausages, livers stored in their own fat, marinated chops and whatever else. The shop on the square sells them all.

There are also three separate bread shops on the square, each with its special breads and focaccias.

My favourite for all produce is Sauro Signori's vegetable and speciality shop that faces the square. Bins of the freshest sort of seasonal vegetables are out in front. Inside you'll find lots of home-made take-aways including a collection of garlic cloves in a piquant marinade, tuna-stuffed little green tomatoes and chilli peppers, gourmet pastas and, as Sauro puts it, 'every fine bean' in Italy. Tuscany is bean country, and here you'll find its best and most freshly dried – no soaking needed – including Sorana, Purgatorio (not really Tuscan, these are mostly from Umbria) and Zolfino. Sauro can give you the history behind every item in his packed little shop.

The Via del Lastrone, a short, narrow little street lined with fourteenth-century houses, leads out from Piazza della Sala. It too is filled with speciality shops, trattorias, pizzerias and coffee bars. La BotteGaia, at number 4, is a little restaurant that attracts a large lunchtime crowd and changes its menu each week. It has a back door leading right onto Pistoia's main Piazza del Duomo, with tables outside at which you can dine during warm months. The restaurant also sells local specialities at its food boutique near the end of Via del Lastrone. At I Sapori della BotteGaia you can buy quality products of the area, including the sausages of a noted producer, Salumi di Marini, of nearby Agliana. Try the very special *mortadella di Prato*; seasoned with spices from the well-known old *farmacia di Santa Maria Novella* in Florence.

Pistoia's entire old centre turns into a vast crowded market two mornings each week: Wednesdays and Saturdays. This is no simple market in a square; rather you'll find street after street and the cathedral square itself crammed with stalls selling every sort of household and personal goods. Food stands include specialities not only of Tuscany, but Naples and Puglia as well.

More interest lies along the streets surrounding the piazzas of the duomo and the marketplace. On Via Cavour is the church of San Giovanni with an impressive block-long green-and-white striped marble facade. Inside the dim basilica-like interior, you'll make out a lovely intricately carved Pesani pulpit and a sublime white visitation by della Robbia. Just down from the main piazza is the not-to-be-missed series of brilliantly coloured della Robbia panels fronting the old hospital which is still Pistoia's main hospital. A set of binoculars can help you to see the intricate detail of the panels. They depict the many acts of mercy ministered by Jesus. Another church, a few blocks away from the main square, is Sant' Andrea, with yet another awesome pulpit, this one by Nicola Pisano and his sons. Another intimate little church – San Bartolomeo – houses an even earlier example of Romanesque sculpture, stiff figures, but with a lot of expression.

The duomo itself is filled with splendid art, beginning with the richly decorated Andrea della Robbia lunette under which you enter. Inside, the richly endowed chapel of St James boasts an outstanding silver altar of the thirteenth century, with almost 650 solid-silver figures. Andrea Pisano designed the octagonal striped baptistry opposite the cathedral; the outside sculptures are splendid examples of the early Romanesque. The inside is imposingly austere, with a remarkable high conical ceiling of simple brick.

Pistoia has an impressive collection of modern sculpture too. Marino Marini was born here; one of his well-known horses occupies the main entrance hall of the town hall next to the cathedral. A gallery of Marini's works, with sculptures and drawings, is in the old Convento del Tau, a few streets away. (Corso Silvano Fedi 30. Open weekdays from 10 a.m. to 6 p.m., Sundays and holidays from 9.30 a.m. to 12.30 p.m.)

A short ride from Pistoia is one of Italy's most impressive modern sculpture parks. Villa Celle is about four kilometres from Pistoia on the road to Montale. Giovanni Gori bought the eighteenth-century villa with its great wooded park in 1969 and made it into an outdoor museum for monumental works by well-known modern artists, including Beverly Pepper, Magdalena Abakanowicz, Alice Aycoch, Dani Karavan, Sol LeWitt, Pistoletto, Richard Serra, Robert Morris and many others. At last count there were more than sixty great pieces in the woods. The forest itself is worth the walk, with its small lake, large old firs and oaks, odd nineteenth-century pavilions and grand avenues to wander through. You'll need a reservation to visit the park. (Villa Fattoria di Celle, Santomato. Reserve by fax: 0573 479486, or by email: goricoll@tin.it)

◆ THE HILLS ◆

The Apennine road from Pistoia up to the Abetone mountain leads to a cool respite on a hot summer's day, when Florence and the cities around it have become horribly crowded and one longs for a cool day in the hills. Local Pistoians, Luccans and Florentines traditionally take their summer's refreshment in these verdant hills of vast pine and chestnut forests. Autumn and winter offer a different landscape and other pleasures as well. The changing colours along the forest roads are wondrous in October and November. During the winter months, Abetone, the highest mountain pass in Tuscany, becomes the largest ski resort of the region. (To travel up here during the snowy season you'll need tyre chains.)

From Pistoia, a single road leads up toward Abetone. San Marcello Pistoiese, the principal town of the mountain, lies about 25 kilometres from Pistoia. Just before reaching San Marcello (you can come back to it on the return trip to Pistoia), a sign on the right points to Gavinana. This cosy ancient mountain village offers your first real view of the awesome mountains above. Gavinana has an appealing square, complete with fountain and equestrian statue of a local sixteenth-century hero, and an impressive lavishly decorated little church – Santa Maria Assunta – that has a number of notable works of art as well: an appealing ancient lion chiselled out of a block of local stone, two lively terracotta bas-reliefs and two carved wooden figures of the angel and Virgin Mary. As you leave you'll notice an ancient stone door in the wall that leads up to the church tower.

Continue through Gavinana on the road marked to Lizzano. It offers more splendid views. By now, you are well up into the cool mountains and reach a kind of primordial gloomy forest, where the bright sunshine suddenly becomes an almost eerie dark shadow. Continue along the narrow road and emerge into the sunlight to Lizzano, a tiny village whose houses along the road have been frescoed with lively modern naive paintings of mountain life. Pass through down to the river Lima. Cross the river and you are on the main road that leads up to the pine forests of Abetone.

The first stop along the river on the road to Abetone is Cutigliano, an old bustling resort town, surrounded by woods and a cool breeze in summer. It's worth visiting at any time of the year. Ambling through its warren of small streets, you come upon a lovely little old municipality building, fronted by an equally attractive fourteenth-century loggia. The facade of the city hall is entirely embellished with coats of arms of every family that has ruled this small town. At the top of Cutigliano is Doganáccia and a funicular railway that travels further up the mountain to its peak. Up here, at 2000 metres above sea level, there are lovely walks over grassy meadows as far as the little lake of Scaffaiolo, a favourite place for overnight hikers to watch the sun rise.

Cutigliano has several produce shops offering local mountain products, including fruit liqueurs and grappa, freshly dried wonderfully aromatic mushrooms and a fine choice of honeys flavoured with the wild fruit of the mountains. Also in Cutigliano is Da Fagiolini, a popular local restaurant. Beyond Cutigliano, on the road to Abetone, at Pianosinatico, there is another fine, unusually interesting restaurant, Silvio La Storia a Tavola.

Abetone is the main winter resort of the area, with lots of ski-lifts and well-developed slopes and trails. The town itself was mostly built after the Second World

War. During its short season of real snow Abetone is quite mobbed on weekends. During the week it's pleasantly empty. Good coffee and pastry shops line the main street, with speciality shops for local products and ski equipment alongside. A favourite after-ski or mountain-hike treat is any number of fresh wild-berry tarts and cream snacks.

The chairlifts in Abetone operate during the summer as well, making it a favourite outing for hikers and berry hunters (who, by local legislation to protect professionals, are limited to only as much as they can eat or stuff into their pockets). During August especially it can get quite crowded, but even then the mountains make a delightful outing.

From Abetone the road continues down over the mountains to Modena (home of balsamic vinegar, Luciano Pavarotti and car-maker Ferrari) in nearby Emilia-Romagna. To remain in Tuscany, turn around and head back down the mountain past Pianosinatico and Cutigliano to the crossroads at Lima. There you can turn right towards Lucca or left back to Pistoia. Near Lima you'll see a sign to a suspension bridge at Mammiano. Take the little detour here. Before the last war, Lima was filled with ironworks, many producing the small arms from which Pistoia takes its name. The suspension bridge was built to connect two plants on either side of the river Lima. It's quite an engineering marvel; at 40 metres long, it just hangs there like a lacy netting. It's been reinforced in recent years but I can remember a frightening trip across on my first visit. It's still scary. From Mammiano Basso (lower Mammiano), off the main road to Pistoia, you get the best view of it. Any number of roads from there take you down the mountain, either towards Lucca or back through San Marcello to Pistoia.

◆ Specialities of the area ◆

Some of the best porcini mushrooms in all of Tuscany come from these mountains, as do the tastiest wild berries, including the small field blueberries called *mirtilli*, wild strawberries (*fragolini*), blackberries (*more*) and raspberries (*lampore*). The berries are found in the woods in abundance during the summer months, although, as with funghi and chestnuts, permits are needed to pick more than a bagful. The forests are public but professional collectors from nearby villages earn a livelihood from picking and selling the fruits. The berries flavour liqueurs and grappa as well as honeys and marmalades. All can be bought in the speciality shops of Cutigliano and Abetone.

Wild mushrooms – one of the glories of Tuscan cooking – arrive in two seasons here. From late June and through July, a limited supply of delicate *castagne porcini* doesn't get much further than mountain restaurants. During the autumn, before the first frost, the main season begins – and ends all too quickly – when fresh funghi are the dish of the day everywhere, and the main local sport as well. By 7 a.m. – when the first light begins – cars are already climbing the narrow roads to the forests. An hour later it's hard to find a place to park. Seasonal and day permits to pick mushrooms in limited amounts are issued inexpensively in most of the hill towns. In the markets for their short season, funghi are costly. A little goes a long way with these heavily perfumed firm mushrooms. They must be wiped clean on top with a moist cloth, and the earth scraped from the stems before they're ready to prepare. The most elegant way of serving porcini is to brush the larger caps with good oil, garlic and salt and grill them over a wood fire. Perfectly firm and fresh porcini and the more delicate *ovoli* are also eaten raw in salads, sliced thinly with equally slim slices of Parmesan cheese, all on a bed of rocket. The smaller, less perfect funghi are chopped and sautéed in olive oil with parsley and garlic; these *funghi trifolati* are served with meat, as pasta sauces and in risottos.

When mushrooms are at their most abundant, a good bit of the crop is laid aside to dry. You can see large slices lying in the open autumn air all over the mountains. Sometimes they are for sale; stop to buy before they go off to market in their little cellophane sacks. It is the moment when they are at their most pungent, still limp and ready for winter storage in a paper bag or airy tin. Pick the ones that seem most healthy, with firm white interiors, brown on the edges. Fresh funghi are also quickly frozen these days. They are nowhere near as tasty as the fresh, but do work as a substitute in cooked dishes.

I've learned a lot from Sauro Signori whose shop in the Pistoia marketplace sells fresh funghi when they're available – even in late spring – and large slices of dried as soon as the season finishes. He taught me about the rare dried white figs from nearby Carmignano that are sprinkled with fennel seeds and dried in laurel leaves, the best chestnut flour and polenta, and the meatiest walnuts from Lari in Pisa's province.

As in other mountain areas of Tuscany, chestnuts are turned into sweet flour, *farina dolce*. The best chestnut flour in these parts, says Sauro, comes from Momigno in the Pistoian hills. The town lies 'below 800 metres and has the best soil and climate' for chestnuts. They are picked in October, laid to dry for at least two months on a netted screen in a drying room (*metato*) with a fire in the corner that keeps a constant low heat, then cleaned of their shells and stone ground in a traditional mill. The flour begins to arrive in Pistoia in December; the supply continues for several months. By late spring it's all gone.

The most popular chestnut-flour dish of the Pistoian hills is *castagnaccio*, the classic semi-sweet cake that combines chestnut flour, pine nuts, raisins, olive oil and rosemary. It is invariably a part of the festive winter meals, especially that accompanying the fresh pressing of olive oil.

The traditional age-old way of using the sweet, albeit heavy, chestnut flour is for *necci*, a generation ago the daily nourishment in every Pistoian farm home. Flour for normal bread was still a luxury. There is a splendid way of preparing them, an art little known among the young today. But one of our young friends, Miranda Vitelli, who comes from a village in Pistoia province, still does. I asked her how. It was impossible to explain and she invited us for a *necci* evening. It's a daunting procedure. And all for a simple mix of chestnut flour and water. It was late January. When we arrived Miranda's husband Paolo was already heating 4-cm-thick stone discs – each the size of a crêpe – in the open kitchen fireplace. About twenty of them sat on the large iron grill, heating for several hours before the procedure would begin. From her storeroom Miranda brought out several batches of dried large chestnut leaves – still green but brittle – that she had picked in September for the *necci* she would make in January. These she gently boiled to give them back their body. For the twenty *necci*, she made a thick batter from a kilogram of stone-ground chestnut flour and water. Only a pinch of salt was added, nothing more.

The stones were hot. Paolo brought out a kind of umbrella-stand bracket, held together by three long wooden columns but otherwise open and just large enough to hold the stack of discs. One by one, with iron tongs, Paolo removed the discs from the fire and into the stand. Miranda covered each with three or four wet chestnut leaves (shiny side up), and poured over a ladleful of chestnut batter. More leaves, this time shiny side down, covered the batter, and on top went another stone. Layer by layer, one stone on top of another, went chestnut leaves, batter, chestnut leaves, until all twenty were stacked into what she called a *castello*. Steam escaped from all sides as the leaves dried instantly in the heat.

Not a minute passed before the *necci* were cooked. One by one Paolo lifted out the stones with his tongs, and we all began to peel off leaves and place the little crêpes on a serving platter. As the stack went to the table the crisp heap of dried chestnut leaves went into the fire and we sat down to eat the little leaf-embossed crêpes rolled with a choice of two fillings, salted *rigatino*, a fat bacon, or sweet fresh ricotta cheese. It was a substantial meal for six. Paolo reminisced about the old days. When his mother was a girl, he said, *necci* were prepared in this way every day for the children's snack when they went off to school and as daily bread in those wheat-scarce days.

Cutigliano holds an annual Festa delle Castagne each November that features both *castagnaccio* and *necci*, which are more quickly baked or fried rather than this elaborate old way of doing them.

A prized little waxy potato is harvested in a single mountain town just under Abetone. *Melo* potatoes are still treasured, but potato farming in the mountains declined and today the *melo* doesn't get much further than the towns around. Area restaurants feature them, especially roasted and served with funghi. There's talk of a revival, and Italy's Slow Food movement is encouraging a DOP protection label for the *melo* that could encourage local farmers to return to it.

Like other mountain areas, the Pistoia's mountains are full of game. The most popular to reach the table are boar and hare. On autumn and winter menus everywhere here, *pappardelle alla lepre*, fresh wide noodles with hare sauce, is a favourite. The same light pasta also comes *al cinghiale*: with a pungent boar ragú.

Another historic winter dish that traditionally marks major winter events in the Apennine foothills is *fegatello di maiale*. The liver of a large pig is cooked in its belly fat and thus preserved to be eaten during the winter. In the Pistoia hills the liver is first mixed with some chopped pork meat, flavoured with fennel, laurel and garlic, then stuffed into the caul, the net-like membrane that surrounds the spleen. The entire package is cooled and preserved in the fat. It solidifies and remains fresh in cold storage the entire winter. I've occasionally seen preserved *fegatello* on Pistoia area restaurant menus. In the mountain area of Monte Amiata, the liver is cooked and served fresh in the same way, tender and pink. In the Pistoia area, preserved as it is, it tends to be tougher, to be sliced like sausage.

Sheep farmers have fared better than potato farmers in the Pistoian hills. These mountains are fertile ground for the hundreds of farmers raising small flocks of sheep. They make a special pecorino, usually at home, from *latte crudo*, unpasteurized milk, that still eludes the restrictive eye of the European market. Much of the shepherding and cheese-making is still done by these small farmers in the traditional way: milk is taken twice a day from grazing pastured sheep and turned immediately into one of the various cheeses. *Ricotta* and *raviggiolo* are eaten fresh, *pecorino* is aged and can be bought at various stages of the ageing period: *fresco* or almost fresh, and *stagionato*, aged for a longer period, harder and more piquant. A dry storeroom serves for ripening and preserving the cheeses. They are very much a local speciality.

◆ Typical restaurants and their recipes ◆

PISTOIA: La BotteGaia

La BotteGaia, Via del Lastrone 4, Pistoia.
Tel. 0573 365602. Best to reserve for both lunch and dinner. On summer evenings ask for a table out the back next to Pistoia's baptistery. Closed Sunday lunch and all day Monday. Prices are moderate.

THIS LITTLE RESTAURANT just off the marketplace in Pistoia's centre has two entrances. The front door leads on to the busy market. The back door takes you out to the splendid Piazza del Duomo that is Pistoia's grand centre. During the warmer months, it is possible to dine here in the shadow of the green-and-white striped marble baptistery facing the grand old city hall and the cathedral tower, an unforgettable experience. In the evening the square is gently lit, and, if you are lucky, you might also dine to the accompaniment of an opera being rehearsed on the piazza. We were especially fortunate one evening to hear and sporadically watch a dress rehearsal for *Rigoletto*. Between courses we wandered over closer to the stage to listen to arias. (There are also noisier jazz evenings; check before you reserve.)

Carlo Malentacchi and Alessandro Ormi, two friends who love good food, opened the restaurant in 1996. They chose a good spot. The restaurant begins to fill just after noon, with students, business people, groups of women out for lunch, market vendors. They continue to pour in until after 2 p.m.; often a table serves three sittings. The two owners also run a little *bottega* at the upper end of the same street that offers specialities of the area, cheeses, *salumi*, wines, marmalades and other sundries. At the restaurant, Carlo and Alessandro at times try to gentrify their fare by adding French (buttery) touches that nevertheless still taste blissfully Italian. They also like to dress up some dishes in their own manner. 'It's an age of specialization,' says Carlo. 'I decided to specialize in good things to eat.' The menu changes weekly, although some favourites are always available.

A warm summer evening meal can begin with a light salad of thinly sliced peaches and local goat's cheese, soft and mild, flavoured with raspberry vinegar and olive oil. The light *pappa di zucchini*, a mash of courgette, bread and basil, is another summer dish. A *crema di zucchini*, another courgette soup with a touch of cream, is more sophisticated and quite delicious.

In the winter they do a lot with chickpeas, a Pistoian favourite. Little pancakes of chickpea flour are topped with fresh tomatoes; *gateau di ceci*, a small cake made from the same flour, comes on a salad of baby greens. At times there's a rolled frittata with the lightest courgette filling bathed in a gentle tomato sauce. Or a creamy risotto with smoked scamorza, a hardened mozzarella-type cheese. For *secondi*, the choices can be a lightly grilled slice of tuna on fresh vegetables, or, another winter favourite of Pistoians, *fegatello di maiale nella rete*, pork liver preserved in fat. It's served with baked beans. Baby lamb chops are a spring favourite; La BotteGaia serves them on a bed of polenta.

An artichoke flan is served on a pecorino-based sauce; a peeled cooked potato is stuffed with ricotta and egg yolk with a shaving of white truffles. Not to be missed are the tagliarini smothered in butter and truffles. On market days there is *tripe alla fiorentina* which comes from 'the best *tripaio* around', a vendor who sells tripe and other innards from a stall in the open-air market out front.

RECIPES FROM La BotteGaia

Courgette cream soup / *Crema di zucchini*

Serves 4–6

½ stick celery, finely chopped
2 shallots, finely chopped
½ carrot, finely chopped
50g butter
500g small dark-green-skinned courgettes, sliced into thin rounds
500ml vegetable stock
60ml cream
Salt and freshly ground pepper
4–6 slices Tuscan bread, toasted
Extra virgin olive oil, to serve

Put the celery, shallots and carrot into a heavy saucepan with the butter and, over a medium heat, sauté until soft. Add the courgettes and cook slowly for another 15 minutes, allowing the courgette to release its water. Add the stock, cook for another 15 minutes and add the cream. Mix well, remove from heat and blend. Add salt and pepper to taste.

To serve, place a slice of toast in each dish, drip a bit of olive oil on to each bread slice and pour the soup over.

Courgette and smoked scamorza cheese risotto / *Risotto di scamorza e zucchine*

Serves 4

½ onion, sliced thinly
50g butter
300g carnaroli or other risotto rice
120ml dry white wine
3 small courgettes, cubed
About 500ml chicken stock, boiling
150g smoked mozzarella cheese, grated
100g freshly grated Parmesan cheese
Freshly ground pepper

In a flameproof earthenware casserole, melt the onion in the butter. Add the rice and cook together for 3–4 minutes. Splash in the wine and allow to evaporate. Add the courgettes and mix well. Add the boiling stock slowly, just covering the risotto with each ladleful.

When the rice is cooked *al dente,* add the grated smoked cheese and mix well. Remove from the heat and add half the Parmesan cheese. Serve immediately, with the remaining Parmesan and the pepper.

Lamb chops in tomato sauce / *Costelette in umido*

Serves 6

1kg baby lamb chops
Salt and freshly ground pepper
Flour for dusting
3 tablespoons olive oil
1 large shallot, chopped
2 cloves garlic, chopped
2 sticks celery, chopped
120ml dry white wine
1 x 300g tin Italian skinned tomatoes

Season and flour the chops. Heat 2 tablespoons of the olive oil in a pan until hot, then add the chops and brown them quickly. Remove and keep warm.

Add the remaining tablespoon of oil and the shallot, garlic and celery to the pan. Pour in the wine, allow to evaporate a bit and add the tomatoes, squashed through your hands. Add more salt and pepper to taste. Replace the lamb chops to cook in the sauce for about 15 minutes, until finished.

La BotteGaia serves the chops on a bed of polenta.

CUTIGLIANO: Trattoria da Fagiolino

Da Fagiolino, Piazza Catilina 9, Cutigliano.
Tel. 0573 68014. Reservations recommended during autumn and summer. Moderately priced. Closed Tuesdays and the month of November.

TRATTORIA DA FAGIOLINO sits on the relaxed main square in Cutigliano. Diners converge on this popular little eating place from as far as Lucca and Pistoia for a lunch or evening meal, even though the twisting mountain road back down the mountain can challenge the hardiest stomach. (A few inexpensive rooms are available at Da Fagiolino for overnight visitors.)

Luigi Innocenti is the third generation of his family to maintain this formidable little inn which specializes in the produce of the area.

Porcini, available from June to mid-July and from September to late November, are prepared in every sort of way. A feast of funghi can begin here with *insalata di funghi* or *crostini ai funghi*, or pasta with funghi sauce. Delicious little home-made gnocchi (also called *topini*, or little mice, in these parts) are seasoned with marjoram and thinly sliced mushrooms. There is a *gran fritto di funghi*, sliced mushrooms dipped in a light batter and deep fried. The *tagliata di funghi di Fagiolino* (a dish that at first glance resembles a sliced fillet of beef, but it's all mushroom!) can be eaten as a main course.

There are other interesting local dishes to consider here as well. Luigi Innocenti's *zuppa di Fagiolino con cipolline fresche*, a minestrone topped with freshly sliced onion, is given a special taste with a bit of prosciutto rind chopped in. His *ravioli al pepolino*, with the traditional ricotta and spinach filling, are covered in sauce flavoured by a local wild thyme called *pepolino*.

Portafoglio alla Fagiolino, a pork roast stuffed with

melting cheese and prosciutto and cooked in a funghi and wine sauce, is a memorable main course. When in season, game is offered too. Chestnut-flour polenta – called *manifatoli* – is served with roasted meats during the winter. In spring, the notable Péscia asparagus is served with a sprinkling of Parmesan cheese.

The best finish to all this is a plate of mixed wild berries accompanied by another house speciality, a light, crisp *biscotti* comprised mostly of air and cornflakes. A glass of *vin santo* arrives with the biscuits.

RECIPES FROM Da Fagiolino

Vegetable bread soup / *Zuppa di Fagiolino con cipolline fresche*

This is another version of the soup so beloved by Tuscans. Similar ingredients to most, but Fagiolino adds fennel instead of the usual rosemary, and a rind (not fat) of ham, which makes it different.

Serves 6

400g borlotti beans, soaked overnight
Salt
2 plum tomatoes
1 small onion, thinly sliced
½ leek, thinly sliced
3 tablespoons olive oil
1 small prosciutto or ham rind
2 carrots, thinly sliced in rounds
2 courgettes, thinly sliced in rounds
1 large potato, cubed
2 sticks celery, cubed
¼ Savoy cabbage, sliced into thin strips

4 kale leaves, sliced into thin strips
1 small bunch dried wild fennel sprigs (or
 1 teaspoon fennel seeds)
1 small bunch basil leaves
6 small slices day-old farm bread
1 red onion, thinly sliced
Fresh extra virgin olive oil and freshly ground pepper,
 to serve

Drain the soaked beans and cook them slowly in a large pan of water. Add salt at the end of the cooking. Purée half the beans with some of the water and the tomatoes. Reserve the purée in a bowl, adding the remaining beans to it. Reserve the remaining cooking water.

While the beans are cooking, soften the sliced onion and leek in the olive oil with the rind of the prosciutto or ham. When soft, add the remaining vegetables. Salt well and cook over a low heat until the vegetables are all soft, about 30 minutes. Add the beans and their purée, the fennel and basil, and cook over a low heat, adding as much of the reserved bean water as is necessary to maintain a fairly thick soup. Add more salt as necessary. Don't allow the soup to become too thin; it should be dense.

When the vegetables are cooked, place the bread in a large oval dish and pour the soup over. Allow to rest for 5 minutes. Slice the red onion over the top and serve with fresh oil and a pepper grinder at the table.

Stuffed pork roast / *Portafoglio alla Fagiolino*

Serves 4

500g boned pork roast
2 slices mild melting cheese, such as Emmental or Gruyère
2 slices prosciutto
4–5 sage leaves
Flour
Salt
15g butter
1 tablespoon olive oil
1 small wine glass white wine
240ml chicken or meat stock
4 fresh porcini mushrooms, chopped (or a handful of chopped dried ones)
1 clove garlic, finely chopped
1 small bunch parsley, chopped

Slice open the roast without cutting it through. Lay the cheese in the middle, not touching the ends. Lay the prosciutto and sage leaves over it, close and tie firmly with string. Dust with flour and salt lightly.

In a heavy pan with a cover, brown the roast in the butter and olive oil. Pour the wine over and allow to evaporate somewhat. Add the stock and mushrooms, lower the heat and cook until the roast can easily be pierced through with a sharp knife, about 1½ hours. Keep an eye on the liquid level and add water if necessary. At the end of the cooking, add the garlic and parsley.

To serve, remove the string, slice and cover each slice with sauce.

Pine nut biscuits / *Biscotti*

Fagiolino offers these light little cornflake and pine-nut biscuits with *vin santo* at the end of every meal.

Makes about 2 dozen

150g unsalted butter, at room temperature
200g sugar
3 large eggs
300g flour
2 teaspoons baking powder
100g pine nuts, toasted
400g crushed cornflakes

Heat oven to 180°C/Gas 4. Line baking trays with baking paper. In a mixer, beat the butter and sugar until well blended. Add the eggs, one by one, beating thoroughly after each addition. Sift the flour and baking powder in another bowl, then add to the butter mixture, beating until blended. Remove the bowl from the mixer and stir in the pine nuts.

Put the crushed cornflakes in a shallow bowl. Take 1 heaped tablespoon of the dough mixture and roll it into a ball in the crushed cornflakes. Place on the baking trays about 3cm apart. Bake until golden, about 20–25 minutes, then allow to cool.

PIANOSINATICO: Silvio la Storia a Tavola ('History at the Table')

Silvio la Storia a Tavola, Via Brennero 181, Pianosinatico.
Tel. 0573 629274. Closed Tuesdays, and 15 days following Easter and in October. Priced inexpensive to moderate. Best to reserve.

PIANOSINATICO IS A LITTLE curve in the road between Cutigliano and Abetone, about ten kilometres before Abetone. Silvio Zanni is a former history professor. His 'History at the Table' is a remarkably unpretentious little place well worth the journey it takes to get there. When you've finished a meal at this inexpensive trattoria high in the mountains of Pistoia, you'll wonder why it doesn't exist in a more accessible major city, or at least around the corner from where you live. There's a good reason. Chef Silvio Zanni grew up in nearby Cutigliano, and after years of teaching in Prato and then Paris, came back home to do his favourite thing: creating splendid things to eat. He takes his role seriously. The jauntily perched chef's toque sits well on his friendly grey head. He claims to have 500 *primi* – first courses – at the ready, many of them invented by him, using only – or mostly – local ingredients.

Silvio graduated with a degree in philosophy at Bologna and taught medieval history for years before seriously turning to the kitchen. He can regale you with talk that mixes food and history, holding forth on Tuscan medieval cooking, citing Brunelleschi's shopping lists or Pontormo diaries. He claims an atavistic right to his culinary skills; his grandfather was a famous Cutigliano hotelier/chef, at a time when the little resort played host to Italy's aristocracy each summer.

Silvio's partner, Andrea Vannuccu, does the serving,

and knows as much about local specialities and the dishes served here. He will tell you about the local wheat that is ground into the special flour used to make pasta and bread. He lists the various local goat's cheeses made from *latte crudo* (raw milk) that have been rewarded with a special certificate from the prestigious Slow Food Presidio.

It's the *antipasti* and first courses that Silvio is most proud of. It's not easy to get through to the main courses. The restaurant usually offers three *antipasti* and five different *primi* as a tasting menu each day. I recommend the tasting menu. If you can save space, the *secondi* of various grilled and roasted meats are also very good. The *antipasto* can be an incomparable combination of the esteemed *melo* potatoes in a truffle sauce, or *crostini* of liver and tuna. *Crostini di funghi* are a special treat during the autumn and in late spring as well. The pasta dishes have mostly been invented in Silvio's kitchen. There's one with a colourful beetroot sauce, another one with red or white onions, a third with carrots and smoked bacon. Ravioli are covered in fresh oil steeped in the ubiquitous wild mint, *nipotella*. In the summer, fresh tomatoes are combined with herbs. The creamed soups include a light chickpea *velluta*, as well as one of fresh peas combined with funghi.

RECIPES FROM Silvio

◆ Liver and tuna crostini / *Crostini di fegato e tonno*

Makes about 30 crostini

1 clove garlic, peeled
2 tablespoons olive oil
5 chicken livers
200g tuna packed in oil, drained well
1 small liqueur glass *vin santo* or port
2 tablespoons tomato purée
Freshly chopped parsley
Salt and freshly ground pepper
1 long baguette, sliced

Heat the garlic in the oil. When the oil begins to bubble, add the chicken livers and tuna. When the livers have lost their red, add the *vin santo* and allow to evaporate. Add the tomato purée and enough water to cover the livers and tuna, and cook for about 15 minutes. Add some fresh parsley, taste for salt and pepper, and blend in a food processor.

Silvio dips the bread quickly in stock before smearing on the paste. It's good but not necessary. You can also serve the spread on crackers.

Summer tomato pasta / *Pasta promodoro estiva*

Serves 4

400g cherry tomatoes
Salt and freshly ground pepper
350g spaghetti
120ml extra virgin olive oil
1 large handful fresh herbs that can include marjoram, rosemary, sage, thyme, oregano, savory and basil
1 small hot chilli pepper, seeds removed, chopped
50g shaved Parmesan cheese, with more at table

Chop the tomatoes into small cubes and put them in a colander with a sprinkling of salt to drain. Cook the pasta in plenty of boiling salted water. In a small pan, heat the oil and add the chopped herbs and chilli. Just as the oil begins to sizzle, turn off the heat. When the pasta is cooked, place the tomatoes in the bottom of a serving dish which you can cover. Drain the pasta and add it to the tomatoes. Add a good sprinkling of salt and pepper, pour over the herbed oil, mix and cover for several minutes. Serve with slices of Parmesan shaved over the top.

Fusilli with a carrot and bacon sauce / *Fusilli con carote e pancetta*

This invention of Silvio's can't really be called traditional, but he certainly is and the pasta is good enough to include.

Serves 4

1½ tablespoons olive oil
100g pancetta or bacon, in small cubes
5 carrots, peeled and coarsely grated
60ml cognac or brandy
30ml cream
350g small butterfly pasta
1 small handful parsley leaves, chopped
Salt and freshly ground pepper

In a saucepan large enough to hold the pasta too, heat the oil and add the bacon. After 2 minutes, add the carrots. Cook over a slow heat until the carrots are cooked. Add the cognac and allow to evaporate. Add the cream and heat to mix well. Remove from the heat.

Cook the pasta in plenty of boiling salted water. Drain quickly, allowing some of the water to remain, then add to the sauce and return the pan to a low heat. Add the parsley and cook together for a few minutes. Taste for seasoning and pour into a heated serving bowl.

Tagliatelle with creamy onion sauce / *Tagliatelle con cipolle cremose*

Serves 6

2 large sweet red onions, very thinly sliced
1 tablespoon olive oil
240ml red wine
1 tablespoon cream
500g egg tagliatelle

In a saucepan large enough to hold the pasta too, sauté the onions in the oil until just soft. Add the red wine, bring to a boil, lower the heat and cook gently until the onions are completely soft. Cook the tagliatelle just for a minute, then add to the sauce. Add the cream and mix well. Cook until the pasta is *al dente* (add water if necessary) and serve immediately.

Butterfly pasta with beetroot sauce / *Farfalle con salsa di barbabietole*

Another Silvio invention.

Serves 6

4 medium beetroot
Salt
4 tablespoons olive oil
3 cloves garlic, finely chopped
120ml vegetable stock
2 tablespoons fresh cream
Small bunch basil, chopped
500g butterfly pasta

Cook the beetroot in a good amount of salted water until they are done but still firm. Peel, cut in half and slice fairly thinly. In a pan large enough to hold the pasta too, heat the oil with the garlic, and when the oil begins to bubble, add the beetroot and the stock. Cook for a minute, mixing well, and add the cream. Set aside.

Bring a big pan of water to the boil, salt it and add the pasta. While it is still very *al dente*, drain and add the pasta to the beetroot. Add the basil and return to the heat for another minute or so until the pasta is cooked through and the sauce absorbed.

◆ Cream of chickpea soup / *Velluta di Ceci*

Serves 6–8

½ onion, thinly sliced
2 tablespoons olive oil
400g chickpeas, soaked overnight with a pinch of bicarbonate of soda, then cooked until soft
1 sprig rosemary
Leaves of 1 sprig sage
500ml vegetable stock (or more)
1 tablespoon tomato purée
1 small knob butter
Freshly ground pepper and fresh extra virgin olive oil, to serve

Melt the onion in the olive oil, then add the drained, cooked chickpeas, along with the rosemary, sage and a quarter of the stock. Cook for several minutes, then remove from the heat and blend. Put the mixture back in the pan, add the tomato purée and enough stock to make a light creamy soup, and heat through. At the end, stir in the butter. Serve hot with pepper and olive oil at the table.

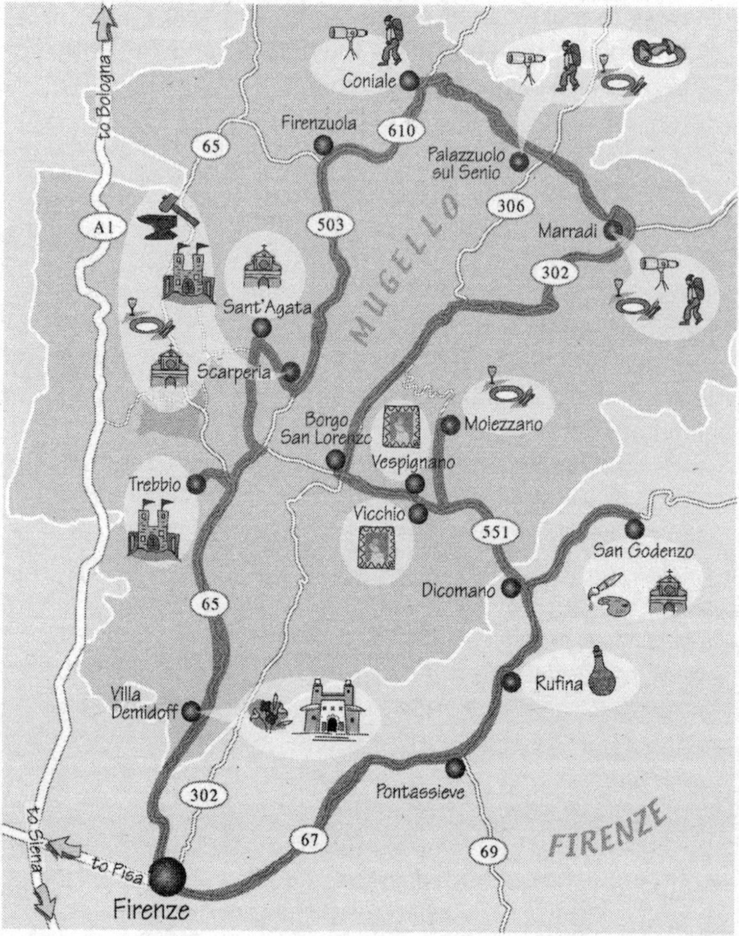
to Bologna
A1
65
Coniale
Firenzuola
610
Palazzuolo sul Senio
306
Marradi
503
MUGELLO
302
Sant'Agata
Scarperia
Borgo San Lorenzo
Molezzano
Vespignano
Trebbio
Vicchio
551
San Godenzo
Dicomano
65
Rufina
Villa Demidoff
Pontassieve
302
67
69
FIRENZE
to Siena
to Pisa
Firenze

Church
Trekking
Crafts
Restaurant
Museum
Garden
Art
Views
Local Produce
Wine
Castle
Villa

5

The Mugello

THE MUGELLO was once the summer playground of the Medici family, who bought most of its southern hills from various noble families in the fifteenth and sixteenth centuries. It lies conveniently just to the north of Florence, in the cool foothills of the Apennine mountains, an inviting retreat in the steamy summer months in the valley. You can still see the fortifications, castles, villas, hunting lodges and bishops' palaces that went up during Medici control. The family even founded experimental farms to bring better nourishment to their Florentine subjects. A flourishing milk industry is the single visible trace of that initiative, but telltale fortress towers and remaining castles become evident soon after you leave Florence.

The Medici remnants are in verdant valleys of the lower Mugello. In the upper hills are Alpine-like landscapes of vast beauty that stretch into Emilia-Romagna. It's one of those places to return to time and again, yet it remains one of the lesser known and little visited parts of Tuscany.

Reaching this awesome beauty can be trying. The valley roads north of Florence are busy with industry, especially around Borgo San Lorenzo and Rufina. But once you get beyond the cement factories and carelessly tossed-together housing estates, you'll find yourself almost alone in one of the more spectacularly beautiful mountain landscapes of Tuscany. It is a land of well-preserved natural parks, perfect for trekking and horseriding. Imposing churches, interesting towns and some tasty traditional dishes add to its attractions. The narrow inside roads are blessedly unspoiled; you drive for long stretches through lovely pastured pine- and chestnut-covered mountains without meeting another car. The most you'll come upon is a warning sign for an unseen cow. (You can also go by rail, on the newly renovated Faentina railway that meanders from Florence up into the hills to Marradi.)

Make a point to visit or at least pass by one of the stately Medici villas and buildings that include Villa Demidoff, Castello di Cafaggiolo, the Palazzo dei Vicari at Scarperia and Castello il Trebbio.

I've tried different ways to get to the Mugello from Florence. There is the most obvious, from the Barberino exit on the *autostrada* to Bologna. My favourite, however, is to head east from Florence to Pontessieve and there turn north through Rufina to Vicchio. Rufina is about a 45-minute drive from Florence, and from there it's a short trip to Dicomano. From Vicchio, head towards Borgo San Lorenzo where a right turn leads up to the mountains, vistas open and you'll reach the remote mountain towns of Marradi and Palazzuolo sul Senio. After that it's back down the mountain to Scarperia and other towns below.

Rufina is not yet really the Mugello; it's the northernmost area where the wines of Chianti are produced. A good bit of commercial Chianti, Chianti Rufina, is bottled here, and you can almost smell the wine as you near the town. The town is mostly interesting for its wine production; there are tastings along the way. Further up the road at Dicomano, turn off for a small detour to San Godenzo, with its noble eleventh-century church of the same name (or San Gaudenzo, as he was originally called). The body of the saint lies in state, beautifully embalmed in an open case. More captivating is the lovely painting by Bernardo Daddi of the Virgin and several saints. San Godenzo had its big moment in the first years of the fourteenth century, when Ghibellini forces gathered here in an attempt to return to Guelfi Florence; Dante Alighieri was among them.

The translucently shadowed valley around Vicchio is Giotto land. He was born in nearby Vespignano where his house is now a small museum (open during summer months: Tuesdays on request, Thursday, Saturday and Sunday from 10 a.m. to 12 and 3.30 to 6.30 p.m. Winter hours are fewer: weekends only at the same times). Some claim that the Renaissance itself burst on to the scene from these low hills. Franco Utili, a lightly bearded gentle Vicchio native who dwells on local lore (and traditional food), described it all to me one day. 'Walk out from Giotto's house,' he suggested, 'into the pastured woodland, and you'll find Ponte di Cimambue – Cimambue's bridge – where Cimambue happened upon the young shepherd Giotto sketching his sheep in the field.' Impressed by his skill, Cimambue invited the boy to his workshop. '*Ecco*, the Renaissance blossomed!' Utili exclaimed. Cimambue was the link, and Giotto began the chain. If you walk through those woods and fields today, he says, you'll see and understand why. I did, and came away convinced.

Fra Angelico also came from Vicchio and in the old town hall there is a museum named after him dedicated to sacred art, open the same hours as the Giotto museum. Another museum to visit is the Museo della Civiltà Contadina, a historical exposition of rural life in this area. (For visiting hours, call the Vicchio *comune* on 055 843921.)

Casa di Caccia, a small restored lodge about twelve kilometres north of Vicchio, houses a restaurant worth the detour; from its pleasant terraced dining room you have a view of the entire valley of the lower Mugello.

From Vicchio and Vespignano, the main road leads west toward Borgo San Lorenzo. Skirting the city, you can turn right on to the provincial road through Panicaglia that brings you through pleasant landscapes to the upper Mugello, to Marradi and Palazzuolo along the Senio river, the area I love best. From the wide valleys in the lower Mugello you rise into the high mountains over narrow passes through meadowed pine and chestnut forests and dazzling views on all sides. This is the Toscana Romagnola, green mountains with rounded peaks that roll off into distant Emilia-Romagna. Head first for Marradi, then across the mountain landscape to Palazzuolo sul Senio. Both towns are perfect little Alpine Italian villages, preserved almost in the state they were hundreds of years ago. And both boast admirable restaurants. In Marradi is Il Camino, with its reputation as the best restaurant in the area. Palazzuolo has Locanda Senio, a cosy inn just off the main old square in the fourteenth-century town centre.

From Palazzuolo another beautiful, almost deserted road with singular mountain and valley views runs up to Coniale and back down to Firenzuola, a bleak little old town with a big history, which was almost bombed out of existence during the Second World War. Garibaldi, fleeing his enemies, made his way across these passes in the freezing winter of 1848, traversing the Apennines in an arduous trek from Livorno to Ravenna. The inscription on the facade of one city hall assures visitors that, fleeing from the French army,

Giuseppe Garibaldi slept here one night '*assieme con la moglie*' (together with his wife).

Firenzuola retains the old Porto Fiorentina and arcaded streets and has reconstructed *palazzi* to give you an idea of what it once was. There is also a little museum dedicated to *Pietra Serena*, the velvety grey travertine stone, quarried and worked here, that faces and fronts so many lovely Romanesque churches. (Museo della Pietra Serena, Rocca di Firenzuolo, tel. 055 8199434 or 5.)

The drive back down towards the valley through another mountain pass brings you to Scarperia, once the main trading town of the Mugello. In the eighteenth century a modern road was built over the parallel Futa pass, today part of the main *autostrada* link between Florence and Bologna, and Scarperia was left by the wayside. Its remnants of greatness remain, however, and thus the town has become something of a minor attraction. Walking up the narrow old main street you come upon an oversized and commanding castle – the Palazzo dei Vicari – looking as though it was simply parachuted into this street of an otherwise low-built medieval town. Awesome, even overbearing, it is a perfect display of the architecture of power. (As an architect, mused my husband upon first laying his eyes on this enormous stone building, 'Stalin had nothing on the Medici. Their taste was better though.') The Palazzo dei Vicari, built by the Medici to house their appointed bishops, wears their coats of arms ornately across its front like an ageing general, proudly decorated but overweight. The palazzo's overwhelming tower and thick crenellated walls – fronting a small piazza and dwarfing the Romanesque church of saints Jacopo and Filippo – seem to possess the entire town even today. Off to the side on the piazza, the little gothic chapel of Santa Maria has a fifteenth-century vaulted ceiling and a lovely old Madonna.

The palazzo houses a museum for another of Scarperia's historic traditions, the hand production of sharp knives. Fine hunting knives have been crafted in Scarperia for hundreds of years, developing into a first-rate artisan cutlery industry that is still a mainstay of its economy. On both sides of the road leading up to the Palazzo dei Vicari fine handmade cutlery shops offer their wares, selling a wide range of kitchen knives, handsome carving sets and well-honed table knives, all irresistibly tempting to buy. Just around the corner from the palazzo, you can watch knives being crafted in the factory shop of Saladini. Owner Pierre Baldini will be happy to show you around and sell you anything you want from his ready supply on the second floor. (Saladini, Via Solferino, 19.) From there you can wander the back streets of Scarperia.

Scarperia celebrates a major festival, the Diotto, on every 8 September, to honour its bishops and commemorate the founding of the town in 1306. Replete with medieval costumes and playing tournaments, a procession of banner-waving young men marches through the streets. Banner-waving is something of a Tuscan art. It's featured in town festivals all over the region.

Just outside Scarperia to the north, an authentically restored grand old building of the Borghese family houses the Fattoria il Palagio, once a farm building and now an impressive restaurant and inn.

From Scarperia, head for nearby Sant'Agata, which possesses one of the more notable small churches of the region, the ninth-century Romanesque Pieve di Sant'Agata. Continue on the road to Galliano, but soon turn to the left for the road that brings you to San Piero a Sieve. Follow the signs for Castello il Trebbio, perhaps the most historic Medici house in the area. Designed and built in the fifteenth century by the noted Renaissance architect Michelozzo Michelozzi for Cosimo de Medici, this imposing castle was described memorably by historian Hugh Thomas as a place where a person with a sense of history will be forgiven if he persuades himself that, even though remote, here is the heart of civilization.

There's a fine view of the valley below, where so many great travellers passed, and many continued on to Il Trebbio. 'Imagine Lorenzo de Medici walking under the pergola with Poliziano or Luigi Pulci, his country neighbour, or Dante nearby plotting with the Ubaldini, Giotto walking with his sheep, Becket, Goethe, Montaigne and Boswell travelling past,' writes Thomas. Here also passed Galileo, Leonardo, Michelangelo, Masaccio and many others. The castle, now in private hands, can be visited in groups Monday to Friday. (Tel. 055 8458793.)

From Il Trebbio it's a short drive to Novoli where you'll find a main artery to Florence that takes you past another sixteenth-century Medici villa, once the magnificent home of Cosimo's eldest son. The grand house fell into ruin, and was rebuilt completely as Villa Demidoff in the nineteenth century by Prince Paolo Demidoff, the son of the Russian ambassador to Florence, hence the name. Its splendid gardens are filled with grottoes, water games, grotesque figures by Buontalenti and the gigantic statue *Appenino* by Giambologna. (Both sculptor/architects are also well represented in the Boboli gardens in Florence.) The park is open to the public on weekends between March and October, and plays host to cultural events as well. (Tel. 055 409427 or 409155.)

◆ SPECIALITIES OF THE AREA ◆

Il Trebbio was a vast agricultural holding as well as a hunting estate. The Medici also called their nearby milk farm 'Panna' (which means cream in Italian) and imported Alpine cows to bring nourishment to the Florentines. Descendants of those cows continue to produce milk to this day. We drink Mukki milk and eat Mukki bio yogurt and other dairy products, all of which have evolved from the Medici incentive in the fourteenth century. It's one of the Mugello's major industries. Beef from the Limousin breed of cattle is also a Mugello speciality, and is considered here on a par with the better-known Chianina beef.

As in other regions of Tuscany, various saints' days and holy periods of the year come with traditional foods in the Mugello. During carnival, the pre-Lenten season, fried pastry strips (*cenci*) appear here and elsewhere, as do millet cakes (*migliacci*). The forty days of Lent – the Quaresima – are commemorated here, as elsewhere, with cocoa mini-biscuits shaped into alphabet letters. On Ash Wednesday, in Borgo San Lorenzo, plates of polenta are offered in the main square to begin the fast before Easter. Another traditional Lenten dish, *farinata con gli zoccoli*, adds beans to the polenta, making a hearty soup that turns almost solid. After a day, it can be sliced and fried for a second meal.

In anticipation of spring, on the day of San Giuseppe, 19 March, Tuscans eat sweet fritters of eggs and rice called *frittelle di San Giuseppe*, celebrating the moment the hens begin laying again after their winter suspension. Every area, including the Mugello, has its own variant of the rice fritter. On Easter and Ascension Day come spring lamb and baby artichokes, and ravioli made with potatoes and pecorino cheese. An especially tasty white potato, grown in the area around Firenzuola, goes into this special ravioli of the Mugello, a traditional dish here and in neighbouring Casentino all year round.

In the upper reaches of the Mugello, chestnuts, wild mushrooms and game have always been the necessary sustenance during the difficult seasons. The chestnut is considered the tree of life in mountainous parts of Italy. Without chestnuts and their flour, the mountain people could not have survived winters; chestnuts became the mainstay of the kitchen. And so they are today.

The DOC , IGP and DOP labels on a bag or tin are designations of excellence and a great source of pride to the artisans and producers who earn them. Buyers unfamiliar with them would do well to learn that only extraordinary foods or wines produced in a particular place are awarded these designations. They signify that you're buying something genuine. The *marrone buono*, or good chestnut, of Marradi is designated IGP, meaning a place of geographical protection. We all look forward to the first chestnuts of the season in late September and early October. Autumn has arrived; chestnuts are here. If you're lucky enough to have a chestnut forest, as we do, you gather them from the ground once the hard spiked coating has split and the nut falls out. This simple nut is the *castagna*. A larger, shinier nut, one that probably doesn't grow in your own woods, begins to appear in local markets in and around the Mugello a little later. These are the *marroni* of the Mugello. The difference is like that between prosecco and a fine champagne. While both species get roasted – in the Mugello roasted chestnuts are called *bruciati*, or burned – and boiled, chestnuts are also ground into flour and made into creams. *Marroni* come from trees that have been pruned, nurtured and coaxed over the centuries into producing larger, perfectly shaped beauties. These generally go into elegant glazed desserts. *Marroni* come on to the market later than chestnuts, renewing the excitement of the year's first encounter. The season is a short one; by December all you'll find is dried chestnuts and their flour.

There are famous autumn *sagras* and *feste* of *marroni* throughout the Mugello. Marradi's and Palazzuolo's are the best known. It's a good time to get on the restored Faentina steam-engine railway in Florence and take the special trip up into *marroni* land and its festivals (every Sunday during October). A bus from the Marradi station can carry you on over a scenic road to Palazzuolo as well.

Recently a group of innovative young people in these high mountains have begun a renewal of old food traditions, introducing organically grown products and marketing them as such. It has meant not only some great new products, but also a rebirth of much traditional agriculture here. Land in the upper Mugello is meagre; it's not easy to grow a great deal. Sheep have their small pastures, grains have their limited plots. Large industrial farming is out of the question. In the past farmers barely subsisted.

A number of cooperatives have been set up, young farmers and producers joining together to offer choice products that find a sophisticated market throughout and beyond Tuscany. They all know one another and work together as friends. One group has begun an artisan production of organic pasta products and *farro*. The mini-climate in these mountains, I'm told, is as ideal for the growing of *farro* as that of the Garfagnana. The label is Rio Maggio, and has become a precious one. Another group of friends has created a cooperative that uses ancient methods to make organic cheese from the milk of grazing goats. They turn out a limited number of really fine goat's cheeses, and they've recently broadened the range of goat life in this region with the import of an Alpine goat. Their cows and sheep graze freely on the grassy meadows of the mountain. The fresh ricotta and raviggiolo cheeses are remarkably good; so is the aged pecorino. You can see and buy a fine selection of them at the Agricoop in Palazzuolo.

Marco Minardi calls himself *il porcaro medievale* after his medieval progenitor who allowed his herd of pigs to wander through the woods, calling them home each evening to sleep. With his wife Rosita, he has begun pork production with pigs foraging the fresh grasses of the woods. He turns out fresh pork as well as smoked and dried *salumi*.

As in other mountain regions, a great number of wild herbs and greens go into the food of the Mugello, as well as into flavoured grappas, brandies, digestifs, honeys and marmalades. Venture into La Dispensa della Locanda Senio in Palazzuolo and you'll find home-made grappa flavoured with berries, or juniper or sage or other wild herbs. Chestnut honey and chestnut cream as well as various wild-berry marmalades are also on the shelves in this enticing small shop.

In the autumn and late spring, porcini mushrooms are on every menu. Another popular mushroom here is the *prugnolo*, which appears in meadows just after the snows have melted.

And, as in other wooded regions of Tuscany, many game dishes appear on the menus of the Mugello.

Typical restaurants and their recipes

VICCHIO: Casa di Caccia

Casa di Caccia is in Roti-Molezzano, a suburb of Vicchio.

Tel. 055 8407629. It's open for lunch and dinner every day in the summer; during other months the weekly closing is Tuesday. Closed for 15 days during February. Prices are moderate. Best to reserve.

WITH PATIENCE AND perseverance a 20-minute drive from the main square at Vicchio will bring you to this old cheese-maker's domain, now a restored gathering place for hunters. You'll get the kind of meal hunters relish. A group of young *cacciatori* bought the ruin about fifteen years ago; they spruced it up and turned it over to Mirella Settori, who runs the kitchen along with the entire large restaurant today.

From Vicchio's main square, take the road in the direction of Santa Maria a Vezzano; there are indications to Casa di Caccia all along the way. The view is splendid; after all, this is Giotto country. Continue along the road for about ten kilometres, and signs will bring you to the restaurant. A good stretch of the road is unpaved, but easily passable. You'll come upon the main sign for the restaurant just about at the moment you think you're totally lost. I'd suggest your first time there be for lunch, not only to see where you are going, but for the lovely views as well.

Mirella Settori is a robust, outdoorsy woman who is justly proud of the restaurant she has created and lives above. The restaurant seems to contain her life and passion for the kitchen. Her menu changes not only with the seasons, but with the game that is available on a daily basis as well. *Antipasti* feature prosciutto of wild boar and roe-buck, and a pâté of wild boar served with strawberry marmalade, along with the usual *crostini* and local salami. Pastas are all made in the restaurant kitchen; both the *ravioli di scamorza con olio di tartufi*, made with a cheese resembling mozzarella, and the *ravioli con pecorino*, her version of the noted potato ravioli, are special. The glass-enclosed terrace dining room is bright and cheery, open to the woods and valleys around. Main courses to try are of game, such as hare with a truffled stuffing and wild boar in a wine sauce. Desserts include a *panna cotta* with a sauce of wild berries.

RECIPES FROM Casa di Caccia

Scamorza cheese ravioli with truffle oil / *Ravioli di scamorza con olio di tartufi*

Scamorza cheese is part of the mozzarella family, a bit more flavourful. It dissolves entirely when you cook the ravioli, forming a meltingly creamy filling. Rather than square ravioli, I find it easier to make half-moon-shaped pasta – tortellini – by forming circles with an 8cm glass, filling and then folding in half to press the edges closed.

Makes about 50 ravioli

FOR THE PASTA:

300g plain white flour
3 eggs
1 tablespoon olive oil
Salt to taste

FOR THE FILLING:

900g scamorza or other firm creamy melting cheese
1 egg yolk, beaten
Truffle oil and/or truffle butter
1 black truffle (optional)

To make the pasta, put all the ingredients in a food processor and process until they form a ball. Remove and knead until shiny and malleable, about 10 minutes. Allow to rest under a cloth for at least half an hour.

Grate the scamorza through the largest holes of a food grater. With two forks, mix well with the egg yolk.

Divide the pasta into about 4 balls. While working with one, keep the remaining balls covered. Roll out the pasta as thinly as possible and, with a large-mouthed glass, cut out circles in the sheet. Put a level teaspoon of filling in the middle of each, fold over and pinch closed.

Drop the ravioli into a large pan of boiling, well-salted water, remove with a slotted spoon as they rise to the top, and serve with a good covering of truffle oil and/or truffle butter and, if available, slivered black truffle.

Piquant strawberry marmalade / *Marmellata di fragole*

500g strawberries
3 tablespoons balsamic vinegar
2 tablespoons sugar

Combine all the ingredients into a saucepan and cook over a low heat until the mix reaches a marmalade consistency. At Casa di Caccia the marmalade is served with pâté. It also goes well with a hunk of pecorino cheese at the end of a meal.

Jellied cream with wild berry sauce / *Panna cotta ai frutti di bosco*

Serves 10

FOR THE JELLIED CREAM:
4 teaspoons gelatine powder
120ml cold water
1 litre cream
225g sugar
1 vanilla pod, split in half lengthways

FOR THE BERRY SAUCE:
150g mixed wild berries
75g sugar

For the *panna cotta* (the jellied cream), Sprinkle the gelatine into the water in a small metal bowl and allow to stand for about 10 minutes. Put the bowl into a low pan of simmering water to melt the gelatine entirely, about 1–2 minutes. In another pan, bring to the boil the cream, sugar and the seeds from the vanilla pod. Simmer for 2 minutes, remove from heat and mix the gelatine into the cream. Whisk until well blended.

Fill 10 individual moulds, allow to cool and then refrigerate.

For the berry sauce, boil together the mixed berries with the sugar for about 5 minutes. Blend half, and mix with the remainder.

To serve, turn out the *panna cotta* on to small flat plates and pour the sauce over each.

MARRADI: Il Camino

Il Camino, Viale Baccarini 38, Marradi, near the railway station.
Tel. 055 8045069. Prices are moderate. Closed Wednesdays and a week during June, but otherwise open for lunch and dinner. Best to reserve.

AN ELEGANT FAMILY runs this unpretentious gem of a restaurant. Golden-haired mamma Rita Bassetti is in the kitchen, her long tresses pulled tightly back into a long ponytail. Her daughter Simona, as brunette as her mother is blonde, is sous-chef. Son-in-law Mirko – also golden-flecked – is *maestro di sala*, welcoming guests and enthusiastically detailing each of the several specialities the restaurant offers every day.

Marradi is on the direct route to the Romagna region above Tuscany, and Il Camino's cuisine reflects both areas. This fusion of two great Italian regions is delectable. Sauces seem to be richer, the bread contains salt, unlike Tuscan bread you'll find elsewhere. Most specialities at Il Camino are seasonal, 'of the moment', as cook Rita puts it. Peas are picked in the morning, prepared for lunch; funghi arrive daily. The pasta served is not only fresh, but rolled and cut as you order.

There is a menu, but Mirko avoids giving it out, preferring to tell you about the specialities of the day. Always on hand, and a must, is a trio of warm *crostini* served on soft absorbent bread rather than the usual firmer, crustier, sliced baguette-type bread or toast: liver pâté, creamed asparagus and a wild mushroom stew that is fresh in season and frozen at the right moment for the rest of the year. Mediterranean-style baby lamb is usually on the menu, as are *bocconcini ai funghi*, bite-sized chunks of chicken and funghi stewed together and served on a bed of polenta.

As Marradi is the home of the grand *marrone buono*, the treat is Il Camino's chestnut pudding, best in the autumn when chestnuts are at their freshest.

RECIPES FROM Il Camino

Chicken stew with wild mushrooms / *Bocconcini ai funghi*

Serve this delectable dish on a bed of polenta or puréed potatoes.

Serves 6

3 large chicken legs with thighs
1 onion
1 carrot
2 or 3 cloves garlic
1 bunch parsley
3 tablespoons olive oil

300g fresh, frozen or defrosted wild porcini mushrooms, chopped
240ml hot chicken stock

Have your butcher bone and skin the chicken legs. The meat should weigh about 1kg. Chop into fairly large bite-sized pieces.

Chop the onion, carrot and garlic coarsely, and the parsley more finely. In a pan large enough to hold the entire dish, sauté the onion, carrot and garlic in the olive oil. Add the chicken pieces and sauté for another few minutes until they have lost their colour. Add the chopped mushrooms and cook for 10 minutes over a low heat, then add the chicken stock. Cook more rapidly until the sauce thickens, about 10 more minutes.

◆ Chestnut pudding / *Budino di marroni*

Serves 8

500g shelled chestnuts (about 1kg with shells)
½ teaspoon salt
Peel of 1 lemon
4 eggs, beaten
400g sugar
2 vanilla pods, split open and the seeds scraped out
50g chocolate, melted
2 tablespoons brandy
2 tablespoons rum
120ml milk, plus extra if needed

If the chestnuts are fresh and unshelled, make a cross on the flat side of each with a sharp knife, and place either over a flame in a chestnut pan or in a hot oven until they open enough that the outer shell can be peeled off. Cover with water, bring to the boil, add the salt and lemon peel, and cook over a medium heat until soft. Pass through a food processor or potato masher to make a purée (of about ½kg). Mix in the eggs, and add 300g of the sugar, the vanilla seeds, chocolate, brandy and rum. Add enough milk to make a semi-liquid mixture, mix well and pour into a mould that has been caramelized with the remaining 100g of sugar.

Cook in a slow oven, 130°C/Gas ½, for 3 hours, until the custard has become firm. Turn out and serve.

PALAZZUOLO SUL SENIO: Locanda Senio

Locanda Senio, Via Borgo dell'Ore 1/3, Palazzuolo. Tel. 055 8046019. The restaurant (it is also a small six-room hotel that is open year round) is open continually from May to October and in the other months from Thursday to Sunday. It's a small place, with only eight tables, and always wise to telephone beforehand. Prices are moderate to high depending on what you eat and drink.

ERCOLE LIGA IS the generous, gregarious and knowledgeable host of this warm and welcoming locanda. He and his wife Roberta have turned their place into a perfect nest of lovingly prepared home produce, which Ercole deliciously describes in his own series of small publications. He designs and prints descriptions of his menus, their history, often their recipes, in four languages. It's fun to talk to him about food. Ercole is a

Romagnolo by birth, and moved to Roberta's Tuscan mountains after his studies and ten years as a businessman in Milan.

Ercole is one of the enterprising young entrepreneurs of the upper Mugello who are bringing back tradition as they fight for the environment. He runs a small *dispensa* across the road where he sells Roberta's jams and his own grappa and mountain liqueurs together with the produce of his friends. Every morning Roberta bakes a variety of breads for the restaurant, including, beyond the normal crusty unsalted Tuscan variety, one with chestnut flour, Parmesan cheese rolls, flat rosemary rolls, grape-studded foccaccia, sweet chestnut and plenty of others. There are little fried puffs of dough called *crescentine* that have their origins in Ercole's home district of Romagna and are served with three bowls of spreads. One spread is a soft, locally produced goat's cheese, *raviggiolo,* another a homemade chestnut paste and the third a sauce of sharp tomatoes. You open the hot little puff, smear on some cheese and over it either the sweet chestnut or the sharp tomato. Either combination is very good.

The menu at Locanda Senio is all mountain food. Several kinds of *menu degustazione* at a fixed price are available, an opportunity to taste the specialities of the moment. One is a 'medieval pork' meal, the pork arriving from the nearby *porcaro medievale*.

First courses are the best. A light salad of various mountain greens and aromatic wild herbs is dressed with salt and fresh olive oil, and surrounded by tiny cubes of freshly deep-fried potatoes. You can also have *tagliatelle di farro* from Rio Maggio in a sauce of local ricotta cheese, a rich smooth *pappa al pomodoro,* or a *farro* salad with beans, capers and thyme. *Secondi*, main courses, varied as they are, also concentrate on local mountain fare. Among them are sausages with chestnuts and oranges, pork from the 'medieval' herd of *il porcaro* and goat in tarragon and mint.

Roberta, a self-taught cook, leaves the local mountains behind as she makes a Bavarian cream dessert that would be credible in the most elegant city restaurant. The presentation is perfect: a mint-green moulded cream on a white plate, covered with fresh cream and decorated with mint leaves and little shaved pale-green gratings of mint-flavoured chocolate across the plate.

RECIPES FROM *Locanda Senio*

Tomato bread soup / *Pappa al pomodoro di Locanda Senio*

Serves 6

1 onion, finely chopped
2 tablespoons olive oil
1 tablespoon tomato purée
1kg tomatoes, squeezed of inner juices and seeds and coarsely chopped
3 slices 1- or 2-day old Tuscan bread
2 cloves garlic, chopped
1 bunch basil leaves, chopped
Salt and freshly ground pepper
Extra virgin olive oil, to serve

Sauté the onion in the olive oil, add the tomato purée and the tomatoes, and cook over a low heat until most of the liquid has evaporated. Set aside. Place the bread, garlic and basil in another large saucepan. Barely cover with water and cook for 5 minutes. Add the tomato mix and continue to cook until the entire mixture becomes pulpy. Season to taste. Blend in a food processor, taste for seasonings and serve with fresh oil at the table.

Medieval *farro* salad / *Insalata di farro medievale*

Serves 10

300g borlotti beans, soaked overnight
400g *farro*
150g capers, preserved in vinegar
1 large bunch thyme (or summer savory)
Extra virgin olive oil
Salt and freshly ground pepper

Drain the beans, transfer to a pan, cover with water and cook over a very low heat until totally soft but still holding their form.

Cook the *farro* in boiling salted water for about half an hour, until it is cooked through but still *al dente*. Drain and run cold water over. Drain the beans and mix well with the *farro*.

Wash the capers well, and add to the *farro* with the cooked beans and chopped herbs. Dress with a good olive oil, season to taste and serve warm or at room temperature. Add more oil at table.

◆ Medieval pork roast with juniper berries and pomegranate / *Arrosto di maiale medievale*

An old recipe offered by Locanda Senio, which promises 'to dispel the bad spirits and bring a healthy air to the home'.

Serves 4

1 fillet of pork tenderloin, about 500g–1kg
Salt and freshly ground pepper
15 juniper berries, crushed in a mortar
1 tablespoon seasoned lard, chopped
Juice of 1 or 2 pomegranates, plus some whole kernels

Cut the tenderloin horizontally to make a deep pocket. Season the inside and sprinkle with the crushed juniper berries. Fold back together and tie securely with string.

Melt the lard in a flameproof pan large enough to hold the entire roast, with a cover. Brown the roast all over, then pour the pomegranate juice over it, cover the pan and continue to cook for about 10 minutes. Uncover and allow to cook for another 10 minutes. Remove the meat and reduce the sauce to a gravy.

To serve, slice the meat, pour over the pan juices and sprinkle with pomegranate kernels. Baked leeks and fried artichokes are suggested as accompaniment.

SCARPERIA: Fattoria il Palagio
Fattoria il Palagio, Viale Dante 99, Scarperia.
Tel. 055 846376. Closed Mondays and from 6 August to the end of the month. Priced moderately to expensive.

A VISIT TO Fattoria il Palagio transports you back to earlier times, when large estates had their tenant farmers and their fattoria, the central farm building of the estate. The restaurant was once an administrative centre and a collection point where tenant farmers brought their produce to sell and to tithe a portion to the estate. Fattoria il Palagio was the largest in the area, belonging to the noble Borghese family. The manor house is still next door. The *case coloniche* or tenant farmhouses have been sold off to be renovated as country retreats. Great old cedar trees that date from the seventeenth century still front the fattoria. The large old building has been carefully and precisely restored by energetic new owner Mirella Lorensi with her husband Leonardo Mazzani in the kitchen and son Mirko as administrator. They've converted it into a large restaurant and halls for receptions. Mirko and Mirella will take the interested visitor on a detailed tour, pointing out how the fattoria once worked.

The big halls are beamed and arched in their original state. These were the granaries, with hand-carved stones covering the openings in the floor through which the grain was poured. A clever device separated the small grains from the large. The smaller grains went straight on to the mill to be ground into flour for bread and pasta. The larger were set aside as seeds. Names of tenant farmers, the year and amount of wheat they brought – in *quintale*, or hundreds of kilograms – have been left scratched into the old walls;

one dates back to 1748. Handmade terracotta floors, worn rich with time and oil, are in place, as is the old step just outside the office where farmers humbly awaited their final accounting from the administrator at his desk in the counting house. The wine cellars have been left with their large chestnut-brown barrels, alas now empty, but still commandingly filling the hall. An old glazed terracotta bacchus decorates a wall in the wine cellar, over the spigots of the wine barrels that have been preserved within. Gently arched windows have been uncovered, brick domed ceilings and walls carefully restored.

The renovations were made tastefully and enthusiastically during the first years of the restaurant. Mirella claims she was simply uncovering the magic of the place. At the same time, Leonardo developed his kitchen skills. They'd more or less inherited their purpose, having helped out in the small restaurant Mirella's parents opened in Scarperia in the 1970s. Mirella is a former primary school teacher, Leonardo was a metal worker in Florence. When Mirella's parents retired the two of them took over the smaller restaurant, then bought the fattoria and started remaking it. Today it has become a landmark institution.

The menu at Fattoria il Palagio is Florentine, with a large *antipasto* table at the ready. A variety of *antipasti* includes various *crostini*, grilled aubergine, tomato/mozzarella combinations, prosciutto and sausages, a *ribollita* and other warm soups in the winter, and *panzanella* (bread salad) in the warmer seasons. The Mugello *tortelli di patate* are generously filled, and served in a rich and savoury duck sauce. Leonardo makes a good risotto in a way that can also save time for the entertaining home cook as well (see recipe below). In season the asparagus risotto is especially good.

Main courses include generous helpings of Florentine speciality, *tagliata*, or slices of thick steak, or a Florentine beefsteak or pork cooked in milk. Desserts include the *torta della casa*, always worth trying.

RECIPES FROM Fattoria il Palagio

Wide noodles with duck sauce / *Pappardelle con salsa anatra*

Serves 6 generously

1 duck, boned, cut up into large pieces
2 tablespoons olive oil
1 sprig sage leaves (about 8), chopped
2 cloves garlic, chopped
1 carrot, finely chopped
1 stick celery, finely chopped
1 onion, finely chopped
350ml passata
Salt and freshly ground pepper
500g *pappardelle*
Freshly grated Parmesan cheese

Remove as much fat and skin from the duck as possible. Heat the oil with the sage and garlic, and brown the duck on all sides. Add the carrot, celery and onion, mix and continue to simmer for another 10 minutes. Add the tomato sauce, salt and pepper, and simmer gently for 2 hours. If the sauce begins to dry, add a bit of water. It should remain liquid.

Remove the duck and shred the meat into small pieces. Return the meat to the sauce and keep warm. Boil the *pappardelle* in lots of boiling salted water, drain, mix in the sauce and serve with freshly grated Parmesan cheese.

Asparagus risotto / *Risotto con gli asparagi*

Some years ago, a fine chef in Chianti taught me how to make risotto in a pressure cooker. With his precise instructions, it turned out reasonably well. Leonardo improves on this particular time-saver. He makes his with a parboiled risotto rice, cooking the rice alone in a low oven for 15 minutes before making the risotto. It's a way of avoiding lengthy preparation at the last minute when you are entertaining friends to dinner.

Serves 6

350g parboiled risotto rice
1–1.2 litres vegetable or chicken stock
500g asparagus
1 onion, chopped
2 tablespoons olive oil
50g freshly grated Parmesan cheese, plus extra to serve

Heat the oven to 150°C/Gas 2. Put the rice into a flameproof oven casserole and barely cover with stock. Leave for 15 minutes; when you take it out, it should still be somewhat hard. Set aside until you begin to prepare the risotto. Keep a pan of boiling stock on a low heat. Chop the asparagus into 2cm pieces. Sauté the onion in the oil, then add the asparagus and cook for 5 minutes. Put the pan with the rice on a low flame and add about half the asparagus mixture, along with enough hot stock to just cover the rice again. When the stock is absorbed, add the remaining asparagus and continue to cook gently, adding stock as needed. When the rice has absorbed the stock, continue to add more, little by little, until the risotto is cooked and the rice still firm. Add the cheese, allow to rest a minute and serve with more grated cheese at the table.

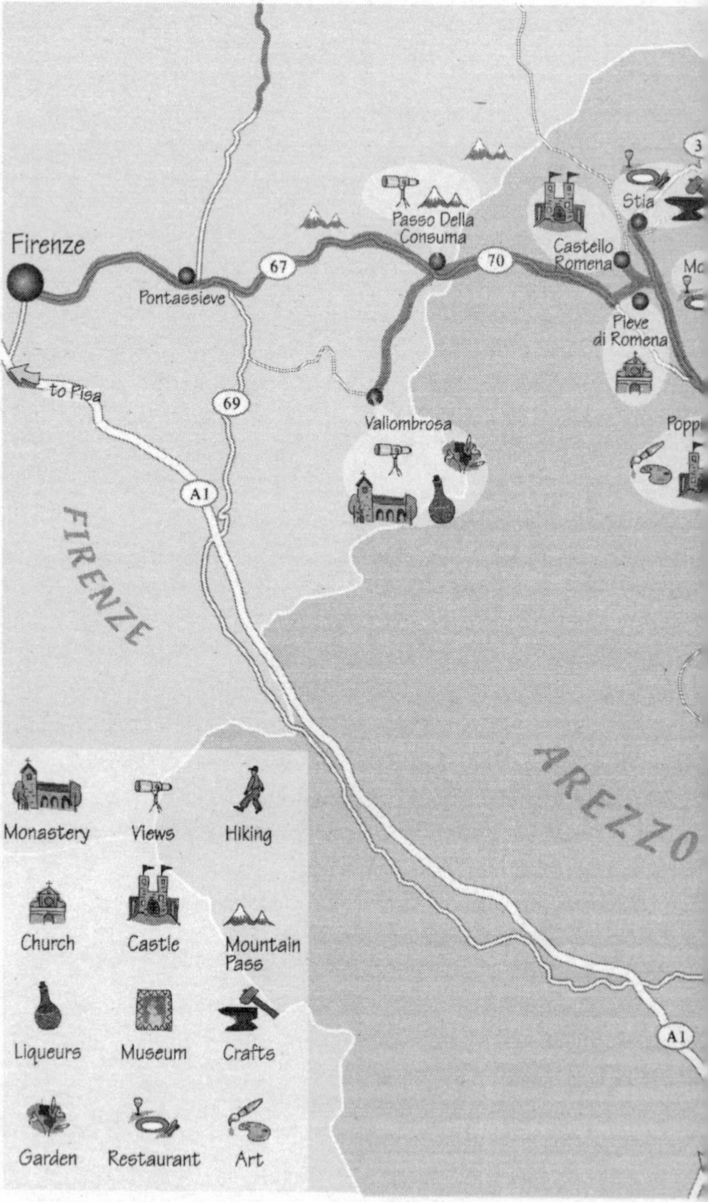

Firenze
Pontassieve
67
Passo Della Consuma
70
Castello Romena
Stia
Pieve di Romena
to Pisa
69
Vallombrosa
A1
FIRENZE
AREZZO
A1
Monastery
Views
Hiking
Church
Castle
Mountain Pass
Liqueurs
Museum
Crafts
Garden
Restaurant
Art

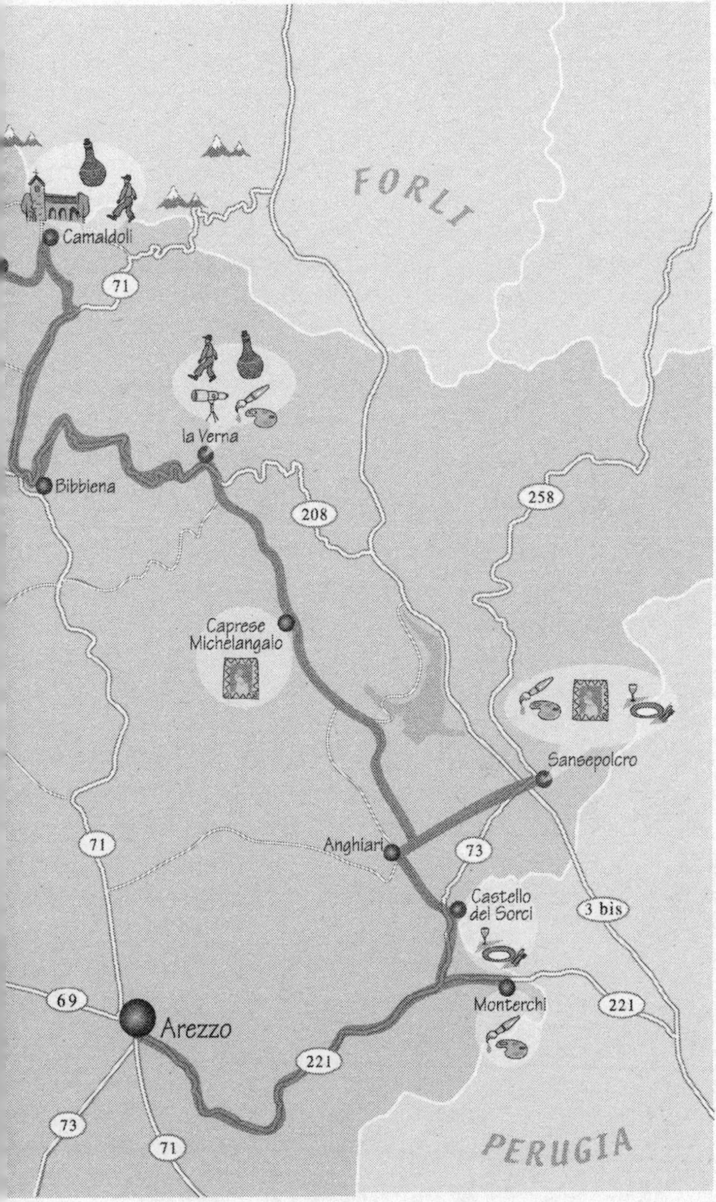

FORLI
Camaldoli
71
la Verna
Bibbiena
208
258
Caprese
Michelangaio
Sansepolcro
71
Anghiari
73
Castello
del Sorci
3 bis
69
Arezzo
Monterchi
221
221
73
71
PERUGIA

6

The Casentino and Tiberina

THE CASENTINO AND Tiberina combine a world of lovely landscapes and retreats, art and good food between the headwaters of two great rivers: from here the Arno flows down to Florence and Pisa before reaching the Mediterranean, and the Tiber begins its journey to Rome and the sea at nearby Ostia. The Passo della Consuma – the easiest mountain pass through the Apennine range – brings you there. It is half an hour's drive from Florence through Pontessieve to reach the pass.

On the other side of the pass you'll find the towns of Stia, Poppi and Bibbiena, the monasteries of Camaldoli and La Verna, the birthplaces of Michelangelo and Piero della Francesca, and the finest examples of Piero's art.

As you climb the pass, the woods open to views of the valleys and towns below. The austere Romanesque abbey of Vallombrosa lies just off the way with its botanical gardens containing an impressive collection of pines and other Mediterranean plants. In less global times, Vallombrosa was the preferred summer retreat for Florentines escaping the city's torrid heat; the legendary art historian Bernard Berenson had his vacation villa here in an old hunting lodge overlooking the mountain range.

The vast national park of Monte Falterona begins as

you descend the pass. It's huge, divided into various forests and parks that extend from the Casentino into the mountains of the Mugello, the upper Tiber valley and neighbouring Emilia-Romagna. Long before it was a national park, Dante wrote of 'the cool rustic waters of the Casentino that trickle down into the Arno'.

Two castles come into view as soon as you head down the mountain to the Casentino. The first, along the road that leads to Stia, is a majestic ruin; upon inspection you can see that it once had fourteen towers surrounded by three walls. The second is the imposing town hall of Poppi, which still looms over the entire valley. Both were once part of the vast domain of the Guidi counts, rulers over a good part of northern Tuscany from the eleventh to the thirteenth centuries. They had originally come down from Lombardy and built themselves fortified citadels here. You still see Guidi traces everywhere in Tuscany, from Cerreto Guidi and Vinci in the Montalbano area to the one in Poppi. Some of these castles were remodelled during the Renaissance by the Medici when Florence – through battle or purchase – moved in to dominate the area and alter the political and cultural landscape.

Two major battles that turned Florence into an important regional power took place in the narrow valleys of the Casentino and Tiberina. One was the Battle of Campaldino in 1289, fought ferociously just under Poppi. Warriors from Florence, Lucca, Pistoia, Prato, Siena, Volterra and even Bologna massed against Arezzo. Dante Alighieri served in the cavalry (and writes about it in the Purgatory). It was an interesting time. The Bishop of Arezzo, it seems, was caught out trying to sell his entire see to the Florentines to ensure a lifetime's annuity for himself and his nephew; he was executed and the Aretinos – i.e. the people of Arezzo –

battled Florence to regain their lost pride. They lost even more, both in men and in territory.

A small arrow to the left as you descend the Passo della Consuma indicates the road to Stia. Follow it, and you arrive at the grand Guidi castle ruin. One of the loveliest Romanesque churches in Tuscany lies just a few kilometres beyond. Another small sign at the ruin indicates the way to 'Pieve di Romena'. This narrow road is definitely the best way to approach the noble simple church. You suddenly come upon the soft, grey, round apse colonnaded with the most delicate Romanesque columns and blind arches. Ask Signora Cipriani at the house opposite (tel. 0575 542027) for the key to see the bare grace and finely decorated column capitals of the church within.

Stia is nowadays best known for its potato ravioli and for the *casentino*, a brilliantly coloured warm wool cloak produced here. Traditionally worn by monks, mountaineers and shepherds during the last century; with the addition of a little fur collar and brass buttons it became the fashionable winter wrap of the Florentine bourgeoisie. Handwoven in the most flattering bright green or orange (the colour of a Sicilian blood orange), the *casentino* is still produced in Stia by a single mill. Two shops on the fine old square – Piazza Tanucci – sell the cloth. No longer rough-loomed and hand-sewn, it is still in great demand and comes in many bright colours and forms: coats, jackets, hats and even slippers. There's a small comfortable trattoria, Filetto, on the same square.

The other imposing castle of the Guidi sits above the old town of Poppi, jutting out against the skyline like a virtual copy of Florence's Palazzo Signoria. The twelfth-century castle is said to have been the model for the larger Florentine palace. After the Battle of

Anghiari in 1440, the Guidi made their formal surrender to the Florentines here. Ponte a Poppi, the commercial centre below the old town, has an inviting bar on its main square, Osteria del Tempo Perso ('Inn of A Lost Time'), where you can learn all about the specialities of the area while you drink your coffee and sample some of them. Cheeses, marmalades, honeys and pork products are all there for the eating, and for sale as well.

From Poppi it's a lovely ride up into the Foreste delle Casentinesi to the monastery and hermitage of Camaldoli. Take the road up through the beech-filled forest through Moggiana where you'll find a well-established trattoria, Il Cedro. The monastery and its hermitage, which date back to the eleventh century, are a peaceful place, at home in sylvan surroundings. The monastery, a cluster of small hut-like houses around a larger building, was founded as a pilgrimage, the monks charged since time immemorial with the responsibility to maintain the environment. This they still do well; they may be the most ecologically minded group within the church. The monks at Camaldoli are strictly vegetarian and grow their own food. They welcome guests and are hosts to interfaith meetings and other spiritual events throughout the year.

Don't miss the impressive old chestnut-panelled pharmacy/bottega at Camaldoli. On sale are balsamic bath oils and other therapeutic lotions and creams, and honey and its by-products. Unlike many other monasteries nowadays, the monks at Camaldoli don't import their potions but produce them here according to their own ancient formulas. Ingredients come from botanical gardens on the grounds dating back to the fifteenth century; a small museum room adjacent to the pharmacy details the medicinal and curative offerings. The Camaldoli monks also run – as they always have – a traditional olive mill, the Pieve di Micciano, where oil is pressed today as it was in the thirteenth century. They decant particularly pleasing oil from the *mosto*, the pulp that is left over from the crushed olives. Their nearby hermitage, Eremo, has an enticing old library to visit.

Bibbiena, another major town in the Casentino valley, has an impressive historic centre. From the piazza of the old town, there are great views of the entire valley. Even better views can be had from the road leading from Bibbiena to Chiusi del Verna and the monastery of La Verna. From La Verna, the road through the Tiber valley leads to Caprese Michelangelo, San Sepolcro and Anghiari.

Try to reach the magnificent monastery of La Verna before the tour buses arrive. If you arrive at a quiet moment, it can be a wondrous experience. Dante called the site the 'rough crag' between the Tiber and Arno rivers. Tradition tells us that St Francis received the stigmata here. You'll find a collection of graceful old buildings and chapels housing dozens of the loveliest porcelain-covered Andrea della Robbia reliefs. A wide piazza looks out over the valleys and mountains around. Walk down to the stream below where there's a shrine to St Francis. It's a magical place.

I asked one of the younger monks at La Verna, Brother Filippo, how they produced all the many magic curative potions, herbal elixirs and exotic liqueurs I found on sale there. He couldn't really tell me; with a wry smile, he suggested I look more closely at the labels. While the herbal liqueurs were still produced according to original ancient recipes, they were bottled somewhere else and the soaps and bath oils were not really different from the sort of thing one finds in health stores everywhere. 'We young priests here,' he said somewhat plaintively, 'no longer even have the ancient recipes.'

The Tiber valley under La Verna gave birth to two of Italy's most revered Renaissance artists, Michelangelo and Piero della Francesca. Caprese Michelangelo is the birthplace of the former. Michelangelo never spent much time here, but did claim that he had sucked in his love of the traditional chiselling tools with his wet-nurse's milk. Caprese was proud enough of its native son to rename the town after him and open a museum in the house where he was born. (Museo Michelangelo, open every day; call 0575 793775 for hours.)

Piero della Francesca was born (and died) not far away, in the small valley town of San Sepolcro. Several of his most exciting works hang in the civic museum here. His splendid *Resurrection* and another polyptych of the Madonna and saints make the museum a mandatory stop. Through a large window cut into the museum wall, it's now possible to view the *Resurrection* (Aldous Huxley called it simply 'the best picture in the world') from the square outside. At night it's lit up. (Museo Civico, Via Aggiunti 65, open daily.) Just down the street from the civic museum, at number 30 Via Aggiunti, is the little trattoria, Da Ventura.

Across the valley from San Sepolcro is the old town of Anghiari. The Battle of Anghiari – which finally and firmly established Florentine rule in the area – happened in the Tiber valley between the two towns in 1440. It could not have been such an enormous battle as has been claimed; we know that only one life was lost, when a warrior fell off his horse. It did gain a firm place in the history of art on a wall in Florence's Palazzo Signoria where Leonardo da Vinci began a fresco of the battle. It remained unfinished perhaps because Leonardo had not mastered the art of fresco as he had mastered almost everything else. The incomplete, badly peeling fresco was later painted over by Giorgio Vasari. Only a few preliminary drawings and a copy by Rubens are left to assure us of its original wonder.

Everywhere in this area, you sense the local reverence for tradition. Stop at the *antico frantoio* (old olive mill), Ravagni, located just outside Anghiari. The mill still operates as it has since the fifteenth century. The most heavenly aromatic scent from hundreds of years of oil pressing hits you as soon as you walk in. Their oil-pressing method has changed little. The olives are still hauled by hand up an ancient winding wrought-iron staircase to the top level and poured down into a basin with the widest grinding stones I've ever seen. The mash then goes through old mat-lined presses. It drips out as oil into large vats. The steel vats for storing the pressed oil are the single modern addition. (In the past, huge terracotta jars served this purpose.) Francesco Bartolomei, the young son of the family that has owned the mill since the eighteenth century, shows the visitor around. You can buy their lightly piquant oil at the entrance. There is also an inviting tasting room inside, and an outdoor terrace with tables where you can enjoy the oil with appropriate accompaniment.

Anghiari is an imposing medieval town high on a hill overlooking the Tiber valley and a good place to explore old artisan customs still strong in these parts. The town is well known for its wood and iron workshops, its carpenters, furniture restorers and stone masons, and its handmade textiles and antique shops. The main street is lined with *botteghe* for both olive-oil products and wrought iron.

The annual Mostra Mercato dell'Artiganato, from 25 April to 1 May each year, is an artisans' fair which attracts visitors from all over the region. On 15 August – *Ferragosto* – an open-air dinner and theatrical performance takes place in a small square here. Visitors are welcome.

The tradition of furniture restoration has led to the establishment of an international school attended by students from all over the world. The renowned Busatti linen and cotton textiles are made in Anghiari. The shop in the old Morgalanti Palace still has shuttle looms working in its basement and the showrooms upstairs have an impressive display of traditionally designed handwoven fabrics and tablecloths.

Immediately coming upon the square under the old town you'll find an interesting bread shop, Al Cantuccio. Its *forno a legna* (wood-burning oven) turns out all sorts of bread-based dishes. A few tables at which to enjoy them are scattered about. It is the perfect spot for a light lunch. Cicalino Gennaioli owns the little *forno* with his wife Domitella; he bakes the bread, she cooks lunch. A thin bread fried in boiling oil, the *ciacia fritta,* is served to crowds on Wednesday market days and Sunday afternoons. Pizzas can be had at lunchtime every day; especially good is the one made with just onion and tomato. There's also a *piatto del giorno* – daily special – gnocchi one day, a pasta or soup on another, and sometimes a lovely stewed *tripe* or *ribollita*. Al Cantuccio also serves a winter bruschetta of the popular Tuscan winter kale leaves, *cavolo nero*. The chopped leaves are first cooked gently in a bit of simmering water, then squeezed, salted and sautéed in fresh olive oil and garlic. Fresh bread is toasted over the open fire, rubbed with half a clove of garlic and dipped quickly in and out of the cooking water. The kale is layered on top.

An array of freshly baked raisin-studded, anise-flavoured biscuits is another temptation.

One of the more original restaurants in the area – La Nena – is just up the street. You'll pass another very popular eating place in the former granary on the estate of Castello di Sorci along the road from Anghiari to Arezzo. The same road takes you to old Monterchi, well worth a visit just to view Piero della Francesca's famous painting, *Madonna del Parto*. In years past it could be viewed in its original home, a remote chapel in the middle of a field just outside town. Alas, no more. It could not be restored and properly protected where it was and so was removed to Monterchi, to a museum of its own, with explanations and pictorial details of its full restoration. Follow the signs. From Monterchi the road leads directly to Arezzo.

Specialities of the area

Like so many traditional dishes elsewhere in the mountains, dishes special to the Casentino and Tiberina began as smart ways to make the most of available produce. Eking out even a living was difficult. Vegetables that grew in summer and could be stored through the winter provided most sustenance. Added to this was milk produce, mainly cheeses that varied from soft, fresh ricotta to aged and seasoned pecorinos. Many Casentino dishes originated with shepherds who took their flocks each winter down to the more hospitable areas of the Maremma. Food from the Maremma came back with them to the Casentino. They had to pay duties and taxes along the way, often in the form of small cheeses. The tradition of Tuscany's most special pecorino – sheep's cheese – wandered with them from place to place. Grazing land is perfect here in the warmer months. Casentino shepherds made notable cheeses, and still do so today.

Potatoes and onions, poor man's staples in most places, make appetizing dishes in the Casentino, full of imagination and substance. A local light potato called *patata di cetica* goes into the ravioli; *aquacotta* (cooked water), a dish imported from the mountains of Maremma, originally consisted of little more than onions sautéed in oil and covered with boiling water. With today's additions of seasonal vegetables and herbs, it can be as delicious as celebrated French soups and is a good first or main course.

Rough wheat still goes into local bread and the pasta *bringoli*. The latter are made with just flour and water – no eggs – hand-rolled and pulled into stringy noodles, and sauced with *sugo finto*, or fake sauce, a local speciality. It's made to taste like the traditional ragú, but austerely without meat.

Pasta stuffed with potatoes seemed a dubious proposition until I tried it. In this traditionally poor country, *tortelli di patate* has long been a staple dish. Beef ragú goes over it today; before the last war, meat sauce was added only on holidays. I first discovered potato ravioli in the Casentino at Stia, but it's popular just across the mountains in the Mugello too.

Another dish of the Casentino and Tiberina is the *scottiglia*, an ancient stew of less desirable meat cuts simmered until deliciously edible in a red wine and tomato sauce. Tiny snails – found on bushes everywhere – make another well-considered meal here. The little creatures are cooked for several hours in a rich tomato sauce and then plucked from their shells with a toothpick. The remaining sauce is sopped up with crusty bread.

Wild fennel grows in these valleys in profusion and is used abundantly to flavour dishes. The *porchetta*, a highly flavoured pork roast you'll find at roadside stands throughout Tuscany and which is usually stuffed with rosemary or sage, is here flavoured with wild fennel. One favourite local salami is the *finocchiona*, a pork sausage flavoured with wild fennel seeds. The Casentino prosciutto is exceptionally good, salty and lean. A slice resembles a small brown plate.

The Casentino is also the land of the spicy *peperoncino*, often used instead of black pepper. A typical bruschetta is little more than fresh olive oil on a thick slice of Tuscan bread sprinkled with a mixture of oregano, salt and *peperoncino* flakes.

Like in other mountain areas of Tuscany, beans, chestnut flour and maize find their way into many substantial dishes. Chestnut flour and maize are still ground as they always were, between two often ancient stone wheels. In the autumn and early winter, wild mushrooms also make their way into almost every dish.

If you've never tasted truly fresh beans at the end of summer, Tuscany is the place to go. Beans are available everywhere. Tuscans speak about the simple bean – *il fagiolo* – with an ardour elsewhere reserved for more elegant food. The pursuit of that perfect specimen – the delicious fresh local bean – is fervent. Fresh from the plant at the end of summer, it has a velvet texture and a skin that's almost not there. Dried beans are a big winter staple and cooked into so many dishes that few beans freshly dried at the end of the summer go further than the late spring. In Tuscany there is little time for them to really harden or shrivel. The Casentino boasts a small, delicately flavoured yellow bean, Zolfino, grown in a small area around Poppi and Bibbiena. It is as meltingly smooth as a bean can be. My husband calls this and its Valdinievole cousin, the Sorano bean, 'Tuscan caviar'. Sorano and Zolfino beans are almost unknown outside their regions; the harvest is tiny. The Zolfino can be bought expensively here, and for bean lovers the cost is worth it. No soaking is necessary. It is cooked slowly, at a simmer, in a bath of water, sage, garlic, oil and just a touch of tomato.

Hard biscuits served with *vin santo* are a tradition in these parts, much as in the rest of Tuscany. The biscuits are slightly different here, with raisins and anise the favourite flavorings. The local *panina,* elsewhere a sandwich, is here bread flavoured with herbs and raisins; *berlingozzi* are more like hard doughnuts, flavoured strongly and deliciously with anise.

Typical restaurants and their recipes

STIA: Ristorante Filetto

Filetto, Piazza Tanucci 28, Stia.
Tel. 0575 583631. Difficult to see from the piazza; look under the sign 'folterra', the name of a former restaurant. Open for lunch and dinner during the summer months; lunch in the winter. Closed Thursdays and Saturdays, and the months of June and November. Reservations are recommended for Sunday lunch. Priced moderately.

The Piazza Tanucci in Stia is an elegant old square, ascending gently up to a grand fountain and lovely Romanesque church. Tuscan piazzas that ascend or descend a hill to form a dramatic natural amphitheatre (Siena's Campo is the most famous but there are many others) are especially attractive though no town-planning board would today approve such a plan. Stia's gracious old square would undoubtedly have been levelled by a modern engineer. So gaze upon it gratefully. It's lovely.

Filetto is a comfortably old trattoria about halfway up on the left of the square, with outdoor eating space in summer. It's a perfect place to watch life on the square and eat a typical meal. The restaurant has been in the Francalanci family for four generations. Even on Thursdays, when the restaurant is closed, the owner – and cook – can be found next door serving up local cold meats and cheese at the bar/tabacchi the family owns there.

After the *antipasti*, a most typical *secondo* is *tortelli di patate*, the traditional pasta of Stia. The customary sauce is the ragú, but one can also eat the tortelli in a simple fresh tomato sauce, or just dressed with butter and sage. Other pastas are served with goat (*capra*) or boar (*cinghiale*) sauce. Filetto's *acquacotta* is a spicy bread soup, made with the addition of chopped pork. A wood-burning kitchen fire provides any number of grilled meats, from ham to lamb.

Recipe from Filetto

◆ Potato tortelli / *Tortelli di patate*

Serves 8

FOR THE DOUGH

400g flour
Good pinch of salt
4 eggs
2 tablespoons olive oil

For the filling:

400g mature floury potatoes
2 cloves garlic, chopped
1 bunch parsley leaves, chopped
4 tablespoons olive oil
1 tablespoon tomato purée
2 tablespoons freshly grated Parmesan cheese
Good grating nutmeg
Salt and freshly ground pepper

Combine the dough ingredients, knead until flexible and shiny and roll out into long thin strips to fill for ravioli.

For the filling, boil the potatoes and peel and mash them (through a potato ricer, if you have one). Mix with all the other ingredients – and seasoning to taste – into a light paste. Place a level teaspoon of the paste about every 6–7cm along the pasta strips, cover with another strip of pasta, and slice into tortelli. Make sure each is sealed. You should end up with about 60.

Boil a large pan of salted water and drop in the tortelli, several at a time. As soon as they float to the top, remove with a slotted spoon to a warm bowl. Serve with a meat ragú or *sugo finto* (see below).

MOGGIONA: Il Cedro

Il Cedro, Moggiona di Poppi.
Tel. 0575 556080. Closed Mondays; reservations recommended. Prices inexpensive to moderate.

Not far from lower Poppi, on the road to the forest monasteries of Camaldoli and Eremo, is the little town of Moggiona. There you'll find a typical small restaurant snuggled in against the landscape, Il Cedro.

Mariangela Tassini is the third generation of her family to run Il Cedro. Her mother still does the cooking and follows strictly the basic culinary rules of her own grandmother. Italians often lament the loss of their traditional kitchen but in almost every out-of-the-way Tuscan town, it's possible to find an osteria or trattoria that still clings to traditional ways. In the Poppi area, Il Cedro does it well.

Peperoncino – the ubiquitous little hot red pepper – flavours almost everything, but judiciously. Curiously, nothing you eat seems overly sharp. Black pepper is used sparingly.

The restaurant reflects the simple peasant kitchen that's always existed in this 700-metre-high mountain valley. Main ingredients are the basics: potatoes, onions, seasonal locally grown vegetables. In the winter that also means cabbage, fennel, artichokes and *cardo* (cardoons, celery-like clusters of bitter stalks of wild artichokes). In other seasons the lighter courgettes are eaten, along with courgette flowers, dipped in batter and fried. Pasta is mostly with *sugo finto*, the meatless sauce of the Casentino. A meat ragú, however, goes over *tortelli di patata*, the simple potato-stuffed ravioli. As is typical in the area, Mariangela tells you that even today the tortelli are a dish for celebration.

In restaurants like this, you discover how different dishes with the same name all over Tuscany can be. *Aquacotta* – boiled water – is a good example. Born in the Maremma with the woodsmen boiling sliced onion to pour over bread for their lunch in the forest, it's taken on more sophisticated dressings everywhere. Different restaurants add a variety of seasonal vegetables and funghi when they are around. It is a clever use of the most prevalent vegetables. At Il Cedro it is still basically an onion and tomato *pappa*, topped with a layer of grated aged pecorino cheese.

Il Cedro has its meat dishes, mostly rabbit, local lamb and game in their seasons. In early spring, when wild fennel begins to appear in the fields, rabbits are stuffed with it and roasted on top of slices of it. Fennel seeds are also added, imparting an additional heady anise flavour.

RECIPES FROM *Il Cedro*

◆ 'Boiled water' *Aquacotta*

In winter, use tinned tomatoes in this dish. One large tin should do. The bread should be Tuscan, i.e. not salted, and of rough flour, which holds its shape when soaked.

Serves 4

500g onions
120ml good olive oil
500g tomatoes, peeled, or 1 x 800g tin Italian plum tomatoes
Salt
1 small chilli pepper, or to taste, chopped
240ml vegetable or meat stock
300g stale Tuscan bread, sliced
100g well-aged pecorino cheese, grated

Cut the onions in half and slice thinly. Put them into a pan large enough to hold the tomatoes as well (a wok serves well here), add the oil and sauté quickly over fairly high heat, mixing often, until they are soft and golden, about 10 minutes. Squash the tomatoes into the onions and add salt and as much chilli as you like. Add the stock and remove from the heat.

Layer all the bread in a terrine or oval dish and pour the soup over it. Sprinkle half the grated cheese over the top and put into a hot oven for 10 minutes. Serve with the remaining cheese at the table.

Fake sauce / *Sugo finto*

Serves 4

2–3 onions, finely chopped
Salt
1 whole pepper chilli, finely chopped
3 tablespoons extra virgin olive oil
1 small wine glass red wine
500g tomatoes, peeled, or 1 x 800g tin Italian plum tomatoes
Pasta and freshly grated Parmesan, to serve

Soften the onions, together with some salt and the chopped chilli in the olive oil, over a low heat in a pan deep enough to hold the entire sauce. After about 20 minutes, when the onions are soft and just golden, throw in the glass of red wine. Raise the heat and allow to evaporate. Cut up the tomatoes and add to the sauce. Cook over a moderate heat until the sauce is reduced to a fairly thick consistency, about 10 minutes. Taste for seasoning.

Serve over long thin spaghetti or spaghettini with grated Parmesan cheese at the table.

◆ Fennel-flavoured rabbit / *Coniglio in porchetta*

Serves 6

1 medium-sized rabbit, cleaned and splayed open
Salt and freshly ground black pepper
Olive oil
2 fennel bulbs
4 cloves garlic, smashed
1 tablespoon fennel seeds
Wild fennel branches, if available

Heat the oven to 180°C/Gas 4. Rinse the rabbit again, dry well and rub down with salt, pepper and olive oil, inside and out. Mix the smashed garlic with the fennel seeds. Slice the fennel bulbs, put them in a bowl with a tablespoon of olive oil and some salt, and mix well. Place the fennel in a roasting dish and put the rabbit on top. Fill the cavity with the fennel seed and garlic mixture and, if available, a few branches of wild fennel.

Bake for 50 minutes and test for doneness by pulling a leg as you would a chicken leg. If it comes loose, the rabbit is cooked. During the last 5 minutes of baking, cover the dish with tin foil. The rabbit makes its own juices to spoon over.

SAN SEPOLCRO: Da Ventura

Da Ventura, Via Aggiunti 30, San Sepolcro.
Tel. 0575 742560. Closed Sunday evenings and Mondays. Prices moderate; reservations recommended for Sunday lunch.

MARCO TOFANELLI is another of the young third-generation family members to run a typical restaurant in these parts. His grandfather first opened Da Ventura, and over the years Marco has introduced some innovations, even a special menu for vegetarians. The restaurant is a favourite with families of the area out for Sunday lunch.

Da Ventura offers familiar local dishes with variations designed in its own kitchen. Names might be the same, but either the ingredients or way of cooking them are a bit different. One good example is the familiar Florentine *ribollita*, made with a rich vegetable minestrone rather than the fairly simple bean soup you find in Florence. It's still served in much the same way, over stale bread and heated in the oven.

In wild mushroom season, Da Ventura offers a salad of *funghi ovoli*. You can see baskets of *ovoli* in most Tuscan markets in early autumn. They are pure white funghi that emerge from a bright-orange coating. At first sight, they are firm orange ovals. Later they develop into delicate white mushrooms. The sooner they are picked and eaten, the firmer the mushroom. Marco Tofanelli makes a salad of them with slices of Parmesan cheese and a dressing of lemon and fresh olive oil. If truffles are in season, he'll add a slice or two of those as well; here the truffle is black.

Hand-rolled *bringoli* pasta is light, of plain white flour and water that absorbs sauce particularly well. Da Ventura serves *bringoli* with a sauce of pancetta, sausages and sliced mushrooms called *salsa ghiotta*. (*Ghiotto*, the noun, has a double meaning in Italian; it can mean both a glutton and a delicacy. At Da Ventura I think it means both.)

Antipasti, vegetables and sweets are offered from open trolleys brought to the table. *Antipasti* include sausages of the area, salads, stuffed vegetables, *sformati* (savoury mousse or custard), baked fennel in bechamel and a mixture of onions with orange.

RECIPES FROM Da Ventura

Sausage and mushroom sauce / *Salsa ghiotta*

Serves 6

1 medium carrot, finely chopped
1 stick celery, finely chopped
1 small onion, finely chopped
3 tablespoons olive oil
50g pancetta, chopped
250g sausage meat (2 fresh sausages)
200g fresh champignon mushrooms, cleaned and sliced
500g peeled and seeded tomatoes (can be tinned)
Salt
1 small hot chilli, chopped (optional)
500g *bringoli*, or spaghetti, to serve

Sauté the carrot, celery and onion in 2 tablespoons of the oil in a small pan until soft. Put the remaining oil, the pancetta and the sausage meat into another large pan that will hold the entire sauce, and cook until the meat has become browned and crisp, about 10 minutes. Add the chopped vegetables, lower the heat and sauté until they are just soft, about 10 more minutes.

Add the mushrooms and cook for another few minutes, until they are well coated and just beginning to release their juices. Squeeze in the tomatoes with your hands, add the chilli, if using, and cook for 20 minutes over a low heat. Serve with a simple spaghetti or, if available, fresh *bringoli*.

Mushroom salad / *Insalata di ovoli*

Ovoli are one of the rare wild mushrooms, delicate in taste, firm, egg-shaped and covered with an orange skin before they open. The limited supply can be found in the autumn. I've substituted fresh large, firm field mushrooms, which work wonderfully. The salad should be made at the last minute. Slice both the mushrooms and the cheese with a cheese slicer.

Serves 4

250g fresh large white field mushrooms, cleaned
Salt and lots of freshly ground pepper
100g fresh Parmesan cheese in shavings
1 small bunch rocket
Juice of 1 small lemon
60ml fresh virgin olive oil

Slice the mushrooms about 5mm thick and place in a wide serving dish. Sprinkle over some salt and add the sliced Parmesan and rocket. Add a good grinding of black pepper, sprinkle with the lemon juice, then the oil, mix gently and serve.

ANGHIARI: La Nena

La Nena, Corso Matteotti 10–14, Anghiari.
Tel. 0575 789491. Open for lunch and dinner, closed Mondays and first two weeks of July. Prices are moderate.

THE CORSO MATTEOTTI is Anghiari's main street. It runs steeply up from the main square, and La Nena is at the top. Three food-loving partners – cook Palmira Alberti along with managers Paolo Severi and Sergio Cappetti – do everything here, and know their food well. They took over the long-time trattoria from its earlier owner-cook, who is still known as Nonna (Grandmother) Elvira. Her *sugo finto* still covers the *bringoli*.

Today the partners feel the challenge to find ways to keep the traditions and be innovative at the same time, so they've added wild berries to the porcini mushrooms that make up *risotto galeotto*. It's fun and delicious. The *sformato selvaggino* is a custard of game purée, served with a sauce that contains local truffles and wild mushrooms. More traditional is the *passato di fagioli*, a thick bean soup with the addition of the thinnest home-made noodles. All the *salumi* – the *antipasto* cold meats – are made in the restaurant as well.

RECIPES FROM La Nena

Risotto with mushrooms and wild berries / *Risotto galeotto*

Serves 6

300g porcini mushrooms (can be frozen), chopped
2 cloves garlic, crushed
3 tablespoons extra virgin olive oil
1 small onion, finely chopped
25g butter
400g risotto rice
fairly large wine glass white wine
About 1 litre chicken stock, hot
4 tablespoons frozen wild berries – blackberries, wild strawberries, blueberries – with their syrup.
Sliced truffle, if available
2 tablespoons cream

Sauté the mushrooms and garlic in the olive oil. Set aside.

Sauté the onion in the butter in a pan large enough to cook the whole risotto, and add the rice. Stir for a minute over a medium heat, then pour in the white wine. Allow the wine to completely evaporate, then cover the rice with hor chicken stock. Cook, stirring every now and again, adding more stock as it is needed. After about 15 minutes of cooking, add the sautéed mushrooms and the wild berries with some of their syrup. Continue to cook until the rice is *al dente*. At the last minute, stir in the truffle and cream. Mix well and serve.

Bean soup with tagliarini / *Passato di fagioli cannellini*

Serves 4

250g white cannellini beans, soaked overnight, and drained
3 cloves garlic
2 sprigs fresh sage
Salt
1 medium carrot
1 onion
1 stick celery
4 tablespoons olive oil
60ml tomato purée
Vegetable stock or water
200g fresh egg *tagliarini*
Fresh olive oil at table

Cook the beans at a bare simmer together with 1 clove of garlic and the sage in enough water to cover by about the width of three fingers. Add a good amount of salt at the last minute.

While the beans are cooking, finely chop the remaining garlic, and the carrot, onion and celery, then sauté for 10 minutes in the olive oil in a large pan. Add the tomato purée and 120ml water or vegetable stock. Add the beans and their water, and cook for another 15 minutes until all the vegetables are completely soft. Purée. The soup should be of light creamy consistency to allow the tagliarini to cook easily. If need be, add more water or stock.

Add the tagliarini and cook for another minute, until the pasta is cooked. Serve warm with a good drizzle of fresh oil.

ON THE ROAD TO MONTERCHI: Locanda di Castello di Sorci

La Locanda di Castello di Sorci, on the road from Anghiari to Monterchi.
Tel. 0575 788022. Closed Mondays. Reservations recommended at weekends. Inexpensive.

NOT FAR FROM Anghiari is an impressive old castle, on whose grounds you'll find one of the simplest traditional restaurants in the area inside the old granary of Castello di Sorci.

The locanda is a big family affair. This historic seat of the Sorci family was in bad shape when Primetto Barelli bought it in 1970 and began to turn it into the festive place it is today. Now his children have grown up and all the family is working there. The locanda is a stone's throw from the castle, which is available for larger celebrations.

The menu is fixed, and it's the kind of meal you'd get at an Italian peasant wedding or baptism. It's a grand feast for a pittance: self-service platters put in the middle of the table, piled high, from which to eat as much as you want. Ask for seconds and you'll have them within minutes. Everything served is the typical food of the region: an *antipasto* of local prosciutto, various cold meats, and tomato bruschetta – thick slabs of toast smeared with a purée of peeled plum tomatoes gently spiced with chilli pepper, garlic and olive oil. Two *secondi* come next, one always home-made tagliarini, the other a choice between sauced polenta, risotto and, a favourite of mine, thick chickpea soup laden with *quadracci* or tiny pasta squares. The main course is a variety of *arrosti* (roasted rabbit, chicken, duck, pork, goose and turkey) served up on one big platter for the table. The exception is Fridays, when traditional *baccalà* (salt cod) in a tomato, wine and fresh olive oil sauce is the main course. There are roasted potatoes and salads to accompany, and a bottle of wine to boot. To finish, as much *vin santo* as you can drink, accompanied by some home-made cake, the local *torcole*.

The atmosphere is festive, the sound level overwhelming, especially at Sunday lunch, the day large families celebrate together. Ask for a table on the second-floor enclosed terrace; while a bit narrow, it's the room with the greatest character.

RECIPES FROM Castello di Sorci

Tomato bruschetta / *Bruschetta di pomodoro*

Serves 4

6 Italian plum tomatoes, peeled and seeded, or
1 x 400g tin tomatoes
2 cloves garlic
2 tablespoons olive oil
Good pinch *peperoncino* (chilli) flakes
1 small bunch basil
Salt
4 slices thick farm bread

Chop the tomatoes into small pieces. In a small pan, press 1 clove of garlic into the oil over medium heat. Soon as the oil begins to bubble, add the tomatoes and chilli. Cook until the sauce thickens. Mash the tomatoes in the pan and set aside. Toast the bread. Halve the remaining clove of garlic and rub into the toasted bread. Cover the bread with the sauce and serve at once, while still warm.

Thick chickpea soup / *Passata di ceci*

Serves 4

200g chickpeas, soaked overnight then drained
2 sprigs rosemary
3 cloves garlic
3 tablespoons olive oil
2 large tomatoes, peeled and chopped
120ml chicken stock
100g *quadracci* (1cm squares of pasta)
Salt and freshly ground pepper
Extra virgin olive oil, to serve

Cook the chickpeas slowly in a large saucepan in water to cover by the width of three fingers, together with 1 sprig of rosemary and 1 clove garlic. When cooked, drain, reserving the water, and purée about three quarters of the chickpeas with enough of the reserved water to make a thick purée. Return the purée and the chickpeas to their pan.

Squash the remaining garlic cloves in the oil in a saucepan over a medium heat. When the oil begins to bubble around the garlic, add the tomatoes and the remaining rosemary. Add the chicken stock, and cook for 10 minutes. Purée, and add to the chickpea soup along with the little pasta squares and cook until the pasta is *al dente*, about 10 minutes. If the soup is too thick, add more of the reserved water or chicken stock. Taste for salt, add a good grinding of pepper, and serve with oil at the table.

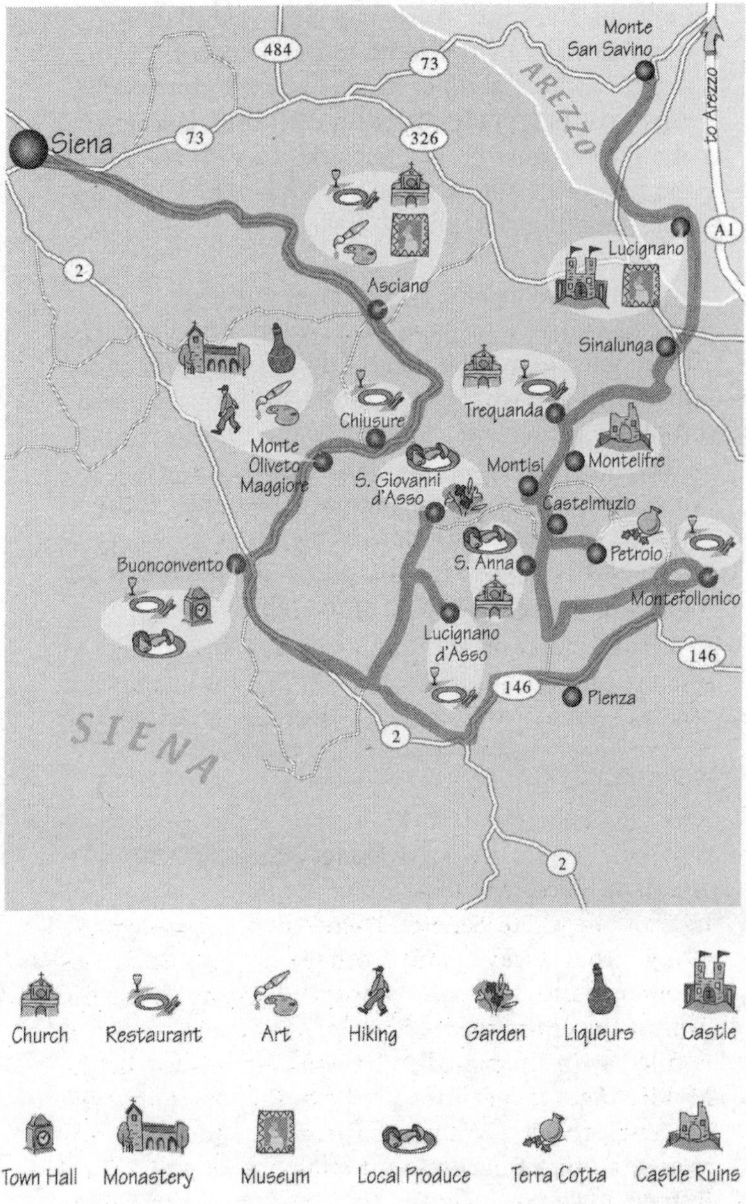
Monte San Savino
AREZZO
to Arezzo
484
73
73
326
Siena
A1
Lucignano
2
Asciano
Sinalunga
Trequanda
Chiusure
Monte Oliveto Maggiore
Montisi
Montelifre
S. Giovanni d'Asso
Castelmuzio
Petroio
Buonconvento
S. Anna
Montefollonico
Lucignano d'Asso
146
146
Pienza
SIENA
2
2
Church
Restaurant
Art
Hiking
Garden
Liqueurs
Castle
Town Hall
Monastery
Museum
Local Produce
Terra Cotta
Castle Ruins

7

Valdichiana and Crete Senese

Valdichiana and neighbouring Crete Senese are Tuscany at its most photogenic. Lying to the east and south of Siena, these are landscapes of almost unsullied beauty. The hilly pastures of Valdichiana blend into the voluptuous, rounded crater-etched hills of the Crete Senese. Few factories and modern housing schemes disturb the rolling pastures and intermittent woods, the contrast of cypress and red earth. Ancient towns dot the olive and vineyard-laden hills.

I have a tendency to divide Tuscany down its middle, not by mountains, woods or valleys, but into east and west of the major Florence/Rome *autostrada*. For whatever reason, trips are confined to one side or the other of the motorway. This one is to the west, leaving the *autostrada* at Monte San Savino to reach a road that passes through Lucignano in Valdichiana, Trequanda and Montefollonico, then goes into the hills of the Crete Senese. There's another Lucignano along that way, and other towns such as Buonconvento, San Giovanni d'Asso and Asciano. Almost the entire route has surprise and little traffic. It is filled with unspoiled hill towns established in the Middle Ages over Etruscan and Roman ruins still evident today. Wander through their narrow streets, admire their frescoed churches, attend a local festival if you're lucky to find one. It is the simple enjoyment of an ancient culture that still lingers.

About ten kilometres south of the *autostrada* exit at Monte San Savino lies the fortified village of Lucignano, a thick-walled medieval enclosure with a perfect concentric urban structure like few others in Italy. Enter one of the four great portals. You'll find a series of ring roads that once housed the various strata of society. The first ring is the imposing Corso Matteotti with its stately townhouses and a major castle – Le Logge – backing on to and forming the outer wall. (The weekly market, on Thursdays, runs completely around this ring road.) Narrow old passageways lead to the second ring, and a third. At the top is the tranquil Piazza del Tribunale. You can also climb the graceful rounded staircase opposite the castle to bring you to the top. You'll meet several lovely Romanesque churches along the way. The civic museum on the Piazza del Tribunale is well worth a visit. It holds one of the more noted shrines of the region, a two-metre high Golden Tree of Life (or *Albero di Lucignano*), a gothic relic of gilded branches, enamels and flowers of crystal and coral. A few fine Luca Signorelli paintings and an impressive early Crucifixion are an addition to the visit.

From Lucignano south, you'll hit a bit of urban sprawl around Sinelunga. Continue on to Trequanda, another fortified town. The castle of the Cacciaconti, a feudal family who once ran the entire area, still dominates the little village. A fine little trattoria just off the main square carries the nickname given to one of the Cacciacontis, Il Conte Matto, or the Crazy Count.

The wonder of the town is a little chequerboard-facade church off to the side of the main (and only) square. Sts Pietro e Andrea is filled with rare treasures, paintings by Sodoma, Giovanni di Paolo and

Sansovino and a splendid walnut urn holding the remains of Bonizzella Cacciaconti, a saintly thirteenth-century member of the ruling family. After her death the good Bonizzella was forgotten for a few centuries, and, but for a miraculous occurrence, might still be so. A swarm of bees is said to have formed a hive in a wall niche of the church. When, years after Bonizzella's death, the villagers went to collect honey from the hive, they discovered her remains just in the back of it, giving off a lovely odour of incense. The remains were removed to her present resting place in the walnut urn. The veneration of Bonizzella continues. The church isn't opened very often, but during the second week of May, when swarms of bees are said to reappear at the spot, it is Bonizzella's moment, and the time to see the lovely single-naved church. At other times, ask at the wine/tourist shop at the corner opposite the church; someone there should know how to find the key.

Near Trequanda are other small hill towns – Montisi, Petroio and Castelmuzio. They seem like they've been there forever, untouched by earthquake, blight or man-made wars. Not quite true, but in each of them a number of charming authentic urban centres remain to wander through and admire: Montisi with its thirteenth-century granary, Castelmuzio, reached by a curving two-kilometre drive through lovely woods, and Petroio, noted for its small workshops for hand-crafted pottery. You'll hit the first workshop as soon as you arrive on the outskirts. A high slim furnace tower tells you you're there; go in through the open doors and discover how the famous large terracotta pots of Tuscany are made. Further on into town, a small museum documents and displays the old terracotta produced here.

Midway between Trequanda and Montisi, you'll be struck by a view of the imposing remains of the old Castello di Montelifre, one of the many strongholds of the Cacciaconti family. In the fifteenth century, the Sienese discovered a nest of conspirators here during battle with the Florentines. An able mercenary chieftain managed to reduce the stronghold to the ruin it still is today. Then, so goes the story, the elders of Siena deliberated how to reward the fine warrior who had saved Siena from great peril. One suggested he receive a precious-stone-embedded gold medal; another urged that he be given high office. After much discussion, they solved the problem by making him a saint. They had to kill him to do so, but thought the solution politically and morally fitting. Such are politics and morality. Within the ruined walls today, there is a little borgo of reconstructed vacation homes.

Further south, off the road to Pienza, lies the ancient monastery of Sant'Anna where *The English Patient* was filmed a number of years ago, partly in the beautifully frescoed refectory, painted in the sixteenth century by Giovanni Antonio Bazzi. Better known as Sodoma, he was mentioned contemptuously by Vasari, who described his licentious ways with young boys, not an unusual practice among some of the best-known Renaissance artists. The name stuck even after Brazzi married and raised a family.

From the terrace at Sant'Anna, there is a lovely view west to the Crete Senese hills. The former monastery now serves as a school. It's possible to stay on the premises and study Italian culture. A small shop selling home-grown wine and produce forms part of the complex.

Before continuing on to the road that takes you up through the Crete Senese, visit the twelfth-century village of Montefollonico, which lies off to the left. Still remarkably intact, the village traces its lineage to Etruscan times, with stone vestiges dating from the sixth century. It is a miniature medieval city. The main alleyways are perfectly preserved. The large old *porta*, almost an antichamber between two arched gates, brings you into town. The Romans pretty well destroyed most of Montefollonico; what you see today are homes and churches built during and after the twelfth century. Montefollonico is also home to one of the better-known inn/restaurants of Tuscany, La Chiusa.

Once you reach the Crete Senese, the change of landscape is remarkable. The bare open pasture is broken only by dramatic craters and evenly spaced tall, graceful, dark cypresses. 'Crete' refers to the clay soil that has hardened over the years. It is the clay soil from these voluptuous hills that provides the area's ubiquitous building bricks whose colour over the years has come to be known as Siena red. The rounded hills are a velvet green, covered by rich pasture that feeds some of Italy's finest cattle and sheep. Only just after it has been ploughed do you see the rich brick-red soil.

As you travel through the Crete Senese, it becomes clear why sheep's cheese and lamb are so special here. The hills never lose their rich cushion of green, except where they drop off into odd crinkly craters. This is fine cheese country. Pasturing sheep can be seen from March through to late autumn.

From Montefollonico follow the signs to Pienza, past San Quirico d'Orcia to Torrenieri. Turn right at Torrenieri on the smaller road that leads to San Giovanni d'Asso. It's along this road that a small sign to the right takes you to the tiny town of Lucignano d'Asso where you'll find one of the best offerings of local cheeses at the little *alimentari*, a perfect place to sample them along with the cold meats of the Crete.

Lucignano d'Asso is little more than a cluster of ancient houses. Upon arriving, you immediately encounter a modest door with an *'Alimentari'* sign above. At first sight it is unassuming, a little shop of staples and vegetables with a second small room containing a few worn wooden tables and chairs. Then you see the vast display of cheeses and sausages. Eraldo Gianneti not only sells the best cheeses of the area but serves lunch here seven days a week. He and his wife are old-timers in these parts, known to everyone. Their son is a sculptor; a few of his pieces lie around at the back. At lunchtime Eraldo's is crowded with eat-in and takeaway customers, entire families, workers, members of the local *carabinieri*. Lunch at Eraldo's means a platter of sheep's cheeses and cold meats served with good country bread and a simple table wine. The cheeses vary: oval and slightly aged *marzolino di Pienza* is the first cheese of spring, sold either plain or heartily flavoured with some local white truffles or sharp *peperoncino*; *roscozino* is a fresh white delicate cheese; *Pienza pecorino delle fosse* is sharper, having been aged in a hole in the ground; another even sharper and longer-aged cheese is *morchiata reserva* with the aura and taste of an old wine. If you want to be sure about a table, call Eraldo beforehand. (Tel. 0577 803109.) Lunch won't be more than a few euros; taking away favourites will cost more. The prosciutto and sausages come from nearby farmers.

From Eraldo and Lucignano d'Asso, head back to the crossroads at Torrenieri and continue along the old Roman highway, Via Cassia, to Buonconvento. The old town of Buonconvento lies alongside the Via Cassia. It's a village of enormous charm, a few narrow streets of medieval, splendidly ornamented red-brick palaces that give the town a fine aristocratic air. You immediately sense that the old borgo well reflects its name, which means a fortunate community of good souls.

At Buonconvento the old Roman highway coincides with the medieval Francigena, the pilgrim route to Rome from northern Europe. Buonconvento was a stopover along the way. Behind the main Via Soncino are medieval alleyways; Via Oscura ends in a delicious little square where summer dinners are held and other festivities take place. A traditional festival of grain threshing is held here in July, and on the third and fourth Sundays of September the Sagra della Valdarbia takes place, when local specialities are offered for tasting and costumed folklore events engulf the town.

Henri VII of Luxemburg – known here as Arrigo VII – is something of a mythical figure in Buonconvento. On the way to his coronation as Holy Roman Emperor in Rome in the early fourteenth century, after causing a good bit of trouble in the area, he died here. Had he lived, a plaque on Buonconvento's city hall assures us, he might have realized Dante's 'grand illusion' to unite and bring peace to Italy. There is a rabbit dish named after him today at Da Mario, a most original restaurant along Via Soncino.

Several interesting shops line the main street. The most tempting is the Dolcezza di Nanni, a bread and pastry shop that grew out of Nanni's old bread *forno* to become an international business that today supplies home-made biscuits and cakes to Queen Elizabeth, Harrods of London and other illustrious clients. Floriana Giuliana, Nanni's wife, and her help are all sunshine, brightly dressed in Floriana-designed smocks with caps to match. Among the wares – in addition to breads leavened with their own yeast – are various fruit and citrus-flavoured cakes, home-made *cantucci* and other biscuits with very Tuscan names, such as *ossi di morto* (bones of the dead) and *brutti ma buoni* (ugly but nice). It's a cheerful shop where local gossip and friendly exchange go on all morning.

Across the street from Nanni is the Cantiniere Ghiotto, where owner Barbara Isolani is happy to tell you where all her local specialities come from and what is special about the different sausages, honeys, cheeses, jams and other wares for sale here. Up the street from here you'll find Trattoria da Mario.

The road from Buonconvento takes you to the noble abbey of Monte Oliveto Maggiore, the major attraction of the area. Travel back through the soothing landscape of the Crete Senese into the tranquil woods surrounding the famous monastery. Monte Oliveto Maggiore is likely to be crowded at times but is surely worth the visit even in high season. The grand fourteenth-century Benedictine monastery is a model of Renaissance architecture with a lovely cloister extravagantly frescoed by Luca Signorelli and Giovanni Antonio Bazzi (Sodoma). The frescoes have an almost modern feel. The long walk down from the great gated entrance to the abbey through the cypress-lined road is lovely; the climb back up is not nearly as challenging as it looks. The monks are still hard at work producing most of the things you'll find in the small shop: honeys, wines, spirits and various elixirs. (I highly recommend the orange honey.) Skin and beauty products sold there are made elsewhere.

From Monte Oliveto it's a short drive to Chiusure, a pretty, old terracotta village, where the Locanda Paradiso (tel. 0577 707016) is an inviting light-lunch stop. The front room includes the regulars at tables in front of the bar, looking like a nineteenth-century Tuscan

Macchaioli painting, *chiaroscuro* with touches of colour. Walk though to another little kitchen room, fire burning, where you can sit and eat a *ribollita* or a plate of *pici* or some of the fine pecorino and sausages of the area.

At San Giovanni d'Asso, you'll find an enticing park, Bosco della Ragnaia, cut out of the woody landscape by Sheppard Craig, an American artist living here. With the help of local youngsters Craig has developed an array of alluring walks and small tranquil spaces in an eight-hectare forest. The walks are lined with blocks of *tufo*, the volcanic rock from which so many Etruscan tombs are built. You don't immediately notice the enormous work that has gone into sculpting a garden in a wood. It's only when you become aware of an umbrella pine that spreads majestically from a lonely, soaring, bare curved trunk that you realize it's all been planned and worked out. The small sculpted spaces are marked by enigmatically engraved thoughts: 'Everywhere you can see a part . . . nowhere can you see all . . .' Four engraved stones on the 'Hill of Painted Posts' tell us, as Craig suggests, how 'things happen': 'Always, Sometimes, Never, Often.' Another terracotta tile reads *aporia*, the Greek word for doubt. The garden isn't gated, entrance is free. The only admonition on the welcoming sign asks the visitor not to smoke.

San Giovanni d'Asso is also the commercial centre for the delectable white truffle of the area. A truffle festival is held every mid-November, and the town has recently opened the first museum in Italy dedicated to the light-coloured tuber. The Museo del Tartufo (Piazza Gramsci, tel. 0577 803101) is open weekends, mornings (10–1) and afternoons (2–6). During season you can also arrange a truffle excursion (phone Assotartufi, 0572 803076).

Another stop – or at least pass-by – in San Giovanni

d'Asso is the *pieve* of San Pietro in Villore, a small eleventh-century church at the end of the old town. It is permanently closed but worth passing to see the facade, a fine example of the many local *pieve*, simple rural churches with an exterior decorated with the earliest kind of Romanesque symbols.

The road from San Giovanni d'Asso to Asciano is another scenic drive through the Crete Senese. As you arrive in Asciano, directly in front of you is the basilica of Sant' Agata. High on an imposing staircase, the church is set well above the town. Here is the main town of the Crete Senese, though it's no longer the great commercial centre it once was. In the past, artisans and farmers sold their wares, and their skills, at the weekly market. You could hire a *segatino* here, a man who would cut your overgrown grass with his small moon-shaped *falcia*, or sickle. Here too the potter sold his terracotta pots, the hat- and shoe-makers sold their goods and tanners their sheep hides. Remnants of what once was can still be found on the second Sunday of every month at a handicraft market.

A walk down the main street, Corso Matteotti, brings you past the old civic tower and its imposing clock to Palazzo Corboli, an old noble home that now houses the civic museum. Within you'll find a handsome collection of sacred art, including a work by Duccio, a crucifix by Giovanni Pisano and two beautiful wooden angels of the thirteenth century. It is an impressive collection. (Museo Civico Archeologico e d'Arte Sacra, Corso Matteotti, open all year, but call to make sure. Tel. 0577 19524.) Next door, in the same palazzo, is Locanda del Ponte del Garbo, serving local specialities and Neapolitan pizzas.

From Asciano, the old Laurentana road passes through the last of the Crete Senese and leads you to Siena.

◆ Specialities of the area ◆

Some of the world's finest beef comes out of the Valdichiana. The hefty white Chianina steer – named after the local Chiana valley – has become one of the more prolific beef breeds everywhere, but nowadays is bred less in Tuscany itself. The breed, known for its succulent, less fibrous meat, spread throughout Tuscany and later around the world from its origins near Trequanda. The Chianina provides the beef-lover's dream, the famed Florentine beefsteak. A restaurant that serves real Chianina will note the fact on its menu.

Once upon a time Chianina steers pulled Etruscan ploughs, and were praised by Roman poets and sculpted by Roman artists. Only a few years ago, you still saw yoked pairs of Chianina steers slowly pulling the same wooden ploughs you find on ancient Roman urns. Nowadays, the white steers mostly just loll on the pastures.

The province is home to another unique animal, the Cinta Senese, a wispy black wild pig sporting a wide white band around its middle (hence the name *cinta*, or belt). Nowadays, it is cultivated but remains free-roaming. Cinta pigs have become a protected species and are farmed throughout the Siena area. Ambrogio Lorenzetti included one of these pigs in his famous fresco *Buon Governo* (Good Government), which covers a large wall in Siena's Palazzo Communale. The Cinta feeds in open woodland on acorns and tubers. Slaughtered young, it provides pungent meat that is seasoned with local herbs to make the many preserved pork products of the area. A blood sausage, *buristo*, and a spicy boiled melange of pork parts called *soppressata* are especially tasty. The *finocchiata*, a sausage seasoned with fennel seeds, is firm and rosy, slimmer than in other parts of Tuscany. *Pan'unto* is also something to try, especially in winter; it is little more than a slice of good thick farm bread smeared with the lard of the Cinta Senese and roasted in a wood fire oven, a traditional farm dish.

Lamb and cheese figure strongly in the local cuisine. The sheep of the Crete Senese provide a well-flavoured rack of lamb along with some of the finest pecorino and ricotta in all of Italy. The pecorino is especially known for its aromatic flavour, which results from open grazing on the grassy knolls of the Crete. Added tastes such as hot red chillies and local white truffles are recent innovations. The latest 'designer cheeses' aren't just a fashion; they have added variety and quality to ubiquitous Tuscan cheeses. Sardinian shepherds can claim the credit for making Siena pecorino so good. They arrived as migrants in the mid-twentieth century from their impoverished island. After some were allegedly involved in a spell of lucrative but hazardous kidnappings of rich residents for high ransoms, the Sardinian shepherds, on abandoned farmlands, revived the ancient art of unadulterated cheese-making that dates from the Etruscans. The late-arrival Sardinians have now become well-to-do landowners and sheep farmers throughout the area. A large variety of delicious new cheese brands is now produced here, from fresh white ricotta and *raviggiolo* and mild pecorino to the sharper, aged variety that can be both eaten at the table or grated on to pasta. They come red- or black-rinded. The red means *semistagionato*, or aged for about three months; black-rinded is the more mature cheese of Pienza, aged for at least six months. There's one great cheese aged in a cave, '*del grotto*'. Cheeses of all ages are served with a variety of marmalades and honeys as a nice sweet course to finish dinner.

The Crete Senese is also one of Tuscany's prime areas for the white truffle, Bianco di Crete Senese, which provides a lucrative livelihood today for farmers around San Giovanni d'Asso. The season begins in September and goes on to December. The major moment is in mid-November at the truffle festival held here. Tuscan truffles, especially those of San Giovanni and San Miniato, now rival those of Piemonte. You'll find wild mushrooms here too, especially porcini, on autumn and winter menus.

The pasta speciality of the area is *pici*, a slim pasta hand-rolled and elongated in alternating movements by practised hands. The skill has been inherited from centuries of forebears. It resembles the *bringoli* of Casentino and the Tiber valley, just a touch more delicate. The width of *pici* differs from cook to cook and community to community, even within the province. I've eaten it rolled to the size of half a little finger in Pienza, and in matchstick widths nearby. *Pici* is usually served with a pungent garlic and tomato sauce called *aglione*, or a less savoury ragú, but it goes well with every kind of sauce.

Typical restaurants and their recipes

TREQUANDA; Enoteca Ristorante il Conte Matto

Il Conte Matto, Via Marėsca 1, Trequanda.
Tel. 0577 662079. Price moderate, closed Tuesdays and month of January. Reservations recommended.

IL CONTE MATTO, or the Crazy Count, is just off the main Garibaldi square in Trequanda. It has belonged to the Arrigucci family since 1983, when Chiara and Davide's grandmother closed her bar to open the first (and still only) restaurant in this small town. It is just down the street from the Cacciaconti castle on the main square. The restaurant specializes in the favourites of the area during the seasons they appear. Uncle Libio Graziani runs the kitchen, applying the basics and improvising the recipes of Grandmother Tosca's original *cucina*. Chiara, who runs the dining room, calls her grandmother's dishes still the best of the menu.

An *antipasto* of local *salumi* made from the wild Cinta Senese pig begins a meal; the local prosciutto, pancetta and *salumi* laced with seasoned fat seem more savoury in these parts. There are also *crostini di cacciotta,* toasted bread with a slice of melted soft cheese sprinkled with local truffles.

I found the summer version of *pappa al pomodoro* the lightest I've eaten anywhere. The simple vegetable and tomato broth is full of delicious vegetable tastes and crusts of bread. The hand-rolled *pici* come with whatever sauce you choose; one is as simple as fried garlic, super-fresh olive oil, breadcrumbs and salt.

RECIPES FROM Il Conte Matto

Aubergine custard with tomato and basil sauce / *Sformatino di melanzane con pomodoro e basilico*

You can prepare this textured custard in a baking dish or 4 large individual moulds.

Serves 4

500g peeled and coarsely chopped aubergine
Salt and freshly ground pepper

2 tablespoons olive oil
180ml double cream
1 entire egg, plus one yolk
3 heaped tablespoons freshly grated Parmesan cheese, plus extra to serve
750g ripe tomatoes, peeled and seeded
1 tablespoon red wine vinegar
3 sprigs basil, chopped, with some entire leaves for garnish

Put the aubergine into a colander, mix some salt through it and leave to rest for at least 30 minutes to rid it of any bitter juices. Squeeze it dry in a towel, and sauté gently in the olive oil until soft. If need be, add a bit of boiling water and allow to cook out. Blend the aubergine, cream, eggs and cheese together in a food processor.

Heat the oven to 150°C/Gas 2. Put the mixture into individual moulds or a baking dish, and place in a bain-marie of boiling water. Bake for 30 minutes in individual moulds or 45 minutes in a baking dish. Test for doneness by sticking a sharp knife into the custard. If it comes out clean, it's done. Cool well.

Meanwhile, blend the tomatoes and basil together in a food processor, then pour into a bowl. Mix in the vinegar, and season to taste. At the moment you want to serve, turn out the mould on to a serving dish, pour over the tomato sauce, garnish with fresh basil leaves and serve with more sauce and grated cheese. You can also serve directly from the mould, with the tomato sauce on the side.

◆ Summer tomato soup / *Pappa al pomodoro*

Serves 4

1 large onion, chopped or sliced coarsely
1 stick celery, sliced
2 cloves garlic, sliced
1 carrot, sliced
2 tablespoons olive oil
1 bay leaf
1 bunch parsley leaves, chopped finely
1 small hot red pepper (*peperoncino*), seeded, chopped
120ml white wine
1 litre vegetable stock
5 sprigs basil leaves, chopped
300g tomatoes, peeled and sliced (about 4)
Salt and freshly ground pepper
3 small slices Tuscan or country bread, cubed and toasted
Freshly grated Parmesan cheese
Extra virgin olive oil

Sauté the onion, celery, garlic and carrot in the olive oil for about 5 minutes. When they begin to soften, add the bay leaf, parsley and red pepper. Pour in the white wine and let it evaporate. Add the vegetable stock, bring to the boil, and stir in the basil and tomatoes. Lower the heat and cook for 30 minutes. Place the cubed toasted bread in the bottom of a soup tureen, pour over the soup, add Parmesan cheese and a dripping of olive oil and serve warm or at room temperature.

MONTEFOLLONICO: La Chiusa

La Chiusa, Via della Madonnina 88, Montefollonico. Tel. 0577 669668, fax 0577 669593. Email: info@ristorantelachiusa.it. Closed Tuesdays. Prices are high. A meal – without wine – is expensive. Reservations are in order, especially during holiday season.

LA CHIUSA would be my choice for the extravagant stop along the way. The restaurant/inn – in a beautifully restored old olive mill – sits under the small village of Montefollonico, with a view from its windows of nearby Pienza and Montepulciano. There are fifteen rooms to let, some of them with jacuzzi and open fire-place in the bathroom.

Owner/chef is Dania Mansotti, a chic and lively Florentine. She manages her kitchen dressed straight out of a fashion magazine. The food is stylish too. Dania turns traditional local fare into highly refined dishes. Lamb is coated with rosemary, garlic and pancetta before going into the oven in a bath of red wine. Beef is large and thick, cut from the fine Chianina of the area. Mansotti spent a good part of her youth by the sea and, while a good distance from the sea, La Chiusa is notable for its seafood. *Zuppa di teste*, an incredibly rich broth, is made with heads of scampi and served over toasted wholewheat bread slices topped with a sliver of Parmesan cheese and two large scampi. The soup is a meal in itself.

Dania's thick puréed chickpea and pasta soup is topped with crayfish for an added taste. The freshly made *pici*, half a little finger round, are coated with a special ragú. A local woman rolling *pici* in front of your table is a featured presentation in the dining room. Artichokes, a major winter and early spring product of the area, are stuffed with puréed artichokes and capers, and served on a large platter generously dripped with a syrupy reduced balsamic-vinegar sauce. Sweet balsamic vinegar, not too long ago known only in the Emilia-Romagna region of Italy, is nowadays a mainstay of kitchens throughout Tuscany.

Dania showed me how to reduce balsamic vinegar to syrup, a lesson well learned. A jam thermometer is a necessary tool in order to save the sauce from turning into hard and brittle sugar. Begin by pouring 500ml vinegar into a small saucepan. Bring it to a boil and keep a watchful eye on it as it cooks down. After 15 or 20 minutes, it will begin to coat a spoon. Measure the heat with the thermometer. When the liquid reaches a soft ball consistency (115°C), remove it from the heat and cool it. It keeps for ever.

RECIPES FROM La Chiusa

Artichoke hearts stuffed with artichoke purée / *Carciofi ripieni*

If you have leftover stuffing, add some mayonnaise and serve as a pâté on crackers with drinks before dinner.

Serves 6

2 large lemons, to acidulate the water
10 large globe artichokes, with their stems
6 tablespoons extra virgin olive oil
2 cloves garlic, smashed
2 tablespoons breadcrumbs
3 tablespoons capers, if possible packed in salt (drain and soak in cold water whether in vinegar or salt)
Salt and freshly ground pepper

240ml dry white wine
120ml reduced balsamic vinegar syrup (see above, page 248)

Fill two large bowls with cold water and add the juice of a lemon to each, saving the emptied halves to rub into the artichokes. Slice the stem from each artichoke and rub the cut edges with a lemon half. Peel each stem to the light inner core, slice and toss into one of the water-filled bowls.

Pluck off the outer leaves from each artichoke until you reach the pale-green softer leaves inside. Trim around the bottom.

Slice into 6 of the artichokes from the top to about 5cm high, scoop out the centre with a sharp knife and toss the artichokes into the second bowl of water.

Cut the remaining 4 artichokes into quarters, and remove the fuzzy core. If they are very large, cut in half again. Add to the stem pieces in the first bowl of water.

In a large sauté pan, heat 3 tablespoons of the olive oil and add the smashed garlic cloves. When the oil around them begins to bubble, add the drained stem and artichoke pieces from the first bowl, and cook for about 10 minutes, adding about half a glass of water and allowing it to cook out. The artichokes should then be fairly soft. Purée the entire contents of the pan and set aside.

Mix the breadcrumbs into the purée. Drain the

capers from their soaking water and purée them. Add to the artichokes, taste and season.

Remove the remaining 6 artichokes from the water and dry well, gently pressing the leaves outwards to form a good cavity. Fill each with stuffing and place in a pan just large enough to hold all 6. Pour half a glass of water around the hearts, and then enough wine to bring the liquid up to a touch beneath the filling. (Don't get the filling wet.) Drip the remaining oil over the top, seal closed with some foil and cook gently for about 15 minutes, until the hearts are cooked. Keep warm.

With a small spoon, drip some rounds of the balsamic syrup on each serving plate and place the artichoke in the middle. Serve warm.

◆ Roast leg of lamb / *Agnello al forno*

Serves 6

1 leg of lamb (about 1.5kg)
50g pancetta, chopped
3 sprigs rosemary
2 garlic cloves
Salt
2–3 glasses dry red wine

Bring the lamb to room temperature. In a food processor, blend the pancetta, rosemary, garlic and salt to taste together into a paste, and rub all over the lamb.

Heat the oven to 200°C/Gas 6. Put the lamb in a deep roasting dish and bake for about 30 minutes. Remove from oven, pour the red wine over the lamb. Lower the heat to 180°C/Gas 4 and return the lamb to bake for another 30 minutes.

Remove the lamb to a serving platter and set aside. Over a high heat, reduce the liquid remaining in the dish to a sauce consistency. Serve in a separate sauce boat to pour over the sliced lamb.

BUONCONVENTO: Da Mario

Da Mario, Via Soncino 60, Buonconvento.
Tel. 0577 806157. Closed Saturdays. Inexpensive, advisable to book in advance.

DA MARIO is a family restaurant par excellence. Mario Pallassini died some years ago, but his wife Alfa – now nearing ninety – still runs the kitchen. Grandson Christian invents new dishes, such as ragú of rooster crests (I did not ask how many roosters lost their crests for one ragú) and a rabbit stewed in red wine, in homage to Henri VII, who died in Buonconvento in the fourteenth century. Christian's mother Anna and her sister Nara alternate between the kitchen and the dining room, mixing with the regulars. Two other grandsons run the upstairs and downstairs dining rooms, and in the summer are out back serving in the large courtyard.

You are never quite sure here who is family and who is paying. A few single men come for lunch and dinner every day; others – usually workers on a local building site – arrive in groups for the evening meal. Beyond that there are local and foreign guests who've discovered the good simple food of this very basic but imaginative trattoria. The room downstairs fills early, latecomers are accommodated upstairs. Everyone hugs hello and goodbye. All in all, it promises a fun evening.

There is a single menu above the refrigerated showcase just outside the kitchen. Few look at it. Most eat what Nara or Anna suggest. Try one of Christian's new concoctions, which usually turns out to be a perfect combination of ingredients (such as a thick bean and mussel soup, the mussels floating in their boatshells amid the beans). More courses include a soothing lentil and rice soup, or tagliatelle with hare sauce. The *pici* are topped with *aglione*, a savoury sauce of concentrated tomato laced with garlic. You can also have the *pici* with simple ragú. Another of Christian's deliciously innovative dishes is a guinea hen in citrus sauce. There's also a pork fillet richly sauced in balsamic vinegar. Just listen to what's offered and dine on the dish of the moment.

RECIPES FROM Da Mario

Pici with thick garlicky tomato sauce / *Pici aglione*

Serves 6

500g *pici*, or thin, fresh pasta
2 x 400g tins Italian plum tomatoes (about 500g fresh tomatoes)
4 cloves garlic
120ml extra virgin olive oil
Salt and freshly ground pepper
Toasted breadcrumbs

Drain the tomatoes. Cut them open to release inner juices. Blend and drain again. Smash and finely slice 2 of the garlic cloves and put them into a heavy pan with the oil. When the oil begins to bubble around the garlic, add the tomatoes and a good amount of salt and pepper.

Coarsely chop the remaining 2 cloves of garlic, and add to the sauce. Cook for about 15 minutes, until the coarsely chopped garlic is softened and the sauce nice and thick. Add more salt and pepper to taste.

Cook the *pici* in well-salted boiling water until just *al dente*, drain and mix with the sauce. Top with toasted breadcrumbs and serve.

Loin of pork in balsamic vinegar / *Maiale al aceto balsamico*

Serves 6

1 onion, sliced
3 tablespoons olive oil
60ml balsamic vinegar
Pinch of sugar
1 small sprig sage leaves, chopped
1 loin of pork, about 800g
Salt and freshly ground pepper

Sauté the onion in 1 tablespoon of the olive oil, add the vinegar and sugar. Cook until the onion is completely soft, then blend in a food processor and set aside.

Heat the sage in the remaining oil. Brown the loin on all sides and cook for 5–6 minutes. Remove the pork and slice into 3cm slices. Put back into the pan, pour over the balsamic dressing and cook until the pork is done, another 5 minutes.

◆ Rabbit in wine vinegar / *Coniglio di Arrigo VII*

Serves 6

1 rabbit, cut into 8 serving pieces
Salt
Extra virgin olive oil
3 cloves garlic
4 sprigs rosemary
240ml red wine vinegar
120ml chicken stock
1 bunch parsley leaves, chopped
6 thin slices toasted Tuscan bread

Prepare this dish in a heavy pot wide enough to take the rabbit pieces in one layer. Salt the rabbit and put it into the pot. Pour 2 tablespoons of olive oil and 2 chopped garlic cloves over the rabbit, mixing to coat the rabbit pieces entirely. Add 3 sprigs of rosemary. Brown over a medium heat, turning the pieces over so they brown evenly.

Pour the vinegar over the rabbit. Increase the heat to high and boil to reduce the vinegar by about half, then add the chicken stock. Lower the heat and cook gently, partially covered, mixing often. Add water if necessary as the dish cooks to prevent burning and keep the rabbit moist. Towards the end, add the fourth sprig of rosemary. Chop the remaining garlic clove finely with the parsley leaves and add when the rabbit is cooked, in about an hour.

To serve, place a slice of toast on each plate, with a piece or two of rabbit on top and a good dousing of sauce. It can also be served with rice or mashed potatoes.

Guinea hen in citrus sauce / *Faraona in agrumi*

Serves 6

1 large guinea hen, in 8 pieces
Salt and freshly ground pepper
2 navel oranges
2 unwaxed lemons
3 tablespoons olive oil
1 small onion, chopped
2 sprigs sage, chopped
2 cloves garlic, smashed and chopped
120ml cognac

Remove the fat, and wash and dry the guinea hen. Salt and pepper the pieces. Slice the zest from the oranges and lemons, slice the zest into thin strips and drop into boiling water for about 30 seconds. Drain. Juice the oranges and lemons.

In a large pan with cover, heat the oil with the chopped onion, all but a little of the sage and the garlic. Allow to bubble for a minute and add the guinea hen. Brown the pieces well on all sides. Add the cognac and let it evaporate. Add the juice and zest of the oranges and lemons and cook over a medium heat, covered, for about 30 minutes, until the guinea hen is almost done.

With a slotted spoon, remove the guinea hen and

reduce the sauce over high heat for a few minutes until it is thick. Replace the hen pieces, reduce the heat and cook slowly until the meat is completely tender, about 15 minutes. Taste for salt and pepper, place the hen pieces on a serving dish and pour the sauce over.

ASCIANO: Locanda del Ponte del Garbo

Locanda del Ponte del Garbo, Corso Matteotti 126–128, Asciano.
Tel. 0577 710011. It's a pension too, thus is never closed. Inexpensive.

GIOVANNI VEGLIO (Gianni) and his wife Giovanna opened their restaurant here after years of owning Italian restaurants in Latin America and Germany. They wanted a small friendly town in Tuscany, found Asciano and opened Locanda del Ponte del Garbo. The restaurant adjoins the eighteenth-century Palazzo Corboli, the museum of sacred art in Asciano. Gianni Veglio is a displaced Sicilian from Salerno, and you find flavours of his origins tapping into the food here. He brings his incomparable mozzarella and ricotta cheeses from the south twice a week; his pizzas are thick and hearty as in Naples, and come in tastes that are just a bit different, like a whiff of pineapples added to prosciutto, mozzarella and tomatoes – Tuscan food with a southern touch.

Gianni is the cook, Giovanna runs the large dining room. The *fegatini* (chicken livers) for the bruschetta are made with white wine, a tasty variation on the usual red. There are interesting soups on the menu, including both broccoli and potato creams. Mostly the menu features local specialities, *pici* (with an anchovy sauce) and wild game of the area. You'll find fish on the menu as well.

RECIPES FROM Locanda del Ponte del Garbo

Chicken liver bruschetta / *Fegatini bruschetta*

This particular version of a very Tuscan *crostini* or bruschetta has a special tang. If it seems too acerbic, add a bit more cream.

Serves 6

250g chicken livers
White wine vinegar to marinate
2 tablespoons olive oil
1 shallot, chopped
Salt and freshly ground pepper
120ml dry white wine
1 tablespoon cream
6 slices toasted Tuscan or country bread
18 capers in salt, soaked

Soak the livers in vinegar to cover for 30 minutes. Drain and pat dry. Heat the olive oil with the shallot. When the oil begins to bubble around the shallot, add the chicken livers, chopped up a bit, and sauté. Add a good bit of salt and pepper. After a minute or two, add the wine and cook for about 15 minutes, until the wine has evaporated and the livers are cooked through. Chop well, either by hand or in a food processor. Add the cream and mix. Spread the liver on the toast and top each toast with 3 capers.

Broccoli soup / Zuppa di broccoli

Serves 4

500g broccoli
2 tablespoons cream
40g slivered almonds
Salt and freshly ground pepper

Peel the broccoli stems and chop them coarsely. Break up the florets. Bring a pot of salted water, just enough water to cover the broccoli, to the boil and add the broccoli stems and florets. Cook until soft, around 10 minutes. Drain, reserving the water. Blend the broccoli with a bit of its water and put back into the pot. Add the cream, and as much water as needed to make a dense soup. Put the almonds in a mortar and pound into a paste. Add the paste to the soup, along with salt and pepper. Heat and serve.

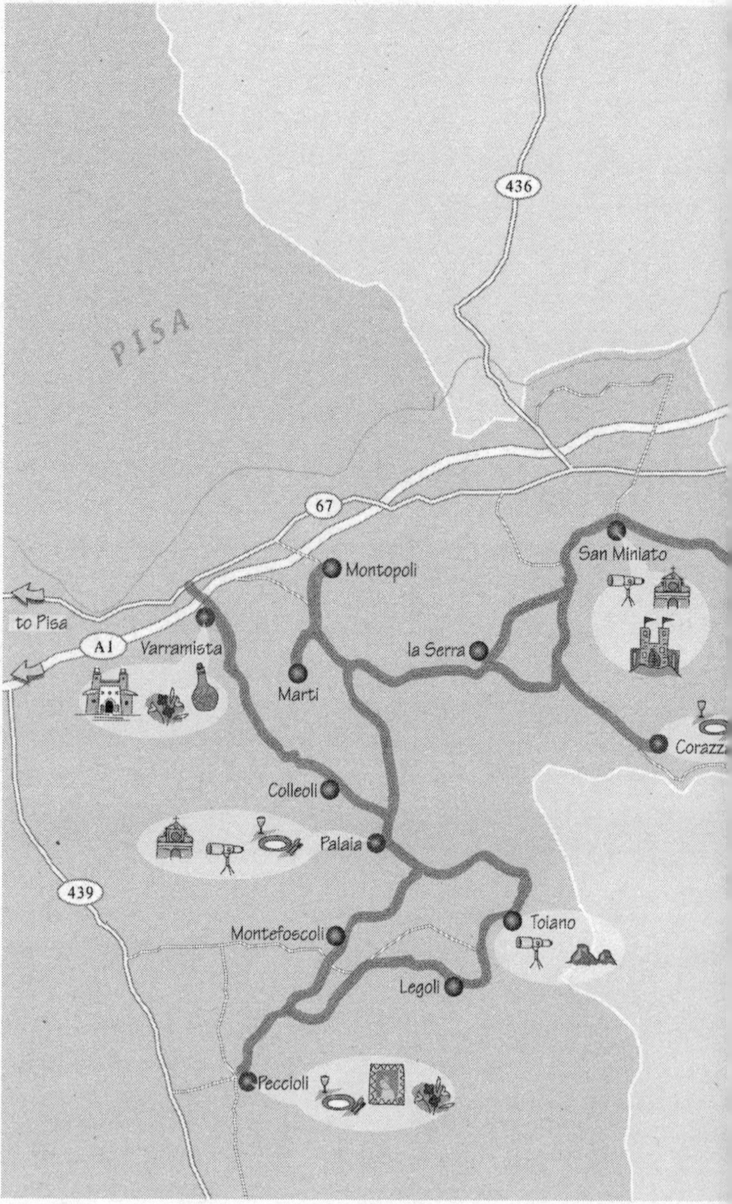

436
PISA
67
Montopoli
San Miniato
to Pisa
A1
Varramista
Marti
la Serra
Corazz
Colleoli
Palaia
439
Toiano
Montefoscoli
Legoli
Peccioli

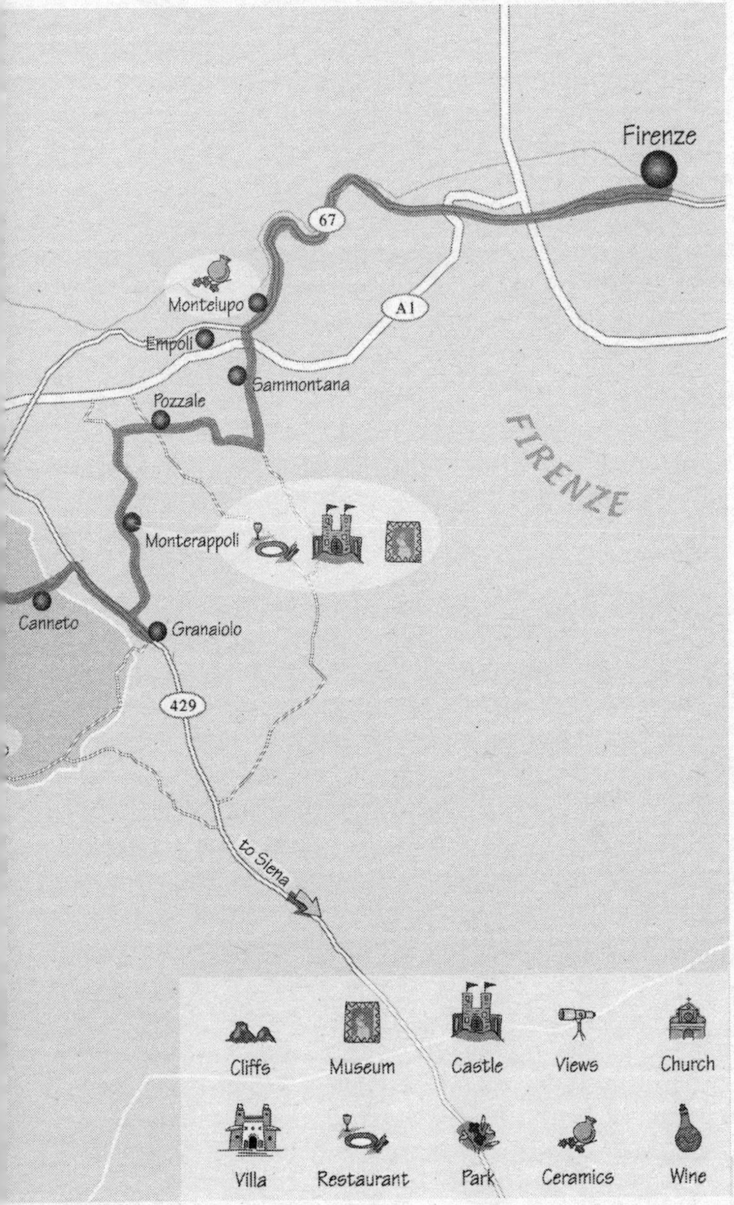

Firenze
67
Montelupo
A1
Empoli
Sammontana
Pozzale
FIRENZE
Monterappoli
Canneto
Granaiolo
429
to Siena
Cliffs
Museum
Castle
Views
Church
Villa
Restaurant
Park
Ceramics
Wine

8

Montelupo Fiorentina and the Truffles of San Miniato

THE VALLEYS to the west of Florence teem with small industry, not particularly enticing for the tourist. But go beyond the crowded valley to find pleasant hills and old hill towns. Montelupo, where this trip begins, is the centre of Tuscany's artisan ceramic industry. San Miniato, the next stop, has come to rival Piemonte in its rich truffle production. Montopoli's aristocratic past under Florentine rule endows its narrow streets with elegance. Palaia and Peccioli in Pisa's Val d'Era hold some nice surprises as well. The trip is almost entirely through little-travelled countryside.

Montelupo Fiorentina is a short drive down the Arno along the Florence (Firenze)–Pisa–Livorno (Fi-Pi-Li) *superstrada*. It is my favourite place to buy wedding gifts. The town and its immediate surroundings are filled with small artisan workshops making highly decorative, old-fashioned platters, jars and bowls with traditional patterns in much the same way as was done during the Renaissance. The high art of tin-oxide glazed ceramics – *maiolica* – arrived in Pisa from Spain with Moorish traders during the thirteenth century; as Montelupo and its river clay – necessary for the production of *maiolica* – lie along the old Roman road linking Florence and Pisa, you can surmise a connection. It was only later, during the Renaissance, that ceramic decoration became the high art form you see in museums today. The new tableware had a civilizing influence too. During the Renaissance the rich tossed away the old boards from which they ate and replaced them with the elegant new tableware.

The original designs, colourful and intricate, are meticulously hand-copied all over town. My favourite workshop is Tuscia, along the road from the Florence highway to town, at Via Chiantigiana 264 in Lastra a Signa. It is fascinating to watch the skilled artisans painstakingly dabbing and painting throughout the day. The old patterns are rendered more or less faithfully. Check the originals in Montelupo's archaeological and ceramics museum in the centre of town on Via Sinibaldi (tel. 0571 51352, open Tuesday to Sunday, 10–6), then pick up something similar at a reasonable price at Tuscia and elsewhere. At the end of June there's a big international ceramics fair. In addition, many Sundays throughout the year – March to October – are given over to an open-air ceramic market.

Montelupo is the beginning for a nice tour to the west through olive- and vine-laden hills brightened in summer by radiant sunflowers. It's a bit tricky to manoeuvre the minor roads away from the industry- and traffic-infested Arno valley, but with some attentive map reading it should be no problem. It took me several tries, but I finally worked out a route that is indeed lovely and takes you first to the ancient town of San Miniato and its truffles.

From Montelupo take the road to Sammontana. Continue on through Villanuova, and when you reach the traffic lights at Pozzale, take a left turn. You cannot go straight across, which is what you'd like to do, but it doesn't really matter. Go left and follow the road through Monterappoli to Grenaiolo, where you'll begin to see signs to San Miniato. Follow the signs over the hills. While struggling to find an asphalted route over the hills, I stopped a friendly-looking man in Monterappoli and gathered a nice historical footnote. 'How might I find the loveliest and most quiet road to San Miniato?' I asked. An odd request, he obviously thought. It would be longer through so many curves, he protested. I assured him I wanted an unfettered landscape that would not take me through the roads surrounding Empoli. This prompted him to tell me the story of Empoli's tiny military force attacking San Miniato in the thirteenth century. (The various towns were continually fighting one another.) In order to look menacing and grand, the little band collected all the goats it could find, tied candles to their horns, lit them and with the well-lit animals marched on in grand style taking on the appearance of a huge military force. Needless to say, they won handily.

Following their footsteps, you reach San Miniato from the rear. You'll first catch sight of the town by its tall thin tower topped by three oddly ragged round brick columns. Travel around on the circumferential road to the old centre where there's limited parking on the main Piazza del Popolo. (If you arrive on a festive occasion, or during truffle season in November, it's best to use the ample parking lot under the old wall and walk up to town.)

San Miniato has a big history, albeit a tragic recent past – another footnote. I first visited San Miniato some years ago, still under the shock of a film I'd just seen, *La Notte di San Lorenzo* (*The Night of the Shooting Stars*), made in the 1970s by brothers Paolo and Vittorio Taviani, natives of San Miniato. Much of it was locally filmed. The film retells the disaster that befell San Miniato during the German occupation in 1944.

During that fatal summer, the town was under siege, with battles between the advancing American army and the retreating Germans. Local partisans were fighting alongside the Americans. Most townspeople had fled and the Germans locked the entire remaining population inside the duomo. During the battle, an American shell hit the cathedral, bringing down a major column and causing the deaths of fifty people. In the immediate post-war years after the American liberation, it was easier to blame the Germans, whose fault it actually had been. When the film was made, photos of the actual battle as well as stills from the film were posted prominently all over town. The people of San Miniato were reliving their shock. The film takes its name from the battle between partisans and Germans on 10 August, the saint day of San Lorenzo. It follows the correct sequence of events, but to spare local feelings the Taviani brothers recreated the duomo scene inside the cathedral of nearby Empoli.

The many grand rulers who passed through these hills left an impressive number of beautiful buildings in San Miniato. Ottone I passed in the tenth century, Frederick Redbeard in the twelfth, and later in the same century his son, Henry IV. Local lore tells us that Countess Matilde of Canossa, one of the legendary figures of the time, was born in San Miniato in the eleventh century. Her father Bonificio, the Marquis of Tuscany, not a pleasant man, is said to have lived here at the time. Upon his death by assassination – two older siblings had already died – nine-year-old Matilde became heiress to vast lands that spread from Emilia-Romagna through much of northern Tuscany. She was one of the more powerful women of the Middle Ages, a veritable warrior who consolidated Bonificio's widespread holdings. She negotiated a famous peace between Henry IV and Pope Gregory VII, who was said to have been her lover as well. The Medici later founded the city of Livorno on top of one of her fortresses. Her great citadels and castles can be seen all the way from the Garfagnana and Mugello down to the Val d'Era. Her main residence was in Canossa in Emilia-Romagna, the castle where she hosted Henry IV and the Pope. She's better known there than in Tuscany.

As each ruler passed through San Miniato, and occasionally stayed a while, castles, towers and churches were built in the city. What's left of them still gives the town an important and impressive look. The last emperor to drop in officially was Napoleon III, when he came to see a relative who was running San Miniato. It is a small place, but with a lovely elegant feel and some very grandly decorated churches. Today San Miniato is most famous for its truffles, little brown marvels that rival the better-known Piemonte variety.

From San Miniato it's a short drive to Montopoli in Val d'Arno. Stay along the inner road, don't follow the road down to the heavily trafficked route to Pisa. Leave San Miniato on the road to Serra, and from there to Montopoli. Along the way is a detour to Corazzano – about eight kilometres from San Miniato – and a little restaurant, La Taverna dell Ozio, where you'll find the best of local food.

Montopoli lives its history. Written records carry the town's existence to long before Florentine rule, as far back as 746. The Florentine grandee Gino di Neri Capponi – his namesake still lives in Florence – captured the town from the Pisans in the fourteenth century and erected an impressive tower that still overlooks the surrounding countryside. He also built one of the most elegant villas of the entire Tuscan countryside, Varramista, just outside Montopoli, designed by the noted Florentine sculptor Bartolomeo Ammannati, architect of the Pitti Palace. In recent years Varramista has been owned by the Agnelli automobile family, and has become an important wine-producer.

Around Montopoli's main Piazza Michele da Montopoli are some fine old buildings: the Bishop's Palace, the Podesta's Palace and the Antique Chancellery Palace with its newly restored portico. On the same square the inn/restaurant Quattro Gigli is well worth a visit. It prides itself on an historical menu of recreated Montopoli specialities.

The remains of the earlier tenth-century castle are a short walk off the square. The castle is today only a simple tower; the rest was destroyed in 1944. Down the road is the fine church of Saints Stefano and Giovanni Battista. And there is a new little archaeological museum along the main street, based on collections of another ancient Florentine family, the Baldinovinetti, whose country house in the nearby village of Marti is still lived in by the family.

The road from Montopoli to Palaia brings you to the Val d'Era, a tranquil valley marked by dramatic sandstone cliffs (*chalanti*), eroded through the millennia as an inland sea that once covered the valley gradually receded. It is after Palaia, on the road to the deserted little medieval town of Toiano, that you get the best view of the cliffs.

Walled Palaia, with its two impressive portals at either end of a rather drab main street, has its most interesting features above the second large gate: the Church of Sant' Andrea, built over the ruins of a Roman temple with a lovely brick facade and impressive group of saints by Andrea della Robbia, and a spectacular view from what was once the *rocca*, or castle, at the top of the town. It's worth the somewhat precarious climb along a dirt path up to the little grassy plot just to have the full view of the valley around, all the way to Volterra in the south and the peaks of the Apennine mountains to the north.

The loveliest visit in Palaia is just below the old town: the large Pieve di San Martino, built and signed – on the capitol of a simple column – by the early Renaissance sculptor Andrea Pisano. The high-vaulted awesomely pure interior is entirely of brick, including its well-designed columns and gothic-shaped apse. The church is usually closed, but across the road lives young Giacomo, who knows it well and will open the severely barred side door to show you around and graciously explain all the intricacies of the church. An ancient hand-hewn baptismal font sits in a corner.

On the way to San Martino, just outside the old walls, is a favourite restaurant of the area, Il Pettirosso, with a terrace that takes in the lovely views around. Inside the walls is also a small welcoming wine bar/restaurant, Antica Farmacia, open only evenings. (Via del Popolo 51, telephone for reservations: 0587 622159; closed Wednesdays.)

From Palaia, the road continues to Peccioli. A few kilometres along this road you'll see a sign on the left to 'Borgo Medievale di Toiano'. The six-kilometre narrow road is a worthwhile detour along a ridge that, to the left, is marked by the dramatic spires and etched sandstone cliffs of the once inland sea. Follow the asphalted road; it becomes a navigable dirt track at the very end, and runs directly into the bridge that leads to the deserted little walled village, now, almost unnoticeably, being gently restored. A few houses seem to be occupied; the only sign of life we encountered on a visit was the postman, motorbiking into the village in his bright-yellow-and-blue uniform, obviously to deliver the post to someone. The other single bit of colour was the tiny cemetery at the entrance, eerily kept in a flush of vibrancy with flowers on every tomb. It is apparently maintained by former villagers still attached to the place.

Return to the main road and follow it past the village Montefoscoli to Peccioli, a further excursion into the graceful valleys and surrounding hills of the Val d'Era. A turn-off to the left at Montefoscoli will take you to Legoli, where the small chapel of Santa Caterina set in a grove of Cypress trees was frescoed by Benozzo Gozzoli in the fourteenth century when he escaped from the Pisa plague to these woods. You can go on from here through Pratello to Peccioli, or return along the same road through Montefoscoli. Peccioli is a small old town, with a few surprising attractions in addition to the graceful twelfth-century church of San Verano overlooking the valley. First there's the parking garage, underneath the town, with an elevator that delivers you right to the main square. Second is a museum of rare Russian icons, the collection of Francesco Bigazzi, an Italian journalist who spent years in Russia and donated his collection to Peccioli. The museum is housed in the medieval Palazzo Pretorio on the square (tel. 0587 672877). And then there's the prehistoric park, a walk among life-sized dinosaurs in a private garden that's open to the public as well (Via dei Cappuccini, open all day, 0587 636030). On the Piazza del Carmine, the square at the top of town as you drive in, is the most sophisticated restaurant of the area, La Greppia.

You can continue from Peccioli to Volterra, about twenty kilometres to the south, or return to Florence on the road that joins the superhighway just beyond the estate of Varramista. Drive up through the landscaped grounds to the architectural beauty that was once the residence of Gino di Neri Capponi and, most recently, of the Agnelli family. (Call to reserve: 0571 44711.)

Specialities of the area

The heavenly, intensely aromatic little tuber known as the white truffle is the major important product of the area. Less well known than those of Alba in Piemonte, they are just as good and rather less expensive. White truffles – brown outside, flecked inside – have been coveted for ages. The Romans thought them an aphrodisiac, precious enough to demand payment in gold coin. They are different both in quality and in texture from the black truffle – where one grows, the other does not. Neither ideally lasts for more than a few days, no matter how you try to preserve it. The highest-quality truffle is round and smooth, easily cleaned of the bits of earth that cling to it. It is usually stored in a jar of rice that absorbs a good bit of the aroma and makes a wonderful risotto. The truffle itself is never cooked. It is probably at its best simply shaved over fresh, buttered tagliatelle.

San Miniato's white truffle is treasured in these parts, considered by locals the best in the world. (The 'biggest truffle in the world', weighing over 25 kilograms, was shipped from San Miniato to President Dwight Eisenhower in 1954; it could not have been all that aromatic. In 2004 a London restaurateur paid $52,000 for a San Miniato truffle at auction.) Nowadays, farmers are successfully seeking out truffles all over Tuscany, in the Crete Senese, the Pistoian hills, the Garfagnana, even the Casentino and Tiberina. San Miniato still holds first place. Its truffle fair on the last three weekends of November has become a major annual event, though truffles can actually be found here a good part of the year. The most aromatic noble white truffle has a limited season, from late September to December; others, like the more delicate Marzuolo (or Bianchetta), go on through to April. There's also a lesser variety called Scorzone that can be found even later. But the height of the season is November.

Throughout the year *tartufi* are the talk of the town, in San Miniato and in the surrounding hills as well, where more than 700 professional truffle-hunters are either training their dogs or out scavenging in the woods. Truffling is a local sport. I went off on a training exercise with Bruno Castaldi, a grizzly bear of a man, whose humour and affection for the pup he was training to hunt truffles immediately dispelled any suspicion I might have had that animal exploitation for man's pleasure was at work here. I met this *tartufaio* almost accidentally, struck as I was by a bunch of wild asparagus he was grasping like a bridal bouquet. It arrived from the woods at a restaurant in Corazzano, not far from San Miniato, where I was having my fill of spring truffles. His asparagus were not the trim slim 'wild' variety one finds in early spring markets, but the ones we go out looking for in the nearby forests. I could see from the awkward angles of the asparagus that they were the real thing, as precious in early spring as the porcini mushrooms we forage in the autumn. With great exuberance, Bruno described the risottos and pasta sauces that bring out the best of these little delicacies. Our conversation inevitably turned to truffles, and Bruno invited me out to the woods with his ten-month-old puppy for a lesson in hunting truffles. The truffle woods were directly across from the restaurant.

Bruno has five truffle hounds, and normally takes out two at a time to hunt. The one I met, Tita, is the youngest, a dog of indeterminate heritage who looks like a mini Labrador. Tita adored the hunt. In his deep-pocketed overcoat, Bruno kept a sack of puppy snacks; each time Tita hungrily and happily nosed out a truffle, she was rewarded. Bruno snatched the truffle; Tita munched the snacks. We walked the edge of the forest. The hunt was in fact virtual since Bruno had earlier planted the little tubers for training purposes about 15cm down. Tita, a gentle and affectionate young dog, found them all.

◆ Typical restaurants and their recipes ◆

SAN MINIATO/CORAZZANO: La Taverna dell'Ozio

Taverna dell'Ozio, Via Zara 85, Corazzano.
Tel. 0571 462862. Reservations are necessary for both lunch and dinner, especially during truffle seasons.
The taverna sits on the main road through Corazzano.
Closed Mondays, and at lunchtime during August.
Prices are inexpensive to moderate.

This unobtrusive little restaurant is a splendid place to enjoy a meal of truffles. Corazzano is best reached from San Miniato, a pleasant drive of some ten kilometres through undulating wine country. Simone Fiaschi is the owner/chef, a portly man with a grand resemblance to Pavarotti; he claims a lovely tenor voice as well. Simone comes from a family of *norcini*, once a highly valued (now almost extinct) profession throughout Tuscany: itinerant pork butchers who roamed the countryside, from one farmer to another, slaughtering and seasoning mature pigs in a way that assured preservation and use of every single part of the animal. *Norcini* salted the hind legs (prosciutto) and the front quarters or shoulder (*spalla*), cooked, seasoned and stuffed the sausages, boiled down the blood for the *mallegata* and carved the roasts and the ribs. By the time the *norcino* was finished, meat for the entire year had been prepared to hang and dry in a cool cellar.

Simone, who runs the restaurant together with his wife Silvia, carries on the tradition, preserving his own meats. A glance at the prosciuttos and sausages hanging in his cellar, ageing alongside the cheeses and preserved mushrooms and olives on the shelves, is an invitation to try them all as *antipasto*. A favourite sausage is his *briciolona*, soft and pepper-spiced, looking like the better-known *finocchiona* sausage, but without the traditional fennel seeds. Pasta courses include, in truffle and funghi season, *tagliatelle con tartufi* or *con funghi*, and delicate thistle/ricotta-filled ravioli, with butter and shaved truffle sauce. The wide variety of interesting main courses is unusual, attesting to Simone's delight in creating savoury meats. He prepares different game dishes: wild pigeon – *colombina* – in a rich wine-and-tomato sauce, wild hare – *lepre* – in a combination of a dozen spices, steak of wild goat – *capriolo* – topped with a shaving of truffles, and pheasant in truffle sauce. An entire milk-fed three-month-old pork can be ordered beforehand, stuffed with sage and juniper berries, and roasted in a sweet-sour sauce.

RECIPES FROM Taverna dell'Ozio

Mushrooms preserved in oil / *Funghi sott'olio*

Makes a 1-litre jarful

500ml white wine
500ml white wine vinegar
500ml corn or extra virgin olive oil
Salt and whole peppercorns
1kg small, perfectly white, firm champignon mushrooms

Boil together for 5 minutes the wine, vinegar and a good tablespoon of salt. Slice off the bottom of the stems of the mushrooms and peel or wipe the caps with a wet cloth. Drop them in the boiling liquid for 3 minutes. Drain and spread on a clean cloth or kitchen paper to dry a bit.

Place the mushrooms in a clean glass jar, add about 20 peppercorns and cover with either corn oil or extra virgin olive oil. Simone uses corn oil; I prefer the olive. Store in a cool place. They are ready for eating in a day or two, and last well for about a month if you can resist them that long.

◆ Mixed vegetables / *Caponata*

Simone Tuscanizes this southern dish, and serves it on a bruschetta, or as accompaniment to his roasts.

Serves 4

1 large aubergine
Salt and freshly ground pepper
1 large red onion
1 large red pepper
3 medium courgettes
2 sticks celery
2 ripe tomatoes
120ml fresh virgin olive oil
2 cloves garlic
1 sprig fresh oregano
1 bunch basil

Cut the aubergine into bite-sized pieces of about 4cm square, place in a colander with a good sprinkling of salt, and allow to sit while you prepare the other vegetables. Cut all the vegetables into bite-sized pieces, about 3cm square. Heat the oil in a large pan and gently sauté the onion with the garlic, oregano and basil. After 5 minutes add the other vegetables – with the drained and rinsed aubergine – and cook gently for 30 minutes. Add salt and pepper to taste. Serve warm or at room temperature.

◆ Hare in sweet-sour sauce / *Lepre in salsa dolce/forte*

This rich sauce does not divulge its ingredients easily but the combination of spices is enormously satisfying. Originally from the east, such spices are used quite often in Tuscan cooking, from flavouring preserved olives to enhancing game dishes. If a hare is not available, a rabbit will substitute well, less gamey but very good. Hare is larger than rabbit; a rabbit will serve 4–6.

Serves 6–8

1 hare or rabbit, divided into small pieces and marinated overnight in a mix of ⅓ white wine vinegar, ⅓ water and ⅓ white wine, enough in all to cover
2 carrots
2 sticks celery
1 large onion
1 bunch parsley
3 tablespoons olive oil
2 sprigs rosemary
1 clove garlic
2 tablespoons tomato purée dissolved in 120ml water
A pinch each of the following ground spices, or as many as you can find: coriander seed, nutmeg, cinnamon, anise, cloves and pimento (together about 1 tablespoon)
Handful pine nuts

Finely chop the carrots, celery, onion and parsley and sauté in the olive oil in a pan large enough to hold the entire dish. Remove the pieces of hare from their marinade and dry well. Add to the pan and brown gently for about 5 minutes on all sides, then remove to a plate.

Chop the rosemary and garlic together and add to the pan along with the tomato purée, the spices and the pine nuts. Replace the hare, with any juice that has accumulated, lower the heat and cook slowly, covered, until the hare is tender. Hare will need about 45 minutes, rabbit less.

MONTOPOLI: Quattro Gigli and Trattoria dell'Orcio Interrato

Quattro Gigli is a welcoming little pension on the main square of Montopoli. Two different restaurants occupy a number of rooms in what were once the storage cellars: the elegant Quattro Gigli and the simpler Trattoria dell'Orcio Interrato, both serving traditional foods of the area. The inn is on terraced land, and the cellars look out on to the garden and surrounding hills. In warm weather ask for a table on the terrace with a view of the surrounding countryside.
Tel. 0571 466878. Closed Mondays. Prices are moderate in the trattoria, more expensive in Quattro Gigli.

THE HISTORIC MENUS at both Quattro Gigli and Trattoria dell'Orcio Interrato are the happy result of owner Luigi Bachini's passion for old Florentine manuscripts and local lore. Wife and chief chef Fulvia Puccioni develops and modernizes recipes dating from the fifteenth century. Meals derived from ancient recipes are more likely to be interesting than mouth-watering, but here they work. The two restaurants sit cosily in a warren of cellars and terraces under a fourteenth-century palace all done up in local pottery and old church artefacts.

Don't be undone by the touch of fancy artefact and pretentious service; the tableware may resemble that of a new London restaurant, but the food is traditional and good.

Luigi's old hand-printed books tell of fruit-flavoured game and spices that arrived in Tuscany from the East and from North Africa. The nobility, he notes, ate from the sky, mostly the birds they hunted; the middle classes could afford meat, and the poor – progenitors of today's fashionable *cucina povera* – ate only what they could grow. Butter was for the privileged, olive oil for the farmer. The food at Quattro Gigli is more that of the upper classes, but the Trattoria dell'Orcio Interrato offers simpler fare.

The dining terrace is a delight, overlooking a garden of persimmon and cherry trees and all the fresh herbs that go into the food. The menu changes with the seasons to include only fresh ingredients. An autumn chicken breast, for instance, is poached in almonds and pomegranate juice. *Antipasti* include a terrine of wild boar, accompanied by marmalade of onions and apples; there's a pasta of fresh cheese gnocchi with a fifteenth-century sauce of ground hazelnuts and rosemary; another is ricotta-filled ravioli covered with pear sauce. Home-made fresh pasta, *torcionetti*, come with a rabbit, olive and aubergine sauce. In November the menu takes on the truffle, and there's lots of it here to try. *Trippa di tartufo* is not innards smothered in truffles (as the name may suggest) but thinly sliced crêpes in truffled sauce. *Crostini di tartufo* are covered with a simple light cheese topped with a good grating of truffles. *Pici con tartufi* are thin hand-rolled pasta in a sauce of fresh pecorino cheese and a generous grating of truffles.

Chianina beef and Cinta Senese pork come from the

Lorenzetti farm in nearby Montaione. The *lonzino di cinta* is a seventeenth-century main course; in September it is served over a peach purée not at all sweet, rather quite delicious. Desserts include a white almond cream, served with a lovely spread of fruit sauces.

RECIPES FROM *Quattro Gigli and Trattoria dell'Orcio Interrato*

Fresh cheese gnocchi in a hazelnut sauce / *Gnocchi con salsa di nocciole*

Serves 6–8

FOR THE GNOCCHI

600g goat's cheese ricotta
200g flour
6 egg yolks
Salt
1 teaspoon freshly grated nutmeg

FOR THE SAUCE

75g butter
1 sprig rosemary
100g hazelnuts, lightly toasted and ground
75g freshly grated Parmesan cheese
Pinch of salt
Butter, to serve

For the gnocchi, whip the ricotta until creamy in a food processor. Add the flour slowly, working it well into the cheese. Add the egg yolks one by one and continue to process until well blended. Remove to a bowl, add a good amount of salt and the nutmeg.

The consistency should be a paste that can be scooped by a spoon and dropped into boiling water, neither too solid nor too liquid.

For the sauce, melt the butter with the rosemary over a medium heat. Don't allow the butter to burn, but let the rosemary steep a bit. Remove the rosemary and whisk in the toasted hazelnuts. Add the cream to make a thick liquid sauce. Add a pinch of salt, mix well and heat just to the boiling point.

Boil a large pan of salted water and, working with a teaspoon, drop small balls of gnocchi dough into the water. Allow to cook for a few minutes, until the gnocchi rise to the top. Remove to a warm buttered dish, adding bits of butter to each layer. Pour over the sauce, mix gently, add the grated Parmesan cheese. Mix again gently and serve with more grated cheese at the table.

◆ Sage frittata / *La salviata*

Serves 6 as *antipasto*

Leaves of 5 sprigs sage (about 20 leaves)
6 eggs
100g ricotta cheese
50g freshly grated Parmesan cheese
Salt
1½ tablespoons olive oil

Pound the sage into a paste, either in a mortar or mini processor. Beat the eggs with the ricotta and add the grated Parmesan. Add the sage paste and a good amount of salt, and mix well.

Heat the olive oil in a large frying pan and put in the egg mixture. Turn, or cover, to set. When the frittata is just cooked through, turn out on to a serving plate. Serve warm or at room temperature.

PALAIA: Il Pettirosso

Il Pettirosso, Via San Martino 15, Palaia.
Tel. 0587 622111. Reservations aren't absolutely necessary, but to have a table ready it's advisable to call ahead. In warm weather ask for the terrace, where there's a nice view. Prices are moderate, depending on what you choose. Closed Tuesdays.

GRAND CHEFS may mostly be men, but in Italy, the perfect little trattoria – the one with the best kind of home cooking – usually has a woman running the kitchen. People often joke about the *nonna* (grandmother) in the kitchen teaching the *mama* all her old tricks. And yet in Italy most rural trattorias are just that, created by a woman moved from her own kitchen to one for paying guests. The rest of the family provides service. Many a rural trattoria began in the poor years after the Second World War to help families make a better living than as tenant farmers. Some started as a bar, as a bakery or grocery. Many have since passed from grandmother to mother and daughter – or sometimes son. The best are still preparing food according to the *nonna*'s old recipes.

It was a special delight to discover Il Pettirosso, where a spry grey-bobbed grandmother of eighty-plus years is still working her old favourites for crowds of diners every day. Il Pettirosso sits just outside the old walls of Palaia, a large and bright restaurant with a terrace of equal size shaded by two great box-shaped oak trees. The terrace looks down on the impressive old Pieve San Martino. Luciana Manganelli has been the chef here since she opened the restaurant in 1962; her son Paolo and granddaughter Francesca serve. Francesca's little boy runs around, with various aunts and cousins to tend him. Workers and local business people come for a fixed-price lunch. During summer months the 150-seat restaurant is full in the evenings as well.

The menu is perfectly simple, perfectly Tuscan, more in the Florentine style than any other. *Antipasti* are the usual mixed bag: slices of prosciutto and other cold meats, liver toasts, prosciutto with melon or a salad of sliced tomato and mozzarella. The traditional taste of old-fashioned Tuscan cooking begins with the *primi*, the first courses. In the autumn, there are fresh tagliarini either with funghi or topped with truffles, both made with just oil and a touch of garlic and parsley. Luciana is especially proud of her *pappardelle delle caccia*, wide noodles with a ragú of wild boar.

The beef is the famous Chianina, grilled on an open wood fire. I prefer the *tagliata*, slices of thick steaks covered with either fresh rocket and slivers of Parmesan, or with another delectable stew of local wild mushrooms. Luciana's own favourite is her traditional *cinghiale con olive*, a bit chewy but filled with pungent flavour.

Desserts are again a particularly well-done version of most Tuscan menus: *cantucci* (biscuits) with *vin santo*, *panna cotta*, a fruit salad or, what Luciana thinks she does best, an irresistible *zuppa inglese*, a very typical Italian dessert fashioned after English trifle.

RECIPES FROM Il Pettirosso

Wild boar in olive sauce / *Cinghiale con olive*

Serves 6–8

1kg wild boar, cut into bite-sized pieces
2 cloves garlic
1 onion
1 small bunch parsley
2 sprigs rosemary leaves
60ml extra virgin olive oil
Salt and freshly ground pepper
1 teaspoon mixed ground spices, including cinnamon, nutmeg and pimento
120ml meat stock
240ml red wine
1 x 300g jar Tuscan olives, with their pits

Place the meat in a bowl and cover with cold water. Allow to rest for an hour. Finely chop the garlic, onion, parsley and rosemary. Sauté together in the olive oil in a large pan. When the sauté begins to take on colour, pick the pieces of meat out of the water without draining and add them to the pan. Add salt and pepper, and then the spices and the stock. Cook over a low heat until the stock has evaporated. Add the red wine. Allow to reduce, and add 120ml water. Cook over a low heat until the meat is cooked through and tender which will take about two hours.

Meanwhile, drain the olives and drop into a pan of boiling water for 10 minutes. Add to the stew and serve.

Italian English trifle / *Zuppa Inglese*

This is one of the desserts you'll find everywhere in Tuscany. Best to make the sauce on top of a bain-marie to be sure it does not curdle. Alchermes is an old liqueur of mixed spices developed by the Medici. If not available, Grand Marnier or Curaçao can be substituted.

Serves 10
12 egg yolks
400g sugar
100g white flour
2 vanilla pods sliced open and scraped
2 litres milk
Juice of ½ lemon
1½ packages or 500g Savoyard biscuits
Alchermes liqueur (or Grand Marnier or Curaçao)
Bitter cocoa for sprinkling

Beat together the egg yolks, sugar and flour in a heatproof bowl. When well beaten, add the vanilla and the milk and place in a bain-marie. Cook over a low heat, mixing all the while with a wooden spoon. When the mixture begins to thicken, add the lemon juice and remove from the heat.

Dip the biscuits in the liqueur quickly and lay them side by side in a large baking dish. Pour over the thickened cream and sprinkle the top with cocoa. Refrigerate for at least 4 hours before serving.

PECCIOLI: La Greppia

La Greppia, Piazza del Carmine, Peccioli.
Tel. 0587 672011. Reservations recommended; there are only seven tables. Open for lunch and dinner; closed Tuesdays. Moderately expensive.

EGISTO CAVALLINI opened this elegant little wine bar/ restaurant some years ago with his wife Daniela after twenty years of wandering through restaurants in Switzerland and Florence. He works alone in his kitchen, devising innovative dishes based on produce from the area. The restaurant's seven tables are placed in small coves; the decoration includes a collection of local pottery, and every table is set with heavy stone platters as place mats.

It's a sophisticated menu, with dishes served a tad pretentiously on large designed plates. Interesting *antipasti* include rounds of truffle-flavoured *tonino* cheese on bread baked to a browned melting softness, a baked pecorino served in a casserole, large prawns wrapped in a warm thin slice of *lardo di Colonnata* and, best of all, a dish of stewed beans and porcini served with red bitter raddichio salad leaves. *Primi*, especially the risottos, are excellent. A risotto of small apple pieces together with tiny shrimps and a hint of Calvados is definitely worth trying, as is one with radicchio. The perfect *pasta al pomodoro* flows out of a crusty basket made from melted grated Parmesan cheese.

Meat courses include the usual roasts, with eleven different ways of saucing a fillet of beef. There's also a breast of duck with a sauce of prunes and *vin santo*.

RECIPES FROM La Greppia

Beans with wild mushrooms / *Fagioli con funghi*

Serves 6

500g cannellini beans, soaked overnight
1 small bunch sage leaves
5 tablespoons extra virgin olive oil
4 cloves garlic
250g frozen porcini mushrooms, defrosted and coarsely chopped
1 bunch parsley leaves, finely chopped
Salt and freshly ground pepper

Put the drained beans to cook slowly in a large pot of water together with the sage, 1 tablespoon of the oil and 1 peeled garlic clove. Cook until tender and reserve in their water.

Chop the remaining garlic cloves and sauté in the remaining oil in a pan large enough to hold the beans as well. Add the defrosted porcini, the parsley and salt and pepper to taste. Cook for about 5 minutes, until the mushrooms and garlic are tender.

With a slotted spoon, remove the beans from their water and add to the mushrooms. Mix well, add a few tablespoons of the bean water, and cook together, reducing the juices to a creamy sauce. Serve warm or at room temperature.

Risotto with apples and prawns / *Risotto con mele e gamberi*

Dill is a strange addition here, not at all indigenous to Tuscan soil. Egisto orders it from a local supplier, but I often leave it out, replacing it for colour with chopped parsley. So-called red peppercorns come from a Mediterranean tree.

Serves 6

500g whole fresh prawns
2 sweet red onions
2 green Granny Smith apples, peeled and cored
2 tablespoons extra virgin olive oil
500g risotto rice
1 small wine glasses Calvados
1.2 litres fish stock, kept at a boil
Handful red peppercorns
1 large sprig dill, chopped
1 tablespoon cream

Peel and remove the heads and veins from the prawns. Place the prawns in a bowl, and cook the heads and shells in about 1.5 litres of salted water for 20 minutes. Drain, and keep at a low boil for the risotto.

Chop the onions and quarter the apples. Slice each apple quarter into about 4 pieces. In a deep pot that will hold the risotto, sauté the onions and apples in the olive oil for about 5 minutes. Add the prawns and cook for another minute, mixing.

Add the rice and cook for another 5 minutes, mixing all the while. Pour in the Calvados. Allow to bubble and evaporate for several more minutes. Begin to add the simmering fish stock, just enough to cover with each addition as the rice absorbs. After about 10 minutes, add the red peppercorns and the chopped dill. Continue to cook, adding stock, until the rice is cooked *al dente*. Add a tablespoon of cream, and allow to rest for a few minutes before serving.

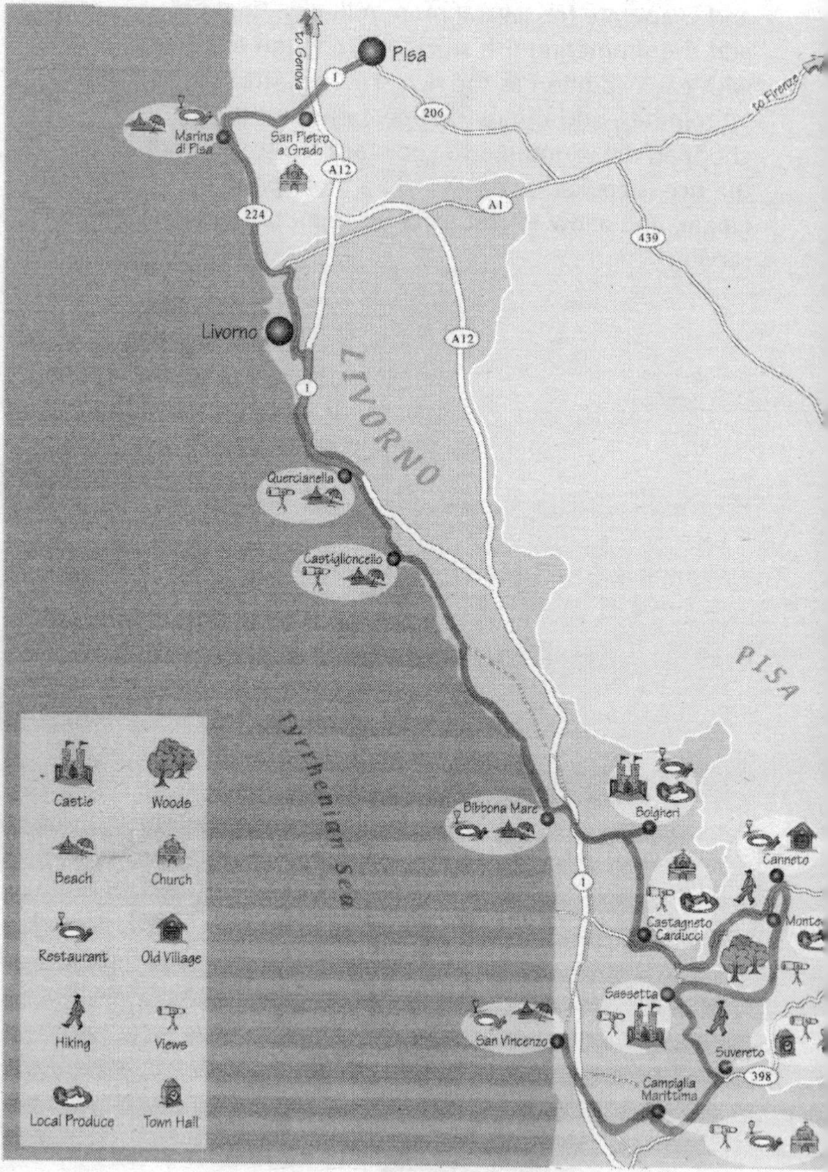

Pisa
to Genova
1
206
to Firenze
Marina di Pisa
San Pietro a Grado
A12
A1
224
439
Livorno
A12
1
LIVORNO
Quercianella
Castiglioncello
PISA
Tyrrhenian Sea
Bibbona Mare
Bolgheri
Canneto
1
Castagneto Carducci
Sassetta
San Vincenzo
Suvereto
398
Campiglia Marittima
Castle
Woods
Beach
Church
Restaurant
Old Village
Hiking
Views
Local Produce
Town Hall

9

Marina di Pisa to Upper Maremma

If you are taken, as I am, with rather dowdy seaside resorts, Marina di Pisa is the perfect place to begin to wander down the Tuscan coast and follow the old Etruscan road into the hills of the upper Maremma. Marina di Pisa lies at the point where the Arno flows into the Mediterranean. It retains a Fellini-like quality of seaside post-war Italy, with few fashionable boutiques and lots of fishermen hanging their lines from worn piers. It exudes its aura of simple hearty tastes and more reasonable prices than most resorts along the shore. It also happens to have a fine fish restaurant right at the mouth of the Arno, Taverna dei Gabbiani.

The north bank of the river is completely taken up by the vast regional park of San Rossore filled with elegant giant Mediterranean umbrella pines, oaks, all kinds of scrub and the grand villa that was once the palatial summer residence of the kings of Italy and now serves the president as his official guest house.

The road along the southern bank of the Arno from Pisa goes directly to Marina di Pisa. The road is lined with an appealing combination of fishing shacks, little boats and vegetable gardens. At a little more than the halfway point, you'll spot a sign on the left, to San Pietro a Grado. It's a church not to miss. The wonderfully harmonious dual-apsed Romanesque basilica rises in the middle of large green meadow. Here is the place where St Peter is said to have preached his first sermon upon reaching the Italian shore. First-century archaeological remains that you see inside lend credence to the story. The interior is as graceful as the facade and the small descriptions of important relics give a good idea of the evolution of the basilica.

As you arrive in nearby Marina di Pisa, the road curves into the middle of town. Side roads to the right lead to the esplanade along the seafront. At the north end is the Arno meeting the sea, and, just opposite, Taverna dei Gabbiani. The drive south from there along the seashore brings you to another seaside resort, Tirrenia, and on to the outskirts of Livorno, a thriving seaport founded by the Medici in the fifteenth century to give some competition to unruly Pisa, which was continually needling the controlling Florentines. The enterprising Medici, anxious to quickly populate the new port, invited all comers to settle there, among them Jews and Arabs fleeing the Spanish inquisition. Livorno provided not only a safe haven for refugees but also a convenient market for the rich booty of pirates in the Mediterranean.

To this day, the food of Livorno reflects its foreign heritage. Couscous arrived here from North Africa. Tuscan food writer Aldo Santini tells us that the ubiquitous tomato – so essential to the Italian kitchen – first arrived in this part of the Mediterranean with Jews fleeing Spain in the fifteenth century. The strange New World fruit – Mexican, actually – was having difficulty being accepted in Spain (or in England, where it also arrived with returning colonizers). True or not, it's a nice story.

Skirt the bustling port city and follow the old Roman road Aurelia that meanders along one of the more beautiful rivieras of Italy, through the lovely resorts of Quercianella and Castiglioncello. It is a coastline of pine- and oak-covered hills dipping down to the sea. Brilliant-yellow broom begins to flower in late spring, the best time to travel here, and carries on through the summer. Swimming is right off the rocks. The coastline becomes flat at Vada and sandy beaches begin again, but the pine and brush forests continue along the coast to Cecina, Bibbona, Donoratico and on. At Bibbona Mare, the seaside resort of Bibbona, you'll find one of the finest seafood restaurants along the coast, La Pineta di Luciano Zazzeri. Just past Cecina, a turn inland takes you to Bólgheri, the beginning of upper Maremma and the so-called Route of the Etruscans – where vineyards and scrub amble up into ancient hill towns, ruins and antiquities.

Bólgheri lies at the end of a majestic five-kilometre drive lined by hundreds of tall slender cypress trees, almost like 'young giants', as the Nobel Prize-winning (1905) Tuscan poet Giosuè Carducci called them in an awed paean entitled 'Davanti San Guido'. The poem begins:

I cipressi che a Bólgheri alti e schietti
Van da San Guido in duplice filar,
Quasi in corsa giganti giovinetti
Mi balzarono incontro e mi guardâr.

Bólgheri's high cypresses, in double file
from San Guido like young giants leaping
as they come to greet me . . . [free
translation]

D.H. Lawrence described the cypresses as the dark shadows of an Etruscan past. The narrow avenue ends at a gracious castle extending over the portal into the small town. It used to be the feudal estate of one of Tuscany's great families, the Gherardesca. At one time, the Gherardesca family owned pretty much all of the land up and down the Tyrrhenian coast. Some of the best wines of Italy have been produced here in recent years, including the noted Sassicaia.

Many of the fields, vineyards and impressive outhouses and stables of the Gherardesca estates are still here to be admired as you approach Bólgheri from the coast. Bólgheri itself is little more than a few piazzas and narrow lanes. It is a pleasant stop, with several nice restaurants, a shop with regional produce and an inviting wine bar/specialities shop called Enoteca Tognoni that offers a good variety of the local game sausages and honeys and the best wines of the area. Honeys (from bees suckled by rosemary, heather, lavender, sunflower, *mille fiori* and orange), bottled vegetables in oil (funghi, aubergine, artichokes and dried tomatoes, to name a few), speciality pastas and *biscotti*, delicious to taste and lovely to look at, are all worth purchasing. Among the restaurants is La Taverna del Pittore, under a pleasant citrus vine at the back of the *enoteca*.

Leaving Bólgheri back down the tree-lined drive, a left turn after about a kilometre brings you slowly up to Castagneto Carducci (the 'Carducci' added last century in homage to the poet), through olive groves and wine fields, past farmhouses that today are mostly second homes of smart well-to-do Florentines and Milanese.

Castagneto Carducci is a pretty little tourist town overlooking the coast below. Wander through the lovely stone lanes, stop in at the little church of Santissimo Crosifisso, where you'll find a wondrous, much venerated fifteenth-century wooden crucifix. The few times I've been there, I found a continuous stream of rather elegant elderly local women come to have an intimate tête-à-tête with the old Christ. There's also a vast sea vista from up here. On clear days you can see the islands of Elba, Corsica, Capraia and Giglio.

From Castagneto Carducci a narrow road continues toward Sasseto, through the protected forest of the Poggio Neri. Even on the brightest June day, the most traffic you'll encounter on this road is the occasional tractor or perhaps a pack of young cyclists. The forest breaks every now and again on to open views of the surrounding countryside. Oaks and chestnuts line the road, and cork trees too, which you can identify by the large rectangles left where hunks of cork bark have been carved out of the trunks. The road looks trickier on the map than it actually is, and leads through fine countryside.

Two kilometres before Sasseto there is a left turn toward Monteverdi, a leisurely detour of about twenty kilometres that will take you on to Canneto as well, a tiny walled enclave that hasn't changed a whit – except perhaps in the livelihood of its inhabitants – in the more than one thousand years of its life.

Before arriving at Canneto, have a look at one of the more ambitious food shops of the area, just at the entrance to Monteverdi Marittimo. You'll see publicity signs heralding Mucci before you come to town. Don't be turned off. When you get there you'll find an inauspicious little doorway announcing an *alimentari*. It's worth the visit. The day I visited, Carlo Staccioli, who runs the shop with his brother Andrea, led me into the back room where I found a scene from another age, audaciously familiar-looking to anyone with a farm in Tuscany. Sides of hairy boar were hanging from the walls. Sausages and hams crowded the little room. I was easily persuaded to try the various house-cured meats. They were fragrantly different. The excellent *prosciutto nostrale* (i.e., their own prosciutto) is marinated in red wine and smeared with roughly ground black pepper and the back fat of the pig before being hung to dry. It was unlike any I've tasted elsewhere. The fennel-flavoured sausage – *finocchiona* – was also special. I followed Carlo down a few stairs into an Etruscan grotto where the odour of ageing cheeses was overwhelming. The cheeses lined the shelves around the room. I especially noted two, my favourite *marzolino*, the pecorino made from the first milk after the sheep's spring grazing begins, ageing in the ashes of burned olive leaves, and the older *pecorino stagionato in grotto*, which had already spent eighteen months in a terracotta amphora before arriving at the Mucci cellar.

On the way out I pinched a large shiny black olive from an open basket. It was amazingly good. Carlo told me these were olives prepared in an old Tuscan manner, dried in the sun before going into their marinade of spices.

A few kilometres on is the old town of Canneto. Enter (by foot only) through the rather important looking two-gated portal and you find a little Romanesque church on your right. That's the top of town. Opposite the church you can walk down one of two narrow little streets, until after about 200 metres they join at the other end in another gate. You can hardly call it a town. It was constructed by shepherds to protect themselves and their flocks from intruders. Each of the houses enclosed a barn as well. The shepherds came home with their sheep and their goats in the evening and herded them into the barns. The two heavy gates leading into the village were shut up tight, ensuring everyone a good night's sleep. Just outside the old city is the trattoria Osteria del Ghiotto, which prides itself on cooking the fine game of the region in traditional ways.

Rather than returning to Sasseto on the ro travelled, follow a smaller road on the out Canneto that points you to Suvereto. After seve metres you'll see a sign pointing to Sasseto. Ta road and soon you'll find yourself back on the ro you left just before Sasseto. Stop for a minute at the historic centre of the town, once an ancient feudal castle that also passed to the Gherardesca family in the fifteenth century. The little borgo sits perched on a cliff overlooking the Val di Cornia leading to the sea. On the second Sunday of October you'll find a delicious *sagra* in Sasseto, dedicated to polenta and a hearty autumnal soup.

The next medieval town through the forest is Suvereto, an imposing fortress town with an old ruin of an Aldobrandeschi castle. This winding road is the best way to approach. Circle the old city wall to the main portal where you immediately peer into an inviting street up into the walled town. Suvereto is the oldest of hill towns in this area, dating back to the Roman era. Its name probably comes from the *sughero* (cork) trees that must have given the town its livelihood even in Roman times. Just outside the main portal is one of the more interesting Romanesque churches of the entire Livorno province. San Giusto dates back to the tenth century; the church you see today has been there since the twelfth. The simple exterior has a handsome entrance topped by a small clover-shaped stone lunette. Inside you'll find an ancient baptismal font surrounded by a glittering chapel of pale-blue and silver mosaic.

There are several little churches to discover within the walls, a convent dating back to the thirteenth century and some wonderful ancient lanes. In one small square – in a truly magical setting – is a fine restaurant, L'Eno-olitica d'Ombrone. Saturday is market day just under the wall. A lively folklore festival in December celebrates the wild boar.

Past Suvereto, further down towards the sea, is another small town to visit, Campiglia Marittima, with a restaurant, La Pizzica, overlooking the dramatically placed church of San Giovanni rising on a lone platform above the town cemetery just below. Beyond is the entire bay.

Along the way towards San Vincenzo is the archaeological park of San Silvestro, where an eleventh-century mining village has been uncovered. Etruscan tombs dot the park. Walking through it is a rigorous experience that will work up the appetite for the next hearty meal. Reservations to visit the park are necessary on weekdays. It is open to all on weekends and holidays, but check for seasonal times. (Tel. 0565 838680.) Returning to the coast at San Vincenzo, you'll find an unpretentious little fish restaurant in a *bagno* right on the sea, Bagno Nettuno.

The Etruscans are the ancient progenitors of Tuscany; even though they occupied much of the Italian peninsula, only Tuscany has inherited the name, the main Etruscan ruins, the most important Etruscan works of art and some food traditions as well. Ruins dot the countryside, including an important one in Venturina along the way from Suvereto to the sea.

The coast is best visited in May or late September, when fewer travellers and holidaymakers crowd the beaches, and a cool breeze freshens the air. In late spring, the wild flowers burst forth everywhere. The soft sea breeze is euphoric. September is time for wine gathering, with the smells of autumn and magnificent dark-green visions of ancient olive trees bursting with fruit. I find the coast enticing in its mild winter as well.

◆ Specialities of the area: fish and shellfish ◆

The Tuscan coastline is famous for splendid fish from a still unpolluted sea, and for the wild game that abounds in little-known corners. Fish and game play an important role in the menus you will find along the way.

From the seas along the mostly sandy coastline from Livorno south to Porto San Stefano come the best fresh fish of Italy, still prepared today in much the same way as in earlier years. But be aware that fish farms have recently sprung up and many fish are raised in salt ponds near the sea. The difference between them is in the eating: organic versus controlled. Purists will always check with the waiter to ascertain that the fish comes directly from the sea. At better restaurants you usually do not have to ask.

By far the most popular fish, served grilled, roasted or baked under a coat of salt, are the delicate, fleshy princes of the sea: *branzino* (sea bass) and *orata* (gilt-head sea bream). Less expensive, a mite bonier but also delicate, are *marmora* (striped bream), *dentice* (dentex) or *sarago* (sheepshead bream). They're all prepared in much the same ways as *branzino* and *orata*.

A favourite meaty fish, always a main ingredient in stews and soups – but also roasted in the oven together with slivers of potatoes, small tomatoes and onions – is the bright red monster called *scorfano* (scorpion fish, or better known as the French *rascasse*). Like another fine-tasting red fish, *cappone coccio* (red gurnard), *scorfano* really looks like a great crusty old red beast. Roasted, it has an absolutely unbeatable juicy quality. The *cappone* is a bit dryer. I once heard *scorfano* called 'the chicken of the sea'. Both *scorfano* and *cappone* – or at least one of them – are essential to *cacciucco*, the local fish stew that is every bit as varied as the French bouillabaisse. (More about *cacciucco* below.) A similar fish and as tasty is *gallinella* (tub gurnard). Another fish usually on the menu in seafood restaurants, mostly served *al forno* – baked – is the oval flat *San Pietro* (John Dory), a rockfish as monstrous-looking as the *scorfano*, but with dull-brown rather than bright-red skin.

Another favoured fish along the Livornese coast is the little *triglia* (red mullet), bony but delicious. It is often filleted into a fine pasta sauce. Tiny *triglie* called *fragolini* are only a few centimetres long and are deep-fried in their entirety. *Triglie alla Livornese*, another local speciality, is red mullet sautéed in tomato sauce. Grey mullet, an entirely different sort of fish, goes by either *cefalo* or *muggine*.

A really ugly, but marvellously tasty, fish is *rospo* (angler or monkfish). Its head is so big that usually only its tail, *coda di rospo*, is seen out of water, even in open markets. It too gets stewed or baked. *Cernia* (grouper) is also popular, found mostly filleted and fried. *Palombo* (smooth hound) is known also as *vitello del mare* (veal of the sea), perhaps because it is usually sliced and served as a small steak.

Still another really fine fish you'll find in these waters, *pezzagnia* (lizard fish), comes up to fishable waters only in springtime to breed, and thus is found on menus only between April and June. If it's there, do order it. It's also called *occhiona* (big eye) because of its enormous round and bulging green eyes. It too is either grilled or baked.

Larger fish are also served *in cartuccio*, tightly wrapped in baking paper with a dressing of just extra virgin olive oil and lemon and baked.

Cacciucco is the best-known seafood dish of the Tuscan coast. It's a truly wondrous combination of many of the above fish with shellfish and crustaceans too. Every seaside restaurant has its own version, but each boasts a distinct variety. It's an enormous bowl of separately stewed fish and shellfish on garlic-rubbed toast in a rich stock made from a blend of smaller fish and the heads of the bigger fish.

Shellfish – *frutti di mare* – abound in these waters. Different sizes or shapes of similar-looking crustaceans go by different names. A glossary is certainly in order, especially among the various kinds of cuttlefish with their big baggy heads and tentacles. Probably the tastiest among the octopus and squid families are *moscardini*, tough little things usually stewed *in guazzetto rosso*, a tomato sauce. The meatiest are *seppie*, cut into rings and served with pasta. *Calamari* and *totani*, the least chewy of them all, are also very popular. *Polpo* is a small octopus, a favourite of Tuscans, cleaned, boiled, chopped and either stewed or, with the addition of celery, made into a delicious vinegary salad.

Cozze are mussels, *gamberi* prawns and *gamberetti* shrimp. *Scampi*, *cicale* and *astrice* are crayfish, usually served with their claws intact. *Vongole*, *datteri* and *arselle* are clams. *Zuppa di cozze* and *zuppa di vongole* are usually on the menu, each chef doing his special broth. A *zuppa di mare*, with clams, squid and mussels, is more of a piquant stew, served on toasted Tuscan bread. There are dozens of different prawns. Most special is the *gambero rosso*, an enormous bright-red prawn that is special to this area. *Aragosti* are lobsters and show up sporadically in these waters. *Granchi* are crabs; the local variety is sweet-tasting and juicy.

◆ Specialities of the area ◆

As you leave the coast for the hills, game replaces fish as the main speciality, especially in the vast wooded upper Maremma. The area is filled with natural parks and its woodland abounds with wildlife: boar, hare, deer and game birds. Much is made of the available meat, from sausages to pasta sauces.

Antipasti include various sliced sausages made of *cinghiale* (wild boar) and other game flavoured with the juniper berry that grows in abundance in the nearby woods. *Beccaccia al crostone* is a stew of woodcock served as *crostini* on small rounds of toasted bread. Pasta sauces include *pappardelle al cinghiale* (wide noodles in a boar sauce) and the same pappardelle with a sauce of *lepre* (wild hare). Main courses can be *cinghiale in salsa* (marinated and stewed boar in red wine and tomatoes) or *in tegame* (simmered in its own juice). *Fagiano al diavolo* (pheasant in the manner of the devil) is flavoured with sage and cooked in white wine. *Tordi* are thrush, usually cooked with sage and white wine. Hare and boar are also cooked *in salmi*: stewed for a long period with herbs and imported spices.

One notable dish, neither fish nor game, is found all along this coast and in the hills too. *Aquacotta*, or cooked water, originated in the Monte Amiata area of the Maremma but in one version or another it is now found all over Tuscany. A simple, modest, hearty dish, *aquacotta* may well be one of the triumphs of Tuscan cooking. Don't leave the region without tasting it. Basically a simple onion broth, *aquacotta* in these parts has the soothing addition of seasonal vegetables, wild herbs and local pecorino, making it almost a *minestrone*. It can be topped with hard-boiled eggs as well.

The upper Maremma is also noted for its rich farmland and spring vegetables, notably the pointed little purple artichokes called *morello*, asparagus and early tomatoes.

◆ Typical restaurants and their recipes ◆

MARINA DI PISA: La Taverna dei Gabbiani

La Taverna dei Gabbiani, Via Tulio Crosio 1, Marina di Pisa. Open for dinner and at times for lunch – summertime mostly – except on Mondays, and a reservation is suggested. Call to make sure about lunch as well. Tel. 050 34180. Can be pricey as fish restaurants are, but it is possible to eat well for less too.

LA TAVERNA DEI GABBIANI lies at the very mouth of the Arno, on the site of the demolished villa from where Gabriele D'Annunzio wooed Eleanora Duse.

Dino Giaconi and his brother Mario run this warm and inviting seafood restaurant. They grew up on this edge of the sea where the family ran a *stabilimento di bagno* on the beach just a few metres away from the restaurant. *Bagni* are concessions along the beach that rent out cabins, deck chairs and showers, usually with a bar and restaurant attached. You can rent space by the day, or for longer periods. At theirs, Dino's grandfather cooked. All over Italy, entire families settle every year for a few summer weeks at a beach. Many choose a *bagno* for its food.

Dino is an inventive chef, who knows and loves his fish. He'll show them off at the slightest hint, with almost a caress. His daily catch is full of shiny, bright-eyed specimens just emerged from the sea. His tubs of *frutti di mare* are varied: *calamari, scampi, cozze, vongole, granchi.* Dino recites his menu verbally as it changes with the daily catch. *Cacciucco* can be ordered beforehand. His *cacciucco* is a meticulous, long process that combines both fish and shellfish, cooked slowly in separate batches and collected in a rich tomato broth that is a meal in itself. (When you make your reservation, mention you'd like the *cacciucco*. It is not something they do every day.)

Nothing goes to waste . . . skins, bones and whatever doesn't reach the diner goes back to the sea, to the gulls – *gabbiani* – that inhabit the rocks just outside the restaurant.

One wonderfully delicious light *antipasto* at this taverna is *mantecata* (mash), usually of *branzino* or *orata*. It's a mousse made with an yolkless mayonnaise and just a touch of extra virgin olive oil to enhance the subtle flesh. Another is a tiny sea snail in a light wine sauce. You pick the snails out with a toothpick. They are delectable little titbits. There's a brush growing along the seashore which the fishermen use to catch these little underwater creatures. The brush is dipped into the water and left there for the snails to cling to it. The fishermen pluck them out of the water on the brush twice each day. The catch is quickly cooked.

As often in small Italian restaurants, the *antipasti* and *primi* – pasta, rice and soup – are the most tempting at La Taverna dei Gabbiani. There are lots to choose from, among them *torta di acciughe e cipolle*, a tart of anchovies and onions, and the *mantecata*, which is served on rounds of thin toasts.

Pastas here are prepared in a way common all along the coast. The pasta – usually spaghetti or home-made tagliatelle – is not thrown into boiling water. Rather it's cooked, almost like a risotto, directly in the sauce.

It's a bit of a trick, especially with long spaghetti or tagliatelle; best to work with the soft fresh tagliatelle. For harder, dry spaghetti, I'd recommend the home cook giving it a minute or two to soften in boiling water before adding it to the saucepan. At Taverna dei Gabbiani, however, the long pasta goes directly into a *soffritto* of olive oil, chopped onion, carrots and celery. White wine goes in next. As it evaporates, the fish and boiling water are added. Water is added slowly, allowing the pasta to absorb each dose. Mixing with two spoons goes on continually. As the pasta absorbs the liquid, the sauce absorbs the starch in the pasta. The result is creamy, well-flavoured pasta. Pasta combinations at Gabbiani, according to season, include asparagus with prawns, short penne with clams and fresh porcini mushrooms, combinations of *calamari* and red pepper, or mussels with fresh artichokes. A blackened risotto, made with *seppie* and their ink, is another speciality.

Recipes from *La Taverna dei Gabbiani*

◆ Fish mousse / *Mantecata di pesce*

Serves 6

1 fresh Mediterranean sea bass, at least 1kg
Salt and freshly ground pepper
3 egg whites
320ml vegetable or peanut oil
Extra virgin olive oil, to serve
12 slices of baguette bread, thinly sliced

Bring a pan of water large enough to hold the entire fish to the boil, salt it and add the fish. Cook for about 15 minutes until the fish is cooked through but still firm. Drain and, before it cools, skin, bone and remove the fleshy meat to a bowl. Break it up with your hands into almost a paste, and allow to cool to room temperature.

Place the egg whites in a food processor, add a good pinch of salt and turn on the machine, slowly adding the oil in a thin stream. As soon as it takes on a thickened creamy consistency, turn off the machine.

Mix the mayonnaise into the fish with a fork, gently and carefully, amalgamating them well. Grind a good bit of pepper into the mixture. Lay on a flat plate and drip some fresh olive oil over it. Toast thin slices of the baguette, drip some olive oil over each and serve with the pâté, allowing each diner to spread his own.

Anchovy and onion tart / *Torta di acciughe e cipolle*

Serves 6

1 large sheet frozen puff pastry, about 350g
240ml bechamel, made from 15g butter, 1 tablespoon flour and 240ml milk
500g fresh anchovies
2 large onions, thinly sliced
Salt, freshly ground pepper and freshly grated nutmeg
60ml olive oil
120ml white wine
60ml brandy
2 eggs, well beaten

Roll out the pastry into a thin sheet to fit a large buttered pizza pan of about 60cm. Prick holes in the pastry and bake for 5 minutes in a 180°C/Gas 4 oven. Remove from oven and set aside. Keep the oven at the same temperature.

For the bechamel, melt the butter, mix in the flour and slowly add the milk. Bring to a boil, mixing all the while, lower the heat and simmer until it becomes creamy and thick. Set aside.

Slice off the anchovy heads, open and remove the bone – an easy operation when you begin at the tail and gently pull it out. Chop the fillets into bite-sized pieces and reserve.

Cook the onions, barely covered with water, until they are soft and the water has completely evaporated. Transfer the onions to a bowl, and add salt and pepper to taste and a good pinch of nutmeg. Add the oil, the anchovies, the wine, brandy and eggs. Mix in the bechamel and taste for seasoning.

Spread the anchovy/onion mixture smoothly over the pastry and bake for 30 minutes until the tart is well set. Serve warm.

Spaghettini with asparagus and prawns / *Spaghettini con asparagi e gamberi*

Dino cooks the thin pasta entirely in the sauce. The home cook would do better to soften it first and then finish it in the sauce. It results in a creamy, rich, almost sweet pasta.

Serves 6

500g large raw prawns, in their shells
3 shallots, chopped
120ml olive oil
120ml dry white wine
3 large ripe tomatoes, peeled, seeded and coarsely chopped
1 small bunch parsley leaves, chopped
500g spaghettini or other thin long pasta
500g asparagus, steamed or boiled until cooked but still firm, and chopped into bite-sized pieces
Salt and freshly ground pepper

Peel the prawns, removing the black vein. Prepare a stock with the shells and heads: put them in a pan with 500ml of water and boil for about 10 minutes. Remove the prawns with a slotted spoon and keep the water simmering. Chop the prawns into bite-sized pieces.

In a large pan, big enough to hold the pasta with the sauce, sauté the shallots in the oil until just transparent. Add the prawns and sauté for 3 minutes. Pour in the white wine. As it boils, add the tomatoes and parsley and cook for another 5 minutes. Add a good amount of salt and pepper and lower the heat.

Drop the pasta into a large pot of boiling salted water, and as soon as it begins to boil again, turn off the heat. Drain the pasta, and add to the pan holding the prawns. Almost cover with the reserved prawn stock, and begin to mix and cook, adding more water as the pasta absorbs it. Add the asparagus at the last minute, with some more salt and pepper to taste. Serve immediately.

BIBBONA MARE: La Pineta di Luciano Zazzeri

La Pineta, Via dei Cavalleggeri Nord 27, Marina di Bibbona. Open all year, except October, for both lunch and dinner. Tel. 0586 60016. Closed all day Monday and Tuesday lunch. Reservations are absolutely necessary; for summer evenings 4–5 days in advance. Lunch is easier. Fairly expensive.

THIS SEAFOOD RESTAURANT – a local favourite – is located on the beach of Bibbona Mare, just south of Cecina. La Pineta (or Zazzeri, after the owner, as most regular clients call the restaurant) is at the end of a pine grove, looking out over the nearby islands of Capraia and Elba. The restaurant might well go unnoticed as just another beach shack, except for its reputation as the finest seafood restaurant around. La Pineta is a special treat, a bit pricey, but sufficiently worthwhile.

Owner and chef Luciano Zazzeri, a trim elegant man, was a fisherman before he came ashore to open a simple fish trattoria. He talks about fish with the restraint of an art dealer who knows he's got a Botticelli in hand, a kind of self-schooled sensibility that says, let the fish sell itself – don't mess with it too much. He has the same attitude to all his other ingredients. His seafood, and his other produce – much of it comes from his father's *orto* (vegetable garden) – have turned La Pineta into a restaurant of simple elegance.

The warm *antipasti* are subtle combinations: a cabbage leaf stuffed with ricotta and fresh anchovies, salad of warm *calamari* in a creamy sauce of olives, pine nuts and white wine or a *sformato* of ricotta dressed with the big red *gamberi rossi* of the area. Asked what makes his *calamari* so good, Luciano will tell you that it's the place they come from and the way they are brought in. He buys directly from fishermen colleagues, and often goes out to fish with them as well.

Zazzeri treats vegetables with the same care. Tomatoes must never be cooked for too long or their sweetness may turn acerbic. Sweet white onions or red *tropea* of Puglia go into the *soffritto* that's the base of *pasta alle triglie,* a delicacy of fresh pasta with small hunks of red mullet. He doesn't believe in garlic or other strong tastes; it's the fish that counts. Few herbs other than parsley get used, but it's lots of parsley.

An oven-crisped flatbread made of fine couscous accompanies the *zuppetta di mare*. *Cacciucco* here is lighter than at most restaurants; the broth is thinner. Ingredients depend upon the catch of the day.

Desserts at La Pineta are good. There's a heavenly Napoleon with cream and caramel, and lots of others.

RECIPES FROM La Pineta

◆ Ricotta mousse with prawns / *Sformato di ricotta con gamberi rossi*

At La Pineta the mousse is made in individual cups, turned out on the tomato sauce and topped with the prawns. At home, I make it in a round baking dish, top it with the tomatoes and surround it with the prawns. It's delicious either way.

Serves 4

2 medium courgettes, chopped coarsely
1 shallot, chopped coarsely
3 tablespoons olive oil
300g ricotta cheese
3 egg whites
Salt and freshly ground pepper
15 cherry tomatoes
9 large red prawns (*gamberi rossi*)
2 ripe tomatoes, sliced, to serve

Sauté the courgettes and shallot in 2 tablespoons of the olive oil for about 10 minutes, until they begin to soften and brown. Remove from heat. Beat the ricotta and egg whites together in a food processor for about 5 minutes. Remove to a bowl and add salt and freshly ground pepper to taste. Mix in the sautéed courgettes. Preheat the oven to 180°C/Gas 4. Butter a round baking dish that will allow the *sformato* to rise (it will immediately fall again, so not to worry) and pour in the ricotta mixture. Bake for about 30 minutes, until the top begins to be golden and the risen *sformato* is firm.

Quarter the cherry tomatoes and cook them quickly in the remaining tablespoon of olive oil. Squash them gently with a fork, and set aside.

Peel the body shell from the prawn, leaving the tail and head. Steam the fish for 3 or 4 minutes until they are just cooked. Put the *sformata* in its baking dish in the centre of a large platter, top with the tomato sauce and surround with the prawns. Garnish with tomato slices, and serve warm.

Fresh pasta with red mullet / *Straccetti con le triglie*

Straccetti are thin fresh home-made pasta; tagliarini works well too.

Serves 4

6 red mullets of about 300g each, cleaned
1 clove garlic
1 small hot chilli, seeded and finely chopped
2 tablespoons olive oil, plus more for drizzling
350g *straccetti* or tagliarini
5 cherry tomatoes, quartered
1 small bunch parsley, chopped

Put the mullets, garlic, chilli, oil and 240ml water into a saucepan large enough to hold the pasta as well, and cook for about 7 minutes, or until almost done. Remove the fish and the garlic. Fillet the fish carefully and return the meat to the sauce.

Cook the pasta for 2 minutes in lots of boiling salted water. Remove and add to the fish. Mix well and continue to cook until just *al dente.* Add the tomatoes, parsley and a drizzle of oil, and serve.

◆ Fresh fish in 'crazy water' / *Gallinella all'aqua pazza*

Serve this either on or with a good amount of country bread. The water may be called crazy, but it's delicious.

Serves 6

1kg fresh *gallinella* (tub gurnard) or other white fleshy fish, filleted
Salt and freshly ground pepper
Olive oil
20 cherry tomatoes, halved
2 red onions, sliced thinly
60ml water
120ml white wine
15 *taggiasca* olives (mixed green and black), pitted

Heat the oven to 170°C/Gas 3. Lay the fillets in a single layer in a baking dish, season them and drizzle some olive oil over each. Spread the tomatoes and onions over, cover with foil and bake for 20 minutes.

Remove the fish from the oven, remove the foil just to add the wine and about 60ml boiling water, cover again and put back in the oven. Cook for another 10 minutes. Remove the foil, add the olives and another drizzle of olive oil. Cook for another 10 minutes, check the fish to see they are ready, and serve with a good country bread.

CANNETO: Osteria del Ghiotto

Osteria del Ghiotto lies just below Canneto's old borgo, on Via di Lardersi.

Tel. 0565 784435. It's moderately priced and small, only seven tables, so best to reserve in cool weather. In warmer months, an outdoor terrace gives more space. Closing day is Tuesday. Also closed in February, and 20 days in November. During the summer, open evenings only.

NADIA MARI is a ferocious little woman who's been turning her own produce into excellent dishes for most of her life. In 1998, with her son Cristiano Ferro and daughter-in-law Sandra, she turned it into a full-time passion. This little osteria in the hills of upper Maremma boasts an authenticity not easily found today. Nothing gets served here that has not been acquired from local farmers and hunters and turned into traditional fare. If you like game and authentic old dishes, there's no better place to find it than Osteria del Ghiotto.

There's no menu. What you get is what's been found during the early morning rounds. Cristiano will tell you what's fresh and what Nadia has done with it, be it wood thrush, wild pigeon or several different sorts of wild mushrooms. Vegetables – they are the freshest – and poultry come from local farmer friends. From November to January Nadia helps her local *norcino* (pork butcher) to prepare the various pork sausages and other preserved meat products that the restaurant serves until they run out in late spring. Later she tries to get similar products from friends. She helps the *norcino* flavour the prosciutto, *spalla* (pork shoulder), *rigatino* (bacon) and *mallegato* (blood sausage). The liver is put into flavoured fat and wrapped in caul to make *fegatello*. The roasts are made into *arista*, thinly sliced, rolled tightly with herbs and preserved in fresh extra virgin olive oil. Other preserved bits of the pork are stuffed into the lower leg to make *zampone* and *contenna di maiale*, traditional stuffed trotters boiled with other meats for *bollito misto* and served at the New Year with lentils.

The wild boar served here is truly wild. It is brought in by local hunters, as is hare. Rabbits and chickens are free range, arriving daily from nearby farms.

Spring features wild asparagus and the small, locally grown purple artichokes called *morello*. Nadia preserves them in fresh olive oil. Not to be missed are the home-made tortelloni, heartily stuffed with a delicious gnocchi-like filling of ricotta and Swiss chard.

It's tough to get a recipe from Nadia; when you ask how much of this or that goes into a dish, she only shrugs and says, 'Quanto basta' (when it's enough) or 'Un bel po' (a good amount). The safest is the one below.

RECIPE FROM Osteria del Ghiotto

◆ Artichokes marinated in olive oil/ *Carciofi sotto olio*

1dozen (or more) baby artichokes (little pointed purple *morello*, if possible)
A mixture of ¾ white wine vinegar and ¼ white wine to cover for cooking
Salt
Handful peppercorns
3 or 4 bay leaves
Extra virgin olive oil to cover

Trim the artichokes down to the light-green leaves around the hearts and cook in the vinegar/wine mixture with some salt for 4 minutes. Remove. Drain and dry well with kitchen paper.

Place in a jar, add peppercorns and bay leaves and cover with the freshest olive oil. Leave for a few days before eating. The traditional way is to cut the artichokes in half and salt them as you eat.

BÓLGHERI: La Taverna del Pittore

La Taverna del Pittore, Largo Nonna Lucia 4, Bólgheri. Open year round except November. Weekly closing Monday. Open for dinner only between 15 June and 15 September.
Tel. 0565 762184. Prices are moderate.

A WILD ORANGE tree rambles over the outdoor tables in front of La Taverna del Pittore. Its perfume engulfs the entire place. The restaurant, owned by the young Gofreddo d'Andrea, has two lovely little rooms inside, with walls covered by the work of local artists. The previous house owner was himself an artist; his evocative landscapes are included among those crowding the walls.

In addition to offering the traditional fare of the Maremma, Gofreddo – with his chef Daniela Macchioni – adds some innovative dishes to the menu. The local version of puffed fried bread – called *zonzelle* – comes as *antipasto*, warm and covered with a thin melting slice of *lardo di colonnata*. Delicious potato gnocchi are bathed in a sauce of melted gorgonzola and taleggio cheeses, highlighted by large juicy halved grapes. *Puntarelle*, a crunchy rough field salad found in winter months along this mild coastline, is lightly dressed with a creamy anchovy sauce, a dish you'll find more easily in Rome than in Tuscany. Lasagne comes in two varieties: one with a creamy young artichoke sauce, the other with *funghi porcini*.

You'll also find the meat specialities of the region, *salvaggino*, or produce of the hunt – wild hare, boar and other game – and Maremma beefsteaks and cutlets. *Maltagliati*, or 'badly cut', are only one of the several freshly made pastas. They are covered with a fragrant duck sauce. Tagliarini (thin fresh pasta) has a pigeon and aubergine sauce, the wide pappardelle come with either boar or hare.

The house treat is a sweet, a Bólgheri speciality, the *cialdone della nonna farcito*: a cone-shaped home-made waffle bursting with whipped cream and covered with either a wild berry or chocolate sauce.

RECIPES FROM La Taverna del Pittore

Pappardelle with hare sauce / *Pappardelle alla lepre*

This popular Tuscan dish can be made with rabbit as well. If you have hare, save the saddle for another use and make this sauce with only the meat from the legs and, if you want, chopped pieces of the liver.

Serves 6

1 onion, chopped
1 stick celery, chopped
1 clove garlic, chopped
1 small bunch parsley leaves, chopped

3 tablespoons olive oil
50g pancetta, cubed
Boned leg meat of 1 hare, cut into strips
Leaves of 2 sprigs fresh thyme
1 tablespoon flour
120ml red wine
240ml hot chicken stock
Salt and freshly ground pepper
500g pappardelle
100g grated Parmesan cheese

Melt the onion, celery, garlic and parsley in the olive oil, add the pancetta and cook for a few minutes. Add the hare pieces and the thyme and cook until the hare is browned on all sides.

Sprinkle over the flour, mix well, cook for another minute and add the wine, mixing well. Allow the wine to evaporate and add the chicken stock. Cover and cook over a low heat for about an hour, until the meat is done thoroughly and the sauce is a nice thick consistency. Add salt and lots of pepper.

Cook the pappardelle in a big pan of boiling salted water. Drain, pour over the sauce and mix in half the grated cheese. Serve with the remaining cheese at table.

◆ Artichoke lasagne / *Lasagna ai carciofi*

Serves 6–8

8 globe artichokes, or 10 baby spring artichokes
2 lemons
60g butter
Salt and freshly ground pepper
Bechamel sauce made from 60g butter, 3 tablespoons flour, 1 litre milk
200g freshly grated Parmesan cheese
1 large ball mozzarella cheese, finely chopped
400g fresh green lasagne sheets

To prepare the artichokes, snap off the outer leaves down to the tender, light inner leaves. Slice off the tops and quarter the artichokes, rubbing the cut edges with half a lemon. Scoop out the fuzzy inner choke and slice each quarter thinly. Drop into a bowl of water acidulated with the juice of an entire lemon. Repeat with all the artichokes.

Drain the artichokes and put them into a large frying pan. Add the butter and water just to cover. Cook over a medium-high heat until the water has totally evaporated and the artichokes are tender. Salt well and transfer to a large bowl. Mix with three-quarters of the bechamel. Taste, add the juice of half the remaining lemon, and more salt and pepper if necessary.

Bring a large pan of salted water to the boil. Have a large bowl of cold water to hand, and the prepared cheeses.

To assemble, butter a large baking dish well. Drop

enough pasta into the boiling water to cover the bottom of the baking dish. After a minute, remove with a slotted spoon and drop into a bowl of cold water to cool. Lay on the bottom of the baking dish. Spread one quarter of the artichoke cream over, then one quarter of each of the cheeses.

Repeat the process for two more layers. Put another layer of pasta on top, and cover with the remaining artichoke cream and cheeses. Add some more salt, and grind some pepper over the top. (The lasagne can be prepared some hours before serving up to this point.)

Heat the oven to 200°C/Gas 6 and bake for about 30 minutes, until a golden-brown crust has formed. Allow to rest a bit before serving.

SUVERETO: Ristorante Eno-oliteca Ombrone
Ombrone, Piazza dei Giudici, Suvereto.
Tel. 0565 829336. Weekly closing is all day Monday and Tuesday lunch. Closed 7 January to 25 February. It's wise to reserve, especially on summer evenings. Moderately priced to expensive, depending on what you eat and drink.

THIS JEWEL of a restaurant is located in one of the most delightful settings imaginable, an old olive mill connected by an ancient wall to the arched twelfth-century municipal hall of Suvereto. The dining terrace is enclosed by both. In the evenings the old palazzo is illuminated, enhancing even more the harmonious quality of the surroundings.

Graziella (Lella) Durante-Bini had little experience

in the kitchen when she married into a family that had been restaurateurs for five generations. She did the logical thing, went to the local Cordon Bleu school and ended up teaching at various Tuscan cooking schools for twenty years. Even today, as she works overtime in the kitchen of Ombrone, she manages a cooking course out of season, twice a week at the restaurant. She likes to play a little with traditional dishes; as a result, Ombrone offers interesting variations on age-old Tuscan fare, what Lella calls 'Cucina Toscana lightly revisited'.

Her husband, Giancarlo Bini, knows as much as anyone about traditional Tuscan products. He is a collector, of information, fine olive oils and wine, exotic teas and rare coffees, chocolates and liqueurs, as well as old tools of the mill. They are all there on display, to savour and to view.

The best way to open a meal at Ombrone is with a tasting of some of Giancarlo's oils on a *fett'unta*, toasted farm bread steeped in fresh olive oil. Here you get a sampling of four or five choice oils that Giancarlo has found.

Fresh herbs, snipped at the last minute, are notable in both *antipasti* and first courses. Galantine of *calamaretto* (little squid) is served with wild herbs; *pomodoro con riso* (fresh tomatoes on rice) is remarkable for its delicate flavouring of different garden herbs. Lettuce soup, with a touch of anchovies, is a spring starter; in the winter local *farro* is combined with split peas. Fine Sienese pork is wrapped in a tuna sauce, a tasty half pigeon is served in a mix of honey and balsamic vinegar.

Before attempting the rich chocolate dessert or baked pear, have a tasting of the pecorino – either fresh or slightly aged – with a choice of sweet-sour marmalades and honey. It's the best old Tuscan way of finishing a meal, especially in those parts where sheep graze and lots of pecorino gets made. Ombrino's sharp pepper marmalade is especially interesting.

RECIPES FROM Ombrone

Lettuce soup / *Zuppa di lattuga gratinata*

Serves 8

4 heads lettuce
2 onions, sliced finely
1 clove garlic, chopped
50g butter
5 tablespoons extra virgin olive oil
6 anchovy fillets preserved in salt, rinsed and soaked for an hour
1.5 litres vegetable stock
1 bunch parsley, chopped
1 small bunch basil, chopped
8 slices toasted farm bread
150g freshly grated pecorino (or Parmesan) cheese
Salt and freshly ground pepper

Cut the hard core from the bottom of each lettuce, remove any old leaves and divide into 6 wedges. Slice each wedge into 3cm widths. Wash and spin dry. In a large soup pot, sauté the onion and garlic in the butter and olive oil. Add the desalted anchovies and allow to melt. Add the lettuce, and when it becomes limp add the stock. Add the parsley and basil and cook gently, covered, for another 15 minutes. Remove from the heat and add salt and lots of pepper. Heat the oven to 200°C/Gas 6. Toast the bread and, if you like, rub each slice with an open half garlic clove. Place 4 of the slices on the bottom of a baking dish, cover with half the soup and a little less than half the cheese. Repeat with the remainder. Bake in the oven for 10 minutes. Serve hot, or warm.

Pigeon in balsamic vinegar and honey / *Piccione con miele*

Serves 4

2 small pigeons or guinea hens, halved
Salt
2 tablespoons olive oil
1 clove garlic, chopped
2 sprigs rosemary, chopped
2 sprigs sage, chopped
180ml white wine
120ml stock
2 tablespoons balsamic vinegar
2 tablespoons honey

Wash and dry the pigeon or guinea hen halves. Salt them well. Heat the oil in a pan with a cover that will hold the fowl and add the garlic, rosemary and sage. When the oil begins to bubble, add the fowl and brown well on all sides. Splash over the white wine and allow to evaporate almost completely.

Add the stock, cover and cook over a slow heat until the fowl is almost cooked, about an hour. Remove the cover, pour over the vinegar and cook over a medium heat until the liquid has a sauce-like quality. Before serving, drip the honey over each of the birds and serve with the sauce.

Chilli marmalade / *Marmellata di peperoncini*

Makes about 750ml

700g small hot chillis
3 red peppers
600g sugar
Juice of 1 lemon
500ml white wine
1 vanilla pod

Clean the chillies and the peppers of seeds and ribs. (Be careful with the chillies; don't rub your eyes!) Put in a pan with the sugar, lemon juice, half the wine and the vanilla pod, split lengthways. Allow to sit for 4 hours. Place on the heat and add the remaining wine. Mix well and cook for 1 hour over moderate heat, mixing often. It should have reduced to a marmalade consistency.

Serve with fresh pecorino or fresh yellow goat cheese.

Farro and split peas / *Minestra di farro e piselli*

Ombrone uses a local *farro* for this dish; I prefer the fat *farro* of the Garfagnana which doesn't have to be soaked. The final dish does not have to be as dry as a risotto; it should have a bit of sauce around it when served.

Serves 4

200g dried split peas, soaked for about 3 hours
1 large onion, chopped
5 tablespoons extra virgin olive oil
200g *farro*
1 head lettuce, sliced and chopped
1 litre hot vegetable stock
Salt and freshly ground pepper
50g freshly grated Parmesan cheese
60g prosciutto, chopped
1 teaspoon balsamic vinegar

Drain the split peas. Sauté the onion for about 3 minutes in 3 tablespoons of the olive oil, add the *farro* and the peas and sauté for another few minutes. Add three quarters of the lettuce, and cook over a low heat for another few minutes until the lettuce completely wilts. Add the vegetable stock, and cook over a minimal heat – barely simmering, in order not to break up the peas – for about 50 minutes, until the peas are soft. If the stock gets totally absorbed and begins to dry, add a little more. Add salt and pepper to taste at the end of the cooking. Mix in the cheese.

In another sauté pan, sauté the prosciutto in the remaining oil and splash in the balsamic vinegar. When the vinegar evaporates, add the mixture to the *farro* and peas and serve with more cheese at the table.

CAMPIGLIA MARITTIMA: La Pizzica
Ristorante la Pizzica, Piazza della Vittoria 2, Campiglia Marittima.
Tel. 0565 838383 Closed Mondays and 15 days in September. Reserve a table on the terrace overlooking the church opposite. Prices are moderate.

ON THE ROAD from Suvereto to the coast at San Vincenzo, just under the old gate of Campiglia Marittima, you'll find the open terrace of Pizzica directly facing the twelfth-century Romanesque church of San Giovanni. Beyond is the sea, with the curved bay of the Argentario and, on a good day, a view of the nearby islands. In the evenings, the church is illuminated, giving it the aura of a stage set. To get the best view, sit on the right of the closed-in terrace; otherwise the great pine tree growing directly in front might block your view.

Renza Venturelli serves the simple food of the region, enhanced by a modern innovation here and there. She has taken over the restaurant from her parents; her mother still cooks alongside Renza. Her grandfather Giuseppe opened the restaurant back in the 1950s, doing all the *casalinga* (home cooking) himself.

A good way to start a meal is with their *antipasto Pizzica,* a mixture of almost pudding-like, soft-cured local *raviggiolo,* sheep's milk cheese, served with a warmed spiced aubergine dressing. The home-made *gnocchi al pastore* is little more than gnocchi on a bed of shaved smoked and aged ricotta with a touch of butter. The *pappardelle in salsa di cinghiale* (wild-boar sauce) features the juniper berries growing in the nearby forests. There's also a thick grilled pork chop served with a sauce of green apples cooked with a bit of cognac and cream.

A special sweet focaccia, locally known as *schiaccia* (squashed) is the speciality of Campiglia Marittima. Made with lard shortening, it is especially light. It is served with *vin santo*, the sweet dessert wine of the area, to end a meal.

RECIPES FROM *a Pizzica*

◆ Aubergine and cheese antipasto / *Antipasto Pizzica*

Pizzica serves the aubergine with the pudding-like *ravaggiolo* cheese. I prefer it with the sweeter and more easily obtainable fresh ricotta.

Serves 6

2 shiny medium-sized aubergines
6 tablespoons olive oil
2 cloves garlic, pressed or chopped
Salt
1 small red, hot chilli pepper, chopped
300 grams *raviggiolo*, or ricotta cheese

Peel and cut the aubergine into small cubes. Put the oil and garlic into a large frying pan. When the oil around the garlic begins to bubble, add 6 tablespoons of water and the aubergine. Cook quickly until the aubergine pieces are soft, about 8 minutes. Add plenty of salt and the chopped chilli. Remove to a serving bowl and serve warm accompanied by the cheese and lots of fresh or toasted farm bread.

Pork chops with apples/ *Costolette di maiale alle mele*

Serves 6

3 slightly tart green apples, such as Granny Smith
3 tablespoons extra virgin olive oil
2 tablespoons cognac
3 tablespoons cream
6 thick pork chops
Salt and freshly ground pepper

Peel and core the apples and slice fairly thickly. Heat 2 tablespoons of the oil in a sauté pan and sauté the apples until just soft and browned. Add the cognac and allow to evaporate for a minute. Add the cream, cook for another minute and remove from the heat.

Salt and pepper the pork chops and brush with the remaining olive oil. Either grill or fry the pork chops, and serve with the apples and their sauce.

Campiglia shortbread / *Schiaccia Campigliese*

Serves 4–6

100g sugar
100g flour
90g lard, at room temperature
1 egg, beaten
100g coarsely chopped walnuts or pine nuts

Put the sugar and flour into a bowl and mix well. Work the lard in with your fingers until the dough is grainy. Amalgamate the egg into the dough, then mix in the nuts. Heat the oven to 170°C/Gas 3.

Grease a pie tin of about 20cm diameter and press the dough flat into it. Bake until the top is golden and the *schiaccia* firm, about 45 minutes. While still warm, cut into squares. At Pizzica the squares are dipped into small glasses of *vin santo* at the end of a meal.

SAN VINCENZO: Bagno Nettuno

Bagno Nettuno, on the beach at Via Costa 3, San Vincenzo. Open from a week before Easter until October, lunchtime and in the evenings.
Tel. 0565 701095. Reservation is recommended.
Inexpensive to moderately priced.

THE LITTLE SEASIDE *bagno* restaurant Nettuno is at the end of a dead-end street on the beach in San Vincenzo. To find it as you drive along the main street from the north, look for a turn to the right called Via Costa which stops dead about 30 metres on. A boardwalk to the left leads to Nettuno. (It is just round the corner from the more elegant and renowned restaurant Gambero Rosso.)

Elio Frassoni, owner and chef, is from Lombardy, but Nettuno is very much a Tuscan restaurant. Rosemary and garlic pervade, put to their tastiest best. The sounds of the sea, the light breeze and soft splashing of waves provide the background music. *Crostini di mare*, a mixture of warm seafood, is served on crisp toast. The *ravioli di pesce* are stuffed delicately with ricotta cheese, *cernia* and *scampi*; the smooth sauce is made of puréed prawn and tomato. A *zuppa* of mussels and clams is served over a tomato bruschetta. The restaurant's *cacciucco* can be ordered in advance for a minimum of four people.

Main-course fish are served simply, either grilled in the pan or *alla piastra*, on a hot brick, with little more than a stuffing of rosemary and garlic, salt and extra virgin olive oil. Elio likes to make a bigger fish *alla Toscana*, gently baked in the oven in a sauce of tomatoes and black olives.

RECIPE FROM *Bagno Nettuno*

Mussels in tomato stew / *Cozze alla marinara*

Serves 4

1kg mussels
3 cloves garlic, chopped
1 small onion, chopped
1 small bunch parsley, chopped
3 tablespoons olive oil
1 small wine glass white wine
500g tomatoes, peeled and squeezed of seeds and chopped, or the contents of an 800g tin Italian tomatoes, drained of juice
Freshly ground pepper
2 sprigs thyme leaves
1 small hot red pepper, chopped
4 slices day-old rustic Tuscan bread, toasted

Soak the mussels for at least an hour in a big pan of cold water. Scrub clean and remove the beards. Discard any mussels that are broken or open.

While the mussels are soaking, prepare the sauce. Sauté the garlic, onion and parsley in the oil for 5 minutes. Add the wine, allow to evaporate and add the tomatoes. If using tinned tomatoes, squeeze them in one by one, breaking them up as you squeeze. Add lots of pepper, the thyme leaves and hot pepper. Cook gently, reducing the sauce to a thick stew. (The mussels will add water and salt.)

Add the mussels and cook over a high heat, shaking the pan, until all the mussels open. With a slotted spoon, remove the mussels to a serving dish and pour the sauce over. Place a slice of bread in each of 4 soup bowls and divide the mussels over.

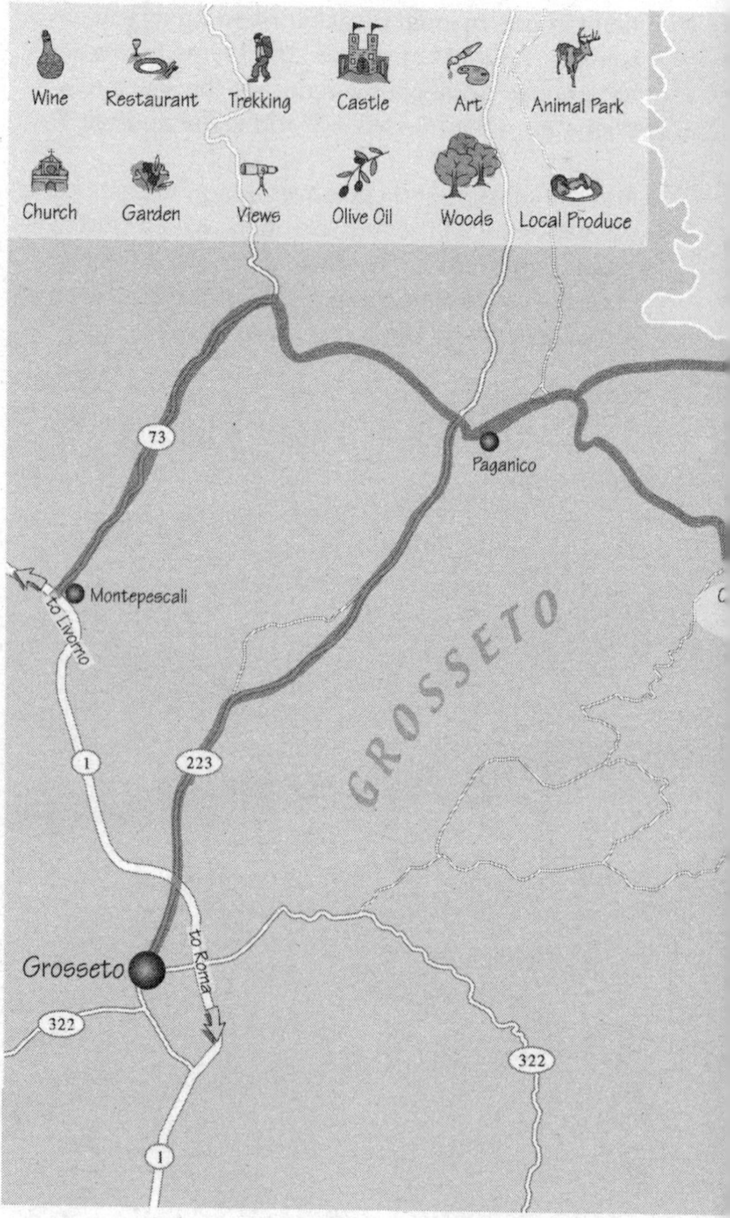
Wine
Restaurant
Trekking
Castle
Art
Animal Park
Church
Garden
Views
Olive Oil
Woods
Local Produce
73
Paganico
Montepescali
to Livorno
GROSSETO
1
223
to Roma
Grosseto
322
322
1

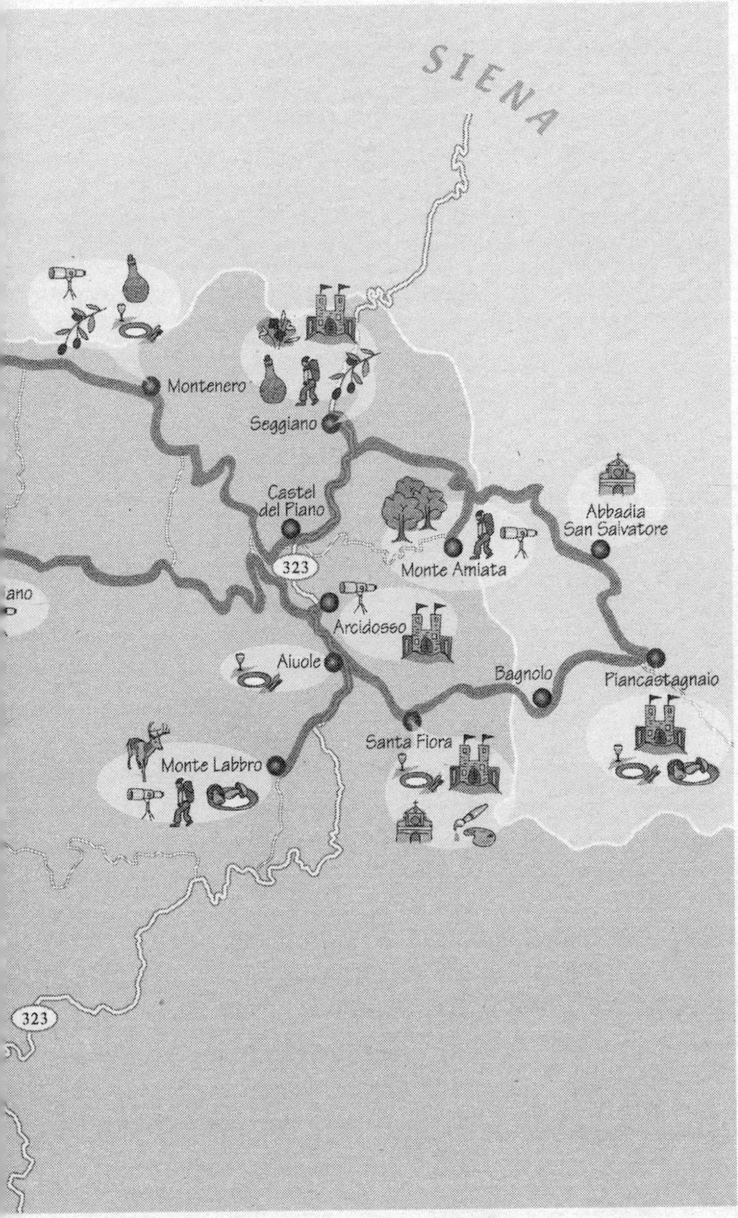

SIENA
Montenero
Seggiano
Castel del Piano
Monte Amiata
Abbadia San Salvatore
323
Arcidosso
Aiuole
Bagnolo
Piancastagnaio
Santa Fiora
Monte Labbro
323

10

The Maremma and Western Slopes of Monte Amiata

As you look up to Monte Amiata from anywhere in southern Tuscany, it seems less a dominating mountain than a long voluptuous island in the sky. The soft summit of beech trees accentuates the roundness. It's hard to imagine that a mere 180,000 years ago, it was a fuming volcano spewing down brim and fire to form huge rocks that today support dramatic hill towns.

The mountain is etched on the horizon of much of central Tuscany. You look at it in the morning to know what kind of day it's going to be. An old proverb tells us, '*Quando l'Amiata mette il capello, devi aprire l'ombrello.*' When Amiata wears a cap, open the umbrella.

Amiata is mostly attached to the lower Maremma, which lies directly under it in the west. It's to the south of the area explored in Chapter Nine and west of Chapter Seven's itinerary. I like best to approach the mountain from the Grosseto coastline. From here, the road climbs gently through the scrub up to the chestnut forests and dramatic hill towns snuggling on the tips of former volcanic peaks.

Before I came to know better, I'd always thought of this lower Maremma as Tuscany's badlands, a Wild West sort of place where cowboys rode off on fabled Maremma horses, to round up their sheep, accompanied by long-haired white Maremma sheepdogs. It used to be an unhappy malaria-infested place, memorialized in a popular folk song, 'Maremma Amara' (Bitter Maremma), a poignant, lilting melody about a dying bird.

A good bit of the flat Maremma remains an extension of the seaside *macchie*, or scrub. But alongside the scrub and brushwood are great avenues of gracious umbrella-shaped Mediterranean pines, majestic cypresses and birch trees. Vineyards and olive groves extend as far as the wooded foothills of the mountain. Amiata itself is laden with hefty, centuries-old chestnut trees that by November give the area one of its most useful nourishments.

Monte Amiata was once a real volcano; dormant for millennia. It is still filled with minerals, hot springs and lots of strange-looking rock formations, many of which are the bases of the clustered hill towns that dot the mountain landscape. Almost as prevalent are huge fortresses and castles. Most were built by the Aldobrandeschi family who came down from the northern Lombardy some time in the eleventh and twelfth centuries. They left massive castles in almost every town you'll see.

A good way to get through the southern Maremma to Monte Amiata is to leave the Livorno/Grosseto *superstrada* at Braccagni, and travel from there to a little-used road that takes you past Sticciano through Stazione Roccostrada to Paganico.

At Paganico, the real trip up to Monte Amiata begins. I recommend the road to Montenero, past Montegiovi to Castel del Piano and up to Seggiano. From Seggiano you can take the road to the summit of Monte Amiata, a lovely narrow forest road that every now and again allows the landscape to show through.

At the top is Vetta Amiata with an enormous iron cross, and a small ski resort just below.

From the summit of Monte Amiata, head down to Abbadia San Salvatore, an old mercury-mining town with the oldest and most beautiful abbey of the area. From San Salvatore, go on to Piancastagnaio, Bagnolo and the amazing castle town of Santa Fiora. Monte Labbro, a soft mountain that many claim has a special spiritual aura, lies just beyond. From there it's a short drive to Arcidosso, the principal town of the Amiato area. The trip back to the coast will take you from Arcidosso through Cinigiano and Sasso d'Ombrone, down to the Maremma coast north of Grosseto.

Each stop along the way has its own special moment, its spectacular view, its verdant forest, a particular church or a hill town of lovely old lanes. The tiny little old town of Montenero, once an Aldobrandeschi estate, has no major fortress, but boasts a handsome little gravelled piazza with a fountain in its centre. It's closed on three sides with small houses and palaces, a little wine museum and an especially good restaurant called Antica Fattoria del Grottaione. Next to the restaurant you can visit the wine and oil cellars of Perazzeta, a major wine producer of the area. Montenero is one of the main stops along the *Strade del Vino* of Montecucco, a Monte Amiata wine zone that received its DOC designation as a distinguished wine area a few years ago.

Alessandro Bocci, owner of the Perazzeta wine cellars, is a native of Montenero (his sister owns the grocery next door – there's an open panel in the wall between them to pass wine on demand). Behind the square is Georgio Franci's *frantoio*, the most prestigious oil press of the area. It's a modern press that works overtime from the first of November all through the winter months. Olives arrive by the ton, the aroma and noise mingle, and you can have an oil tasting in the dining room above the press. From Montenero there's a good view of Amiata, the Val d'Orcia below and, on a clear day, the distant rounded hills of the Crete Senese.

The main road continues to Castel del Piano. From there the next worthy stop is Seggiano, yet another town where you immediately feel the rekindling of old traditions in food and wine. You come upon this beige beehive of a town quite suddenly; it's an impressive view. Just before town, a turn to the right brings you to an interesting modern addition to the landscape: the sculpture garden of Daniel Spoerri. Over a large area of mostly meadow and olive trees, Spoerri – a Swiss artist – has placed some eighty sculptures, of his own and works by other, mostly Swiss, sculptors. My favourite, by Olivier Estoppey, is a flock of 160 remarkably agile geese running from three bulky trumpeters announcing Judgement Day. There's a fine view from here of Seggiano and the massive Castello di Potentino just under the town. You'll also find a small restaurant at Spoerri's sculpture garden serving basic traditional food. Visits to the sculpture garden as well as restaurant must be reserved in advance. (Tel. 0564 95457; fax 0564 950026; closed Mondays.)

The medieval centre of Seggiano is evocative with its small ancient alleyways, portals and stairways. The town is becoming better known for its very special olive oil. It comes from a tree called *olivastra* that produces a light fragrant oil known in Roman times. The oil is now enjoying a revival, thanks in part to the foreigners who have moved into the area. The *olivastra seggianese* grows only here, benefiting apparently from a combination of micro-climate and volcanic earth. You can also find a fine little cheese-making enterprise just at the entrance to Seggiano, the Caseificio Seggiano. It makes a variety of excellent pecorino (sheep's milk) cheeses, from light fresh ricotta to a fine seasoned pecorino aged in the well of a cave.

Castello di Potentino, in the valley just under Seggiano, dates back to Etruscan times. Its earliest documentation is 1042, when it belonged to a count. Today it is filled with fine old English furniture. It belongs to Hugh Greene, a brother of English author Graham, and his family, wife Julia and daughter Carlotta. They have planted vast new vineyards and olive groves. 'It's really we women who are doing it,' Carlotta told me. I came across her just as she was emerging from the olive groves with a small band of what she calls her 'eco-slaves', young college kids who come from all over to live at the castello and work a few weeks or months at organic farming, for which they receive bed and board. They had been picking olives the entire morning. We joined her and her helpmates for a hearty minestrone and cheese before they ventured out again. Carlotta, a writer, is an old acquaintance.

The huge stone castle was a complete ruin when they bought it. Carlotta and her mother have painstakingly restored it during the past eight years and she's more or less given up on serious writing and turned to serious winemaking. Their wine is now one of the finest of the Montecucco DOC area, as is their *olivastra* olive oil. The castle and its winemaking facilities are visitable; there are also a few rooms for rent. To visit, reservations are necessary.

(Tel. 0564 950326; Fax 0564 950014; Email castellodipotentino@virgilio.it).

The road back to Castel del Piano from Seggiano soon has a left turn that will take you through the forests directly up to the summit of Monte Amiata. From there another road takes you down to Abbadia San Salvatore, an old town that still has rusting equipment lying around from its better days as a mercury-mining centre. Here the imperative visit is to the great abbey itself, enclosed in a small square behind a medieval portal. Make sure not to miss it. You'll be stunned as you enter. Few churches are as evocative of the early Middle Ages. It's the oldest church in the area, begun by the Lombards in the eighth century, with a gold-embellished altarpiece and magnificent drystone walls. The church is on two levels, with a monumental staircase leading up to the altar. The real marvel lies below in the crypt. Turn the light on (as you come down the few stairs the switch is on your right). You enter a chamber of slender, gently lit, ancient stone columns, each with its own decoration and capital. Fantastic animals and primitive human icons decorate each, with geometric designs and floral motifs. There's an interesting medieval town centre near the Abbazia that's worth visiting as well.

Nearby Piancastagnaio is a medieval hill town with a rich cultural past, dominated by a perfectly restored, overwhelming *rocca*, a castle that squats like an overlord on top of the town. From its tower, you can look down at the medieval houses as they tumble down the hillside, Humpty-Dumpties pushed off their high wall. The castle was originally built by the Aldobrandeschi family in the twelfth century. In the fourteenth the Sienese took it, and a century later, the Florentines. It still boasts the Medici family crest over its main door. The town takes its name from the chestnut woods all around it and celebrates the ubiquitous nut every 1 November, All Saints' Day, with Il Crastatone, a festival that features all the dishes derived from chestnuts. There are a great many. There's also a fine restaurant, just outside the castle wall, Ristorante Anna. Near Piancastagnaio, on the way to Bagnolo, is a small cluster of houses called Tre Case; there you'll find a huge oak tree that St Francis is said to have rested by. It's one of the largest in Italy, designated as a 'monumental plant'.

Bagnolo is a drive-through town, but with a special mill that still stone-grinds chestnut and corn flours and a *forno* that bakes its bread in the old-fashioned way as well. An old-fashioned flatbread that still gets eaten here is made only in Bagnolo: a *schiacciata di friccioli,* its top sprinkled with fried pork drippings.

Don't miss the remarkable little town of Santa Fiora nearby. It boasts the *pieve* of Sante Flora e Lucilla, a church filled with sublime fifteenth-century della Robbia bas-reliefs, including one that takes its inspiration from Piero della Francesca's beloved fresco of the Resurrection on the wall of the civic museum in San Sepolcro. You enter the town from the top, through the open entrance portal of what was once a Strozzi palace, a large chilly room-like gate that actually has a fireplace at its centre. At the other side of the entrance, you exit into an inordinately large rectangular square fronted by an older structure of the thirteenth century, the castle of the Aldobrandeschi.

The Aldobrandeschi also built the lovely church of Sante Flora e Lucilla. It lies at the end of Via Carolina, a narrow street running down from the right edge of the piazza. Among the other della Robbias in the church are a baptism of Christ and a Last Supper. The *Resurrection* is on the pulpit, complete with sleeping soldiers at the feet of the Christ. Along the same narrow Via Carolina is the restaurant Il Barilotti, a pleasant lunch stop.

In one of the characteristic old streets around the centre, the Via del Fondaccio, many of the tiny houses still have medieval symbols on their lintels, mostly those of the hunt that was always so much a part of life here. If you get to the little church of St Augustine, you'll find a small wooden Madonna and baby said to be by Jacopo della Quercia. In all there is an amazing amount to see in this small town, including evidence of a small ghetto and synagogue dating from the sixteenth century when Jews fleeing Spain found refuge and civic privilege in much of the Maremma.

Just under the old town of Santa Fiora is a small hand-wrought water basin called Le Pescheria (fishing hole), dug by the Aldobrandeschi in the thirteenth century to grow trout, and undoubtedly one of the first fish farms around. Later the ruling Sforza turned it into a park, and it's still enjoyed today as such. Driving past the Pescheria, there is a turn up on to the serene Monte Labbro, with an aura that people around here maintain is pure inspiration and spirit. It boasts therapeutic spring waters, pastures of grazing sheep and some dramatic volcanic rock formations.

Davide Lazzaretti began the first Italian commune here in the mid-1800s as a protest against new taxation on tenant farmers. It was a spiritual endeavour too, and began with the backing of the church. He became too much of a messianic figure, however, and ended up being killed by the *carabinieri* while leading a peaceful march through Arcidosso. He was buried in Santa Fiora, the only community that would accept his body. He's still a much-revered figure in these parts; there is a monument to him on Monte Labbro.

The Parco Faunistico on Monte Labbro is a wild-animal refuge with its own very special restaurant. Antonella Sabatini has prepared lunches and dinners here in the Podere dei Nobili for many years. The restaurant is now run by her son-in-law and daughter, but she is still responsible for the varied menu that includes dishes featuring all the wild herbs of Monte Labbro. Antonella also raises her own vegetables and domestic animals for the restaurant. She serves pastas stuffed with various aromatic herbs, roast chicken with thyme, wild mint, oregano and wild chives, or a turkey breast rolled with various wild salads. Antonella knows all the edible funghi on the mountain, and makes use of all of them. She also includes dandelions, poppies and other weeds that grow in the fields in various dishes at the restaurant.

She has a special way of preparing chickpeas, an old Maremma tradition, she told me. The chickpeas go into a large pot, ashes from the hot fire are poured in on top of them and then boiling water over that. In this way, they soak for at least six hours; she drains and washes them, rubs them dry and the skin comes right off. All this happens before the chickpeas are put to cook slowly in more simmering water. They turn out unbelievably tender, skinless and tasty.

Antonella has no freezer, nothing is from the tin. Her food is freshly made every day. The menu gets decided when she sees what is available, so it's best to call ahead. (Tel. 0564 966867; the park is closed Mondays.) Another restaurant to savour, a treat not to miss, is an inauspicious little inn that lies between Monte Fiore and Arcidosso, at a crossroad that leads to the summit of Mount Amiata. L'Ainole is about seven kilometres from either town.

Arcidosso, just under Monte Labbro, is the biggest town of Monte Amiata, the capital of the area. It's mostly a modern commercial and cultural centre, but its profile against the sky is a noble one. The old *centro storico* is a warren of ancient streets meandering from an old stone portal through narrow streets that bring you to yet another Aldobrandeschi castle. The castello dominates its profile from afar.

The way back down from Arcidosso takes you through to Sasso d'Ombrone and the harmonious hill towns of Cinigiano and Monticello. It's a lovely ride through fields of grazing sheep and even some Maremma horses.

◆ Specialities of the area ◆

There's a saying on Monte Amiata that the daily diet here consisted of '*pan di legna e vin di nuvole*'. *Pan di legna* ('bread of the woods') is the chestnut, the basis of so many dishes here. *Vin di nuvole* ('wine of the clouds') is the clear pure water of the mountain springs.

Today's delicious soup called *aquacotta* is the historical beneficiary of the *vin di nuvole* of the Amiata. This soup comes in variants all over Tuscany. One of the best versions is here where it was born of little more than fresh onions, good olive oil, dried bread and fresh spring water, to provide woodsmen their daily lunch in the forest. The livelihood of the mountain people came mostly from harvesting the woods. The *boscaiolo,* or woodsman, collected and turned the cut timber into carbon. Amiata, like so much of Tuscany, was poor country. When the *boscaioli* went off to chop wood, they carried their lunch with them: an onion or two, and bread. Water came from the clean, pure springs all over the mountains. Leonella Quattrini, who now owns the Ristorante Aiuole near Arcidosso – a memorable restaurant – remembers her grandfather, a woodsman on Monte Labbro, taking his onions, oil and bread from the larder each morning as he went out to chop and bring back the wood.

This was the original *aquacotta*, onions sliced and cooked in a bit of water, flavoured undoubtedly with a good bit of salt and poured over the bread. The soup has developed from there; today every cook has his own version with a variety of seasonal ingredients – Swiss chard, wild mushrooms in the autumn, in summer courgettes and other flavours, carrots and celery, tomatoes and so on. For Sunday lunch, or celebrations, an egg is dropped in at the last minute. Like so many other nourishing soups of Tuscany, *aquacotta* is still served over a slice of yesterday's bread.

Chestnuts provided much of the mountains' basic nourishment – understandable when you realize that a kilogram of chestnuts provides the body with more than 1000 calories. In and around Santa Fiora and Piancastagnaio you'll see securely fenced, century-old, well-tended chestnut groves that produce *marroni*, unusually large dark-brown nuts, from pruned large-trunked trees. The smaller chestnuts – from less-nurtured trees – are dried for several months, then peeled and finely ground into 'sweet' flour that in turn is made into *polenta dolce*, a staple of the kitchen in these parts. Fiorella dei Santis, a *castagnetta* in Santa Fiora, showed us around her grove one day. Her family, she noted proudly, has been nurturing the grove for almost seventy-five years. Some of the trunks have diameters of well over a metre. From October to December Fiorella spends her entire day in the grove collecting, separating and packing the chestnuts for their different uses. Wholesalers come every day with their trucks to collect the heavy burlap bags and take them to markets all over Italy. Other licensed collectors gather their chestnuts in the forests; no one without a licence is allowed.

Chestnut flour is best after mid-December, the moment when stone-grinding begins. Hearty chestnut polenta is served with simple game ragú, fresh ricotta cheese or sausages. There's also a chestnut bread – *fiandulone* – flavoured with rosemary, and a purée made from boiled chestnuts, *la pichiona*. The nuts are also prepared here like those sold on city streets, roasted on the ashes of an open fire in a long-handled hole-punched pan.

The forests are rich with wild mushrooms, *funghi porcini* and others. They sprout profusely under the chestnut trees. I was sitting in a cafe, having a coffee in Cinigiano, and fell into conversation with a group of rugged old men about the hills and their riches. It was autumn. The talk naturally turned to funghi. One old chap told me of his youth in the woods collecting funghi for the noonday soup. He'd go off every day during the season from late September to early November. The mushrooms came home fresh and fragrant in their baskets, his mother cleaned and sliced them, heated some fresh olive oil, threw in some garlic, a few hot peppers, the funghi, some chopped parsley and a little water. A goodly amount of salt finished off the dish as a final act of love. With a slice of the roughest sort of home-made bread to sop it up, it was a daily feast.

During their season, porcini go into many main courses, as do numerous other wild mushrooms: the little yellow *giallarelli* or *finferli*, the orange-topped *ovoli*, and, in springtime, a mushroom that some think is the finest around, the *prugnolo*. In one delicious *zuppa di funghi*, a variety of mushrooms are first sautéed and then puréed. Handfuls of pungent porcini and some water go in at the last minute.

Olive oil is another of the area's singular products. The *olivastra seggianese*, the tree I mentioned above, produces one of the sweetest, most fragrant oils I've ever tasted. It is not a well-known oil, but the small production travels far. Carlotta Greene, at Castello di Pontentino in Seggiano, exports it to England. In Seggiano itself, the first Sunday of December is devoted to a festival celebrating its pressing. Another notable oil here comes from Piancastagnaio, where volcanic ash has formed the particularly fertile soil.

Wildlife is extensive. From mid-September on you may wake to the sounds of a battlefield. Nothing explosive, just a lot of shooting. Birds, wild hare and wild boar are all fair game. You find them on every menu during the winter months, delivered to local restaurants and trattorias by the hunters themselves.

Ricotta is the prime local cheese. It is eaten fresh with chestnut bread or turned into pasta fillings and desserts. Another well-regarded product of the Maremma hills is honey taken from various mountain plants. It goes well with the various sheep's cheese produced from the flocks you often see here grazing on the mountain meadows.

Truffles – both black and white – are newcomers to the diet of Monte Amiata, eaten mostly in restaurants. In the past they were not sought; they were thought to require too much work. Today they flavour cheeses and sauces.

◆ Typical restaurants and their recipes ◆

MONTENERO: Antica Fattoria del Grottaione

Antica Fattoria del Grottaione, Via della Piazza,
Montenero d'Orcia.
Tel/fax: 0564 954020. Closed Mondays. Priced
inexpensive to moderate.

THE LITTLE SQUARE in Montenero is like a big courtyard. Antica Fattoria del Grottaione is located on the left. It's part of the old *fattoria* (administration building) of a once large estate. The restaurant shares an old building with the Perazzeta wine and oil warehouse next door. The entire complex has been well restored. The restaurant with its arched rubbed-brick ceilings is a well-designed and inviting place. Summer dining is on the rear terrace with a view over the rich farmlands of the Val d'Orcia. Flavio Biserni opened the restaurant only a few years ago, after some years in Arcidosso. He is inventive and works hard at new versions of traditional dishes. Autumn brings chestnuts and game: Flavio offers fine *tortelli di castagne* (discs of pasta stuffed with chestnut paste) served with a ragú of *capriolo,* a much-hunted roe-buck. Another dish I especially liked was *polenta con bietole di vigna e salsa di zucca,* polenta made with a special chard that grows in the vineyards between the vines. It has a slight winey taste. After it's cooked the chard polenta is cut into little squares to be covered with a pumpkin sauce. *Zuppa di spinaci e ricotta* is an old Maremma shepherd dish served here in a new entirely soothing version.

Flavio's house wine is the local wine of Montecucco, from Perazzeta next door. It is the basis for his *brasato di cinghiale,* wild boar stewed in wine. Another worthy main course is *baccalà al contadino,* salt cod in a vegetable tomato sauce. It's all in the good tradition of Maremma's rural kitchen.

RECIPES FROM *Antica Fattoria di Grottaione*

◆ Swiss chard polenta with squash and pine nut sauce / *Polenta con bietole e salsa di zucca*

Serves 6

100g Swiss chard leaves, ribs removed
3 tablespoons extra virgin olive oil
Salt
250g quick-cook polenta
20g butter
2 garlic cloves, chopped
500g peeled squash or pumpkin, cubed
350ml chicken stock
1 sprig basil leaves, chopped
50g pine nuts

Put the washed Swiss chard still wet into a sauté pan with 1 tablespoon of the oil and a good sprinkling of salt. When the chard is wilted, remove with its oil and remaining water and blend in a food processor.

Put the puréed chard, the polenta and 1 teaspoon salt into a large pan with 400ml water. Whisking constantly, bring to a boil and add another 1 litre water. Continue to cook over a medium heat, whisking all the time, until the polenta thickens, about 10 minutes. Add the butter and whisk in. Remove from the heat.

Turn out on to a rectangular baking dish and spread smoothly. The polenta should not be more than 2.5cm thick. Leave to cool and solidify, about an hour.

Meanwhile, make the sauce. Put the remaining 2 tablespoons of olive oil into a large saucepan with the garlic and squash. Sauté for several minutes, then add the chicken stock. Cook at a high heat until the squash is completely soft and about 250ml of liquid remains. Add the basil leaves and remove from the heat. Toast the pine nuts gently and reserve. Blend the squash with its remaining liquid, and add the pine nuts.

Before serving, slice the hardened polenta into squares and warm in the oven (or fry if you like) before covering with the heated squash sauce.

Spinach and ricotta soup / *Zuppa di spinaci e ricotta*

This delicious soup is not at all acerbic as it may sound. The water can be a light stock if you like. I prefer it with just plain water.

Serves 6

1.5kg fresh spinach
3 fairly large onions (about 500g)
1 tablespoon olive oil
1 small wine glass red wine
500g fresh sheep's ricotta, broken up
Salt and freshly ground pepper
6 slices day-old farm bread, toasted

Wash the spinach well. Drain and spin dry. Slice the onions thinly and melt them in the oil in a large soup pot over a low heat, stirring often, for about 20 minutes, then add the spinach, bit by bit, until it all fits. As it melts down, pour in the red wine and cook for 30 minutes over a low heat. Add the ricotta and cover with boiling water. Add lots of salt and pepper and cook for another 30 minutes. Place a slice of toast in each soup bowl and pour the soup over.

PIANCASTAGNAIO: Ristorante Anna

Pensione Ristorante Anna, Viale Gramsci 486, Piancastagnaio.
Tel. 0577 786061. Best to reserve, especially for lunch. Closed Mondays, except in summer. Closed 15 days in September. Prices are moderate.

JUDGING FROM THE crowds that gather here daily for lunch, Ristorante Anna is a place for businessmen who like to eat well and for family celebrations. The surroundings, just outside the city wall, up a commercial street from the massive castello, are not very promising. Once inside, however, the feeling is one of being in a good country kitchen.

Giuseppe 'Pino' Sprolli has been working with cook Anna Maria Petrucci for fifteen years, developing a rich menu that changes with the seasons. In autumn and winter, game, chestnut and mushroom dishes dominate along with various hearty soups. Lighter fare comes with warmer weather; *zucchini lasagna* made with both courgettes and their flowers is served with just a simple tomato and basil sauce. Gnocchi come with a pesto of *arugula* (rocket).

Piancastagnaio is in the province of Siena, just over the border with Grosseto, and *pici*, the fresh pasta made south of Siena, makes its way on to Pino's menu. It is served with a simple garlic and oil dressing sprinkled with a good amount of fresh herbs.

The autumn/winter menu is hearty. The funghi

soup with *farro* is a delicious mix of beans, *farro,* a bit of chilli and precious wild funghi from the chestnut forests nearby. Freshly ground polenta comes with a sauce of meat ragú into which some funghi have been dropped.

The classic Tuscan dish, *fegatello,* today found in few restaurants, is a regular favourite at Ristorante Anna. It consists of hunks of pork liver cooked on a bed of fennel seeds. You usually find *fegatello* in meat markets resting in a bed of pork fat; here there's no visible fat, just a tender chunk of liver still lightly pink inside permeated with fennel and rosemary. The stewed wild boar here is as good as you'll find anywhere.

Piancastagnaio is named after its ubiquitous nut, and chestnuts dominate dishes here. The best chestnut dessert in the area is at Ristorante Anna, a light chestnut cake topped with chestnut paste and whipped cream.

RECIPES FROM Ristorante Anna

◆ Pesto for gnocchi / *Pesto di arugula*

More than enough for 6 servings

200g rocket (about 3 full bunches), hard stems removed
1 bunch basil leaves
75g pine nuts
100g freshly grated Parmesan cheese, plus extra to serve
1 clove garlic
1 teaspoon salt
240ml extra virgin olive oil
500g potato gnocchi

Put the first 6 ingredients into the food processor, turn it on and slowly add the oil. Process until smooth. Mix well with the cooked gnocchi and serve with more cheese at the table.

◆ Pork liver with fennel seeds / *Fegatello*

Ask your butcher for the ingredients to this dish. You'll need one pork liver and enough caul fat to wrap the divided pieces.

Serves 4

1 large pork liver, about 800g
Salt and freshly ground pepper
1 section caul fat
2 sprigs rosemary
2 sprigs dried fennel stalks, if available
1 big handful fennel seeds
Olive oil

Heat the oven to 180°C/Gas 6. Divide the pork liver into 4. Salt and pepper each well. Divide the caul fat into 4 sections and wrap each piece of pork in the netting. Secure with a toothpick and place in a baking dish over sprigs of rosemary and, if available, dried fennel stalks. Throw a good handful of fennel seeds over the top, then drizzle olive oil over each piece. Bake for about 15 minutes. The liver should not be overcooked, but still pink inside, and tender.

SANTA FIORA: Il Barilotto

Il Barilotto, Via Carolina 24, Santa Fiora.
Tel./fax 0564 977089. Closed Wednesdays, and from 20 November to 7 December, and from 20 June to 1 July. Reservations recommended. Priced moderately.

YOU'LL FIND this fine little restaurant along Via Carolina leading down from Santa Fiora's main Piazza Garibaldi to the church of Saints Flora and Lucilla. It specializes in traditional local food. The big season is autumn, when game, wild mushrooms and chestnuts dominate the menu. Pierangelo Croci, the owner, sees to it that it's good throughout the year. When local hunters no longer have game to bring him, he concentrates on local spring vegetables – artichokes, courgettes, spring peas. Hearty soups mark the winter season; light, tomato-based pastas are fresh and fragrant during the summer. Other than stews and soups that take longer preparation, every dish is made to order.

Pierangelo's cook Daniela worked in Rome for years before she came to Santa Fiora and Il Barilotto's tiny kitchen. The restaurant, like so many in rural Tuscany, grew out of Pierangelo's father's grocery. His father first added a bar, then a little osteria and, in 1927, received permission for a full restaurant. It's been growing ever since, situated wonderfully and serving good food.

Wild mushroom bruschetta / *Bruschetta di funghi*

A mix of fresh field mushrooms with an added 30g of dried porcini mushrooms works well if fresh or frozen Italian porcini are not available. Soak the dried mushrooms for 30 minutes in warm water, squeeze out the water and chop finely. Add them to the pan after the chopped field mushrooms.

Serves 6

350g funghi porcini (can be frozen)
2 cloves garlic
1 small hot chilli
1 bunch parsley
3 tablespoons extra virgin olive oil
Salt and freshly ground pepper
6 slices Tuscan or country bread, each about 2cm thick

Clean the mushrooms. Chop both the caps and stems into tiny pieces. Finely chop the garlic, chilli and parsley together.

In a pan that will also hold the mushrooms, heat the oil together with the garlic, chilli and parsley. When the oil begins to bubble, add the mushrooms, a good amount of salt and pepper, and cook together for about 10 minutes, until the mushrooms are soft and begin to release water. Remove from heat and check the seasoning.

Toast the bread and divide the mushrooms over the slices.

Maremma 'cooked water' / *Maremma aquacotta*

This typical Maremma dish has travelled all over Tuscany, altered as it goes. This is an embellishment of the original plain onion soup. Traditionally, an egg for each diner has been added when *aquacotta* is served at festive Sunday lunch.

Serves 6

200g dried borlotti beans, soaked overnight then drained
500g onions, sliced
2 sticks celery, sliced
1 small hot chilli, chopped
2 tablespoons olive oil
700g Swiss chard
4 tablespoons tomato purée
Salt and freshly ground pepper
6 eggs (optional)
6 slices toasted Tuscan bread
Extra virgin olive oil, to serve

Cook the beans slowly in water to cover by 2.5cm. When soft, remove and purée half the beans, then return them to the remaining beans and their water. Set aside.

Put the onions with the celery and chilli in the oil in a heavy soup pot. Cook over a very low heat and don't allow the onions to brown. About 30 minutes should do it.

Chop the Swiss chard finely and add to the onions. Mix well and cook for another few minutes. Mix the tomato purée into the beans then add to the soup pot. Add lots of salt and pepper to taste. Add 500ml boiling water and cook for another 30 minutes.

If serving eggs, drop them one by one into the soup, trying to keep them separate. Cover the pot until the eggs begin to firm on top. To serve, place a slice of toast in each soup bowl. Scoop out an egg for each with a slotted spoon, place on the toast and ladle soup to cover. Serve with fresh extra virgin olive oil to drizzle over at the table.

Stewed boar/ *Cinghiale alla Maremma*

Serves 6

3 tablespoons olive oil
3 sprigs fresh rosemary
3 sprigs fresh sage
500g wild boar, cubed
Salt and freshly ground pepper
240ml red wine
300g fresh or tinned tomatoes, peeled and chopped
25 pitted black olives

In a heavy pot large enough to hold the entire dish, heat the olive oil together with 1 sprig each of the rosemary and sage. Brown the meat on all sides. Add salt and pepper and the red wine. Allow to bubble and reduce to about half. Add the tomatoes, reduce the heat and cook slowly, covered, for about 1½ hours, until the meat is cooked through and soft. Add the olives at the last minute. Taste and adjust the seasoning.

◆ Chestnut cream / *Crema di castagne*

Serves 6

500g peeled chestnuts
Milk to cover
120ml cream
125g sugar
60ml brandy
Whipped cream, to serve

Put the chestnuts in a saucepan and add milk to cover by several centimetres. Cook slowly until the milk has almost evaporated, about 15–20 minutes. The chestnuts should be soft enough to put in a blender or through a food mill to purée.

Put the purée back into the saucepan with the cream, sugar and brandy. Cook over a low heat until the sugar has melted. Mix well and pour into a serving dish to cool. Serve with whipped cream at the table.

ARCIDOSSO: L'Aiuole

Aiuole, at Bivio Aiuole, base of Monte Amiato. Tel. 0564 967300. Closed Sunday evenings and Mondays, and all of November. Moderately priced, best to reserve.

RISTORANTE AIUOLE, a delightful restaurant, is about seven kilometres from Arcidosso, on the road to Santa Fiora. It's at the very base of a road to Monte Amiata's summit; from Aiuole the road leads right to the top.

Ugo Quattrini is a large graceful man with a Mark Twain moustache bursting from his gentle face and eyes that twinkle when he talks about the food he serves in his restaurant. He is a man determined to maintain – and recreate – the culinary traditions of the Maremma mountains. The menu here was originally his mother's, carried on and further elaborated upon by her disciple, Anna Soldi, who currently runs the kitchen. It's like a family kitchen, just off the dining room. You can glimpse Ugo joining in to whip up something in a saucepan, or his petite, pretty wife Leonella – she normally sits at the cash register – quickly making a sauce for a particular pasta someone's ordered. Her father was a chef on a grand Italian ocean liner like the *Michelangelo*; he still sometimes makes a grand meal for friends here. Otherwise Ugo advises and serves, comments and exchanges funny stories with diners, most of whom seem to know one another.

His mother Rosanna opened the restaurant/hotel in the 1940s, on Ugo's fourteenth birthday, with dishes that she'd been preparing all her life. Now it's his. There's no menu really; everything served is last minute, or prepared for the day. The restaurant fills for lunch with local diners, from the mayor to local businessmen. Most of them eat exactly what Ugo suggests. At crowded moments, he hops into the kitchen to help. He claims Giancarlo Bini of Suvereto's Ombrone restaurant as his mentor, along with Giorgio Veronelli, the closest thing to a food connoisseur in Italy.

Ugo not only knows food, but he can tell you about the whole area surrounding Arcidosso, an area he thinks of as mystically endowed. The various mountain springs, more than thirty of them, come in three qualities – 'drunken water', 'good water' and 'strong water'. They give special energy and mental health, he says. They also deflate any swollen stomach.

The first time I visited Aiuole, I asked Ugo to give

me a tasting, a sampling of what he thought were his best dishes. We didn't know one another yet. He seated me at one end of the restaurant, and placed fifteen dishes in front of me, one after the other, announcing only the names. I didn't get all the names, but finished them off with a zest I didn't know I possessed. We began with a *minestra*, a *farro* soup lightly touched with freshly ground pepper and the lovely *olivastra* oil. When I questioned the *farro*, assuming this was something transported from the Garfagnana (where it is plumper), he cited a local truism: 'Where there was misery, there was *farro* and chestnut flour.' Next came *gnudi*, a light and airy local speciality, a sort of large puff of ricotta, chard and wild greens, served with a sprinkling of grated aged pecorino and, again, the oil. Another speciality of the house called *fiocchi di neve* (snow flakes) followed, large light balls of ricotta and mashed potato served with grated cheese and oil. Then arrived a large *tortelli* filled with ricotta and spinach and topped with a highly flavoured, fragrant meat sauce. *Aquacotta*, with an addition of freshly harvested beans and a bit of tomato, came next, and then a *zuppa di funghi*. It wasn't porcini season. Ugo confessed that these were mushrooms he'd frozen in previous months. Such were his *primi*, the course that comes after *antipasto*, which, thankfully, I'd not eaten. Now began his *secondi*, the main courses. A bit of rabbit in a caper/anchovy sauce was followed by a deliciously stuffed cabbage leaf, pork in tomato sauce and a five-layered *melanzane parmigiana*.

Next, gratefully, was the final main course: wild boar in a chocolate sauce. I couldn't believe it had some tradition attached. Ugo explained that it was originally made here with the chocolate, raisins and pine nuts left over from the traditional Easter eggs. I asked how such poverty could produce chocolate Easter eggs. It was a splurge, Ugo said, and the *avanzi* – leftovers – had to get used up. With all this I drank the house wine, a lovely Montalcino.

Samples of four desserts arrived on a single plate. They were, hard to believe, an almost weightless end to a long meal. The one I liked best was a dish of fresh ricotta, tasting almost like thick cream, topped by a delectable caramelized chestnut paste. Afterwards, Ugo and I sat down together to a glass of golden, almost orange, grappa that he told me, when I asked to buy a bottle, was forty years old and made from the fabled Sassaicaia wine of Bólgheri.

RECIPES FROM L'Aiuole

◆ Nude ravioli / *Gnudi*

This is the filling for a ravioli that is made into a dumpling, without the pasta wraparound. Thus the term 'nude ravioli', or as it's known in this area, *gnudi*. In the Casentino the dumplings are called *gnocchi di Casentino*. At L'Aiuole they are made without flour and light enough to melt in the mouth, not an easy task for the home cook. It's safer to put a bit of flour into the paste, allow it to rest overnight before forming the small balls. Fresh herbs and field greens such as nettles and young dandelions get added to the greens at L'Aiuole. Ugo serves them with just a dressing of fresh olive oil and Parmesan cheese. They also go marvellously with a butter and cheese dressing or a simple tomato sauce.

Serves 8

1kg fresh spinach or Swiss chard combined with field greens, cooked and squeezed dry of water
400g ricotta cheese
3 eggs
150g grated Parmesan or aged pecorino cheese
Salt and freshly ground pepper
A good grating of nutmeg
100g flour, plus more for coating the *gnudi*
Extra virgin olive oil and more freshly grated cheese, to serve

In a food processor, purée the greens with the ricotta. Add the eggs and grated cheese, salt, pepper and nutmeg. Transfer to a bowl and sift in the flour. Allow to rest overnight.

Pour some flour on to a plate. With a teaspoon, scoop out enough of the paste to make a small walnut-sized ball and roll in the flour Place each ball on baking paper to rest for an hour.

Drop the *gnudi* into a large pot of well-salted boiling water. When they rise to the top, lift them out gently with a slotted spoon on to a serving plate. Sprinkle with more cheese, drizzle over some olive oil and serve.

Stuffed cabbage leaves / *Cavolo ripieno*

Serves 6

1 large white cabbage
500g pork sausage meat
3 tablespoons freshly grated Parmesan cheese
5 sprigs basil, chopped
1 bunch parsley, chopped
Salt and freshly ground pepper
A good grating of nutmeg
3 eggs
350ml tomato purée

In a large covered pan of boiling salted water, simmer the cabbage for 30 minutes. Remove to a colander and cool. When it's cool enough to handle, gently separate the leaves, cutting away the core from the bottom as you go to make it easier. The outside leaves will be almost impossible, but it gets easier as you reach the inner leaves. There should be at least 12 leaves, but the stuffing will probably fill even more. Reserve the core and the unusable leaves.

Mix the sausage meat well with the cheese, basil and parsley, some salt, pepper and nutmeg. In a food processor chop the unused core and leaves of the cabbage, and add to the sausage. Gently beat the eggs and add, mixing everything really well.

Heat the oven to 180°C/Gas 6. Loosely fill and close each of the cabbage leaves and place one next to the other in a baking dish large enough to hold all the stuffed leaves. Pour over the tomato sauce and bake for 30 minutes, basting if need be. Serve warm.

Rabbit in caper/anchovy sauce / *Coniglio con capperi e acciughe*

Serves 6

1 large rabbit
1 liver of the rabbit
2 cloves garlic
2 sprigs rosemary
2 sprigs sage
2 tablespoons olive oil
240ml white wine
1 tablespoon capers preserved in vinegar
3 anchovy fillets

Cut the rabbit into small serving pieces and the liver in half.

Finely chop together the garlic and leaves of 1 sprig each of the rosemary and sage. Heat with the oil in a pan large enough to hold the rabbit. As the oil around the garlic bubbles, add the rabbit and liver. Sauté until the meat has lost its colour.

Add the white wine and allow to evaporate by at least half. Remove the two pieces of liver and blend together with the capers and anchovy fillets. Put the mixture back into the pan, add 100ml water and cook, covered, over a low heat until the rabbit is cooked through. At the end of the cooking, add the leaves of the remaining sprigs of rosemary and sage. Serve with polenta or mashed potatoes.

Afterword

WE'VE LIVED IN Tuscany now for more than thirty years. Almost as soon as we'd settled into our new old farmhouse, I remember being warned by foreign friends who'd been here longer than we, that Italy was no longer what it once was. It is a lament we continue to hear often, with greater stridency as the years pass. My Italian friends continuously caution me that Italy is not the rosy picture I conjure up. This almost goes without saying. But I hope this book will help to convince them that it's not as bad as all that, and with an open eye you can still find the traditions that make this country so dear to so many of us.

Of course things change. The Esselunga supermarket arrived the same year we did . . . and for my first few summers here I think I was one of the few that ventured in. The communist party ran a cooperative chain of small supermarkets where local people bought staples occasionally, but here in red Tuscany they boycotted inroads of capitalism on the food front, as well as resisting anything but a recognizable freshness of produce. Even today, as supermarkets and huge discount malls thrive – and even the coop has gone private – daily and weekly markets continue to be the centre of domestic and social life in the small towns that make up most of the country.

Seemingly uncontrolled urban blight and industrial pollution pervade the valleys and city outskirts, traffic comes to a daily standstill on the *autostrada* leading into town, political life is a Byzantine miasma, the products of 'progress' abound. But when we first arrived, our town had no ambulance service, no refuse collector – but for Emilio who came to pick up our rubbish bags once or twice a week and whom we rewarded with a bottle of *vin santo* and a tip twice a year – and a postman who came only when there was enough mail to deliver. Now we have a four-storey health clinic and a fleet of ambulances, paid for and built with local voluntary funds, refuse vans and disposal bins (to where we must now deliver our rubbish), and a mail service that brings us our daily English-language newspaper before noon.

When we first arrived so many old farmhouses were still abandoned, the beautiful hills were marred by overgrown vineyards and neglected olive groves. Houses were shuttered and bleak. In the evenings it was dark all around but for the dim light from neighbouring hill towns.

Today we look out in the evening at brilliantly lit, restored old farmhouses and well-tended olive groves and vineyards. Properties have been bought up by shopkeepers and business people from the densely populated valley below and by non-Italians like us. Farms are once again producing. I often think that we *stranieri* – foreigners – have done our bit to bring old traditions back to Tuscany. Few of our Italian neighbours still make their own wine, and they have leased their olive groves to others. We plod on, making our wine, picking our olives, tidying up the landscape and at times even working the land ourselves.

But the village hasn't changed a whit, other than welcoming in newcomers of all hues and accents. The real population remains the same, 135 souls. It is a small, well-tended village, gently nestling into a hill open to the valley on one side and the Apennine foothills on the other. Two gates at either end of a single winding street are all that remains of an ancient defensive wall. (One remnant of a defence tower sits under an entangled mass of green at the edge of our parking area.) The street is lined with red-roofed little stone houses, a few old *palazzi* and one truly grand villa of the former feudal overlord which is now a Swiss pension. A little offshoot of the main road winds up steeply toward the church, past the old Benedictine convent that dominates the skyline. There were still seven ancient nuns living in *chiusura* (seclusion) when we arrived; now it's been abandoned for years. A few yards further up the little road spreads out into a small perfect piazza with its twelfth century Romanesque church and bell tower, and the Palazzo Pretorio, its splendid front encrusted with coats of arms. The palazzo now houses the area archives and is the venue for occasional art shows, concerts and lectures. The piazza itself is the place for lots of events, including picture-taking of the many couples who choose this beautiful church and its setting for their biggest day.

We used to have a little bottega about midway through the village, the only shop for basics and a few fresh vegetables. Housewives picked up their daily needs here, exchanged gossip and paid bills at the end of the month. The village children came every morning to fetch a *panino* or *schiacciata,* a snack to take off to school. Bread arrived from the next door *forno a legna,* (wood-burning stove) during the morning hours; we ate it before it cooled. A butcher from the town below delivered meat to every home each day and took orders for the next day. The *forno* was just under the old gate (it still is, almost as good but no longer wood-burning) and a daily pick-up truck comes by in the morning to sell fresh vegetables, but the little bottega and daily deliveries of meat have succumbed to 'progress'. With prosperity arrived the usual crush of cars, two for most families.

Other than this, not a stone has been added to the village within the walls during the years we've been here. The Belle Arte commission in Florence has inflexible rules that govern every threatened change. No one can add a centimetre, change the colour of a facade or cut a window where none has been before. New buildings are banned. The green zones remain green. Amazingly the breathtaking view from our terraces over the foothills towards the mountains is still essentially the same as it has been since the sixteenth century. The single threat on the horizon is a proposed car park – convenient for no one – to be carved from the olive groves on the far side of the hill under the church cemetery. Perhaps the Belle Arte commission will veto that as well. I do hope so.

Index

Index of Recipes

List of Restaurants by Area

The Maremma and Western Slopes of Monte Amiata